W9-CJN-800

ck out on comp :

THE WAR OF STEEL AND GOLD

The Development of Industrial Society Series

Henry N. Brailsford

THE WAR
OF STEEL AND GOLD
A Study of the Armed Peace

IRISH UNIVERSITY PRESS
Shannon   Ireland

First edition London 1914
Second edition London 1914
Third edition London 1915

This IUP reprint is a photolithographic facsimile of
the third edition and is unabridged, retaining the original
printer's imprint.

© *1971 Irish University Press Shannon Ireland*

All forms of micropublishing
© *Irish University Microforms Shannon Ireland*

ISBN 0 7165 1767 1

T M MacGlinchey Publisher

Irish University Press Shannon Ireland

PRINTED IN THE REPUBLIC OF IRELAND BY
ROBERT HOGG PRINTER TO IRISH UNIVERSITY PRESS

The Development of Industrial Society Series

This series comprises reprints of contemporary documents and commentaries on the social, political and economic upheavals in nineteenth-century England.

England, as the first industrial nation, was also the first country to experience the tremendous social and cultural impact consequent on the alienation of people in industrialized countries from their rural ancestry. The Industrial Revolution which had begun to intensify in the mid-eighteenth century, spread swiftly from England to Europe and America. Its effects have been far-reaching: the growth of cities with their urgent social and physical problems; greater social mobility; mass education; increasingly complex administration requirements in both local and central government; the growth of democracy and the development of new theories in economics; agricultural reform and the transformation of a way of life.

While it would be pretentious to claim for a series such as this an in-depth coverage of all these aspects of the new society, the works selected range in content from *The Hungry Forties* (1904), a collection of letters by ordinary working people describing their living conditions and the effects of mechanization on their day-to-day lives, to such analytical studies as Leone Levi's *History of British Commerce* (1880) and *Wages and Earnings of the Working Classes* (1885); M. T. Sadler's *The Law of Population* (1830); John Wade's radical documentation of government corruption, *The Extraordinary Black Book* (1831); C. Edward Lester's trenchant social investigation, *The Glory and Shame of England* (1866); and many other influential books and pamphlets.

The editor's intention has been to make available important contemporary accounts, studies and records, written or compiled by men and women of integrity and scholarship whose reactions to the growth of a new kind of society are valid touchstones for today's reader. Each title (and the particular edition used) has been chosen on a twofold basis (1) its intrinsic worth as a record or commentary, and (2) its contribution to the development of an industrial society. It is hoped that this collection will help to increase our understanding of a people and an epoch.

The Editor
Irish University Press

THE WAR OF STEEL AND GOLD

A STUDY OF THE ARMED PEACE

BY

HENRY NOEL BRAILSFORD

THIRD EDITION

WITH AN ADDITIONAL CHAPTER

LONDON
G. BELL AND SONS, LTD.
1915

FIRST PUBLISHED IN MAY, 1914.
SECOND EDITION, DECEMBER, 1914.
THIRD EDITION, JUNE, 1915.

CONTENTS

PART I—Descriptive

PART II—Constructive

PREFACE

TO THE THIRD EDITION

A BOOK which attempts a study of the armed peace may seem superfluous amid general war. But the true causes of the present struggle lay already in the protracted rivalry that preceded it. The strain of the Serajevo murder broke the bonds of public law and goodwill, only because a decade of diplomatic strife had left them frayed and worn. The argument of this book, which traces this strife to the pressure and rivalries of economic expansion beyond the frontiers of Europe, deals only incidentally with European questions of nationality. These have been amply discussed in the able books of Dr. Seton Watson, Mr. Toynbee and others. It seems to me doubtful, however, whether they could have made a general war, had not colonial and economic issues supplied a cruder motive for the use of force. For us the Serbian question stands out from the Eastern battlefield as a straight issue of national right, but it was none the less an economic motive which directed German ambitions to the Near East. The political aspirations of the Slavs were in fatal conflict with the economic ambitions of the Germans. France hopes in this war to complete her nationality by the recovery of Alsace, but she is also defending her acquisition of Morocco. The immense issues that centre in Turkey, China, and Africa are all of them governed by the economic motive. The exclusive attention which public attention in this country has devoted to the issue of nationality has its dangers. It abandons to professional diplomatists and interested groups precisely that field of foreign policy which stands most in need of illumination by critical thinking and idealistic construction. By ignoring these economic problems of Imperialism, we risk a relapse after this war into the sordid rivalries of armed peace.

In a fresh chapter I have added " a postscript on Peace and Change," which develops the constructive proposals of the first edition. The chaos of our international relations is more desperate than it seemed a year ago. The evil is too gross for timid remedies. The lesson from this war is that the only alternative to an endless struggle for a Balance of Power, is the uniting of Europe in a Federal League. I have, with much diffidence, attempted to sketch an outline of such a League.

A few additional notes are distinguished by the letters P.S. I have made some corrections in the text, but no changes of substance.

H. N. BRAILSFORD.

May, 1915.

CHAPTER I

THE BALANCE OF POWER

A TRAVELLER who journeyed from London to Constantinople would remark in the changing landscape an eloquent variety of expression. No face could pass more obviously from confidence to caution, and from caution to fear than the plains and valleys through which his train would carry him. In the straggling villages, the little groups of isolated cottages and the lonely farm-houses of England and France or the Low Countries, he would read the evidences of an ancient civilisation and a venerable peace. Here violence has departed from men's lives, and whatever wrongs and mischiefs scourge society, the dread of the marauder and the bandit has ceased to vex them. They build with the knowledge that the highways are safe, and even the lonely places secure. In Hungary, and still more in Servia, the change begins that marks the transition to the East. The villages are more compact, the scattered cottages less numerous, the remote farm-houses have a look of newness. Here in quite recent generations the Turk was master, and the confidence which made the populous countryside of Western Europe has been slower in

9

coming. With the crossing of what was yesterday the Turkish frontier, the last phase declares itself. The broad landscapes lie open, tilled but untenanted. Outside the towns and the villages no one has dared to settle. Fear is the master-builder, and it is on the mountain tops or in sheltered glens that he has set villages where men herd together, gregarious and apprehensive. When the first Macedonian peasant builds himself a cottage out of sight of town or village, we shall know that the disappearance of Turkish rule has altered men's lives and changed the face of the country.

Landscapes do not lie. It is by the readiness of a population to build in lonely places and to abandon the security of a village where neighbours form a garrison, that one best may judge the success of a government in preserving internal order and peace. A like test may be applied to the relations of peoples. Seven years ago, Great Britain for the second time in a generation, refused to allow the construction of a Channel Tunnel. Year by year King's speeches may declare in the conventional formula that our relations with other Powers are friendly. At intervals our representatives may attend Peace Conferences, and our King exchange hospitality with all the monarchs of Europe. That refusal to construct the Tunnel revealed a lurking fear stronger and more sincere than all the amiable professions of *ententes* and ceremonies. There spoke the fundamental instinct of the people of these islands, and it was an instinct as imperious as that which forbids the Turkish peasant to inhabit a lonely farm-house. It proclaimed the dangers of modern Europe ; it

pronounced war and invasion a possibility to be
reckoned among everyday perils, as clearly as the
Turkish landscape spells brigandage and the nullity
of law.   In vain the experts showed how completely
the French entrance of this tunnel would be commanded by the guns of our fleet, how easily its
exit on our soil might be controlled, how perilous
for an invader would be the attempt to use it, how
readily it could be closed or flooded at the first
approach of tension or danger.   Public opinion,
official and unofficial, unmistakably announced
that it meant to run no risks.   Yet a Liberal
Government was in power.   Sir Henry Campbell-
Bannerman was attempting to lead Europe in a
movement for the reduction of armaments.   Nothing
could have served his purpose so well as a gesture
of confidence, a flinging open of our island gates.
The fear which forbade the construction of the
tunnel could be explained only on one of two grounds.
Either public opinion dreaded that our intimate
understanding with France, of all European countries
the least aggressive, might in some measurable time
give place to an enmity so harsh as to tempt the
French to embark on some sudden and perfidious
scheme of invasion.   Or else it feared that within
the same measurable period—the " our time "
in which we pray for peace—France might be so
utterly crushed by a German conqueror, that the
tunnel might be used by him for a descent on our
coasts.   The wildness of these fears and the
remoteness of these risks gave the measure of the
insecurity in which this country believes itself to
live.   The project of the Channel Tunnel is once

more under the consideration of the Government. The Liberal party is still in power, building Dreadnoughts and talking peace. Our friendship with France has stood the test of time. Our relations with Germany have become normal and even cordial. But it seems doubtful whether even now the project will be sanctioned, and if sanctioned it should be, the chief reason will be that a fresh terror, due to novel forms of warfare, has in the interval begun to prey upon our minds.[1]   Fear vetoed the scheme then ; it is just conceivable that a rival fear may advocate it now.   A Europe in which such alarms may be seriously entertained by great masses of educated and civilised men is a continent dominated by the nightmare of war, a society in which nation no more trusts nation than man trusts man under a lawless oriental despotism.   The refusal to construct a tunnel betrayed our knowledge that we live in an epoch of militarism, as clearly as the Japanese, when they refrain from building stone houses, betray their knowledge that they inhabit an earthquake zone.   Here, too, on our frontiers and channels, fear is the master-builder.

Fear is always apt to seem a ridiculous affection. Yet it would be a random judgment which would pronounce this caution merely irrational.   Only by the gross stupidity or deliberate treachery of the defenders, or by some. inconceivably diabolical cunning of the enemy, could the tunnel be seized and used to our hurt ; but in war all these factors

[1] P.S.—The refusal to sanction the Tunnel was maintained.   Our experience of submarine warfare suggests that even from the purely military standpoint, it might have been wiser to construct it.

must be considered, more especially stupidity. It is only twelve years since France was the enemy, the butt for Mr. Chamberlain's threats, the foe whom the *Daily Mail* wished to " roll in mud and blood," while Germany was the " friend in need," whom Mr. Chamberlain invited to join us, with the United States, in a Pan-Teutonic alliance. In a world subject to such brusque changes, no friendship is eternal, and nothing permanent save the mutability of national rivalries. Since the century opened, five wars in thirteen years have reminded us how distant is still the dream of an enduring peace. In three of these wars Great Powers were engaged. Our own South African campaign was followed by the Russo-Japanese war, and Italy by making war on Turkey for the possession of Tripoli gave the signal for the two wars of the Balkan Allies against Turkey and each other. Nor is it only by the spectacle and experience of actual war that the sense of insecurity is stimulated. A war that has just been averted leaves behind it its legacies of alarm and revenge. Five times at least during these thirteen years has a war been on the verge of breaking out between European Powers, and in four of these five crises the war, if it had been declared, must have involved more than two Great Powers. Twice the Moroccan question gave occasion for such a crisis—once in 1905 after the Kaiser's visit to Tangier, and again in 1911 after the Agadir incident. Had France been engaged in war with Germany at either of these times, there is no doubt that our Fleet would have supported her. Twice at least have the affairs of the Balkans led to the same risk. A war between Austria and Russia in consequence of the annexation of Bosnia was averted in 1909, after mobilisation had begun, only by the delivery in St. Petersburg of a German warning which resembled an ultimatum. In the autumn of 1912 the Austrian and Russian armies were again partially mobilised, and faced each other across their common frontier. They escaped a war partly because the Austrian plans had been divulged to Russia by a traitor on the Austrian General Staff, and partly because Germany and Great Britain united their efforts to keep the peace. The fifth crisis was more singular and more secret than any of the rest, because it occurred between two nominal allies. There was in the early phases of the Italian war with Turkey, a real danger that the military and clerical party in Austria, with the Heir-Apparent at its head, would force Baron von Aerenthal's hands, and bring about a sudden Austrian invasion of Italy. It is possible in surveying such a record as this of perils averted to draw an optimistic conclusion. Five times in this short period has a military caste or an aggressive interest essayed to make a war between two equal members of the European family. Five times has the effort failed. Some force there has always been, whether the public opinion of the nation concerned, or the pressure of neutral states, which has averted the calamity. It is a pettifogging reading of history which would pretend that it was some precarious intervention, now of the Kaiser or again of Sir Edward Grey, which availed to keep the peace. Individual statesmen in such crises are the servants and voices

of the general will. Civilised opinion already regards
war as an obsolete barbarism, and in these five crises,
albeit indirectly and by means apparently accidental,
it has imposed its resolve that war shall cease, at
least among the six Great Powers. The Balkan
Peninsula is in its moral and economic development
some generations behind the rest of Europe, and the
Transvaal, Japan and Turkey were all of them
outside the charmed circle of European fraternity.

It is possible to admit this conclusion, and yet to
doubt whether we are near a period of security or in
sight of the end of militarism. The philosophic spectator, impressed by these repeated failures to make
war, may draw the conclusion that the obscure and
beneficent causes which averted these five wars will
always serve to keep the peace in the European
homeland. But that is not the conclusion of statesmen. They act indeed on the assumption that a
peril averted is only a peril postponed. Consider
for a moment the paradoxical spectacle which
Europe presented after the rapids of the two Balkan
wars had been safely passed. It had been a commonplace among students of international politics
that the Balkan question could not be settled, nor
the heritage of the Turk divided, without a war
among the Great Powers. The thing was done.
Macedonia was partitioned, Albania created and
the Turks confined to a small corner of their ancient
empire, and peace none the less was kept among
the Powers. Nay, more, a Concert was created
which, in the Albanian question at least, contrived
to act, and to act beneficently. In the Conference
of London we even seemed to have the nucleus

and model of a permanent European Council. It is true, indeed, that the concert failed miserably to avert the second war, and to modify the settlement which followed it. But it had at least availed in a momentous and complicated crisis to keep the peace among the Great Powers. If peace can survive such dangers, we might have concluded, she may survive anything. But while the journalists were all congratulating Sir Edward Grey, the soldiers proceeded to arm. Russia began by greatly increasing the numbers of her army on a peace footing. Through M. Poincaré she then imposed on France a return from two to three years' service for her conscripts. Germany, informed betimes of what Russia was preparing, increased her army before the French project had even been submitted to the Chamber, and thereby rendered its adoption inevitable. Great Britain, if Mr. Churchill has his way, is about to follow with an enormous naval increase. These are the permanent consequences of a crisis which seemed superficially to mark our progress towards peace and international organisation. The more successfully we escape war, the more hotly do we prepare for it. We eliminate a question which for three generations has made perennial anxieties for European statesmen, and the result is only to add to our armies and our fleets. Morocco, Tripoli, Albania, Bosnia, Macedonia, Persia—all these outstanding questions diplomacy has settled in the past seven years. It grows every year harder to guess what there is left to quarrel about. First with France, then with Russia, and at last even with Germany, we have closed our accounts and settled our differences. And still our armaments increase. It seems to be more costly to settle our quarrels to-day, than it used to be to nurse them. With nothing left to fight about, our chief concern is that we may have something to fight with.

Too often a show and form of peace has been preserved only because one party to the quarrel was acutely aware of its unpreparedness for war. There lies the seed of strife in these recent harvests of peace. When France yielded in the former of the two Moroccan crises (1905), dismissed M. Delcassé, called the conciliatory M. Rouvier to power, and consented with an ill-grace to the summoning of a European Conference, it was not because public opinion demanded peace, but rather because the emergency found her with her army unready, and her magazines empty. When Russia in March, 1909, much against her inclination and apparently against the tendency of her public opinion, counselled her protégés, the Servians, to return a soft answer to the hectoring of Austria, her Minister of War defended this unpopular course in the Duma on the ground that the army over which he presided was disorganised and unprepared. It is not the will to keep the peace which staves off war from crisis to crisis, but a sense of the overwhelming risks of battle. The play of alliances has powerfully reinforced the argument from prudence. Germany, by standing behind Austria, imposed peace on Russia. Great Britain, in Mr. Lloyd George's Mansion House speech (1911), warned Germany in effect that her fleet and probably a portion of her army stood behind France.

There is in these expedients for averting war neither
finality nor security. A Power which has been
forced by the deficiency of its own armaments to
accept a diplomatic reverse, at once sets to work to
beggar itself in the effort to recover its lost prestige.
Nor does it always happen that a Power is able to
gauge, before the decisive moment, either its own
weakness or its enemy's strength. Nicholas II.
no more foresaw Tsushima than Louis Napoleon
foresaw Sedan. A moment of national vanity, a
passing caprice in which fashion amuses itself by
despising the enemy, as the Russians despised the
Japanese and our own Imperialists derided the Boers,
suffices to make a war. Modern warfare has indeed
long since entered on the phase of scientific prevision
and calculation. Potential adversaries can keep
few secrets from each other. Every admiralty can
tell what weight of shot and shell every ship in the
enemy's fleet can hurl upon its own vessels. Every
naval and military budget is printed and published,
and studied as carefully by the enemy's experts as
by the Parliament at home. It is known approximately within how many days each Power can fling
a given number of army corps across its frontier.
The more elaborate the organisation, the more superfluous is an actual trial of strength. For the old
recurrent wars of flesh and blood there has been
substituted a continuous war of steel and gold. It
never pauses even in time of peace. Behind every
acute diplomatic discussion there goes on a calculation with maps and balance sheets and statistics.
The incessant competition knows no term or relaxa-
tion as to which Power can mass the larger number

of recruits under the colours, provide for their rapid
movements by the most efficient transport, outrange
the enemy's field-guns, or outbuild the enemy's fleet.
The computing of these elements tends to replace
actual warfare. The old world fought ; the modern
world counts. But there are always unknown factors
in the problem. Where is the expert who does
not cherish some fond illusion about the superiority
of a gun, a rifle or a type of ship ? Who shall balance against some material disadvantage the moral
factors which may outweigh it—the superiority of
officers and men in intelligence, in education, in
patriotism and in endurance, or the genius of a
commander ? If the issue of a war could always be
foreseen, there would never be a war, but the
miscalculations first of the Turks and then of the
Bulgarians forbid us to suppose that modern military
science is much nearer than the old haphazard practice to that accuracy in preliminary calculation
which might abolish war. In the last resort, a
slightly inferior Power may hope, by a sudden attack
without a formal declaration of war, to gain a
preliminary advantage which will balance some
deficiency in numbers or armaments.

Alliances give no security that the stable equi-
librium will be maintained, and the armed peace
kept. " Treaties," as Lord Salisbury once put it,
" are mortal." Alliances may be renewed from
term to term, but seals and signatures are no guarantee that their provisions will be faithfully observed.
Calculations of self-interest inspired them ; the
same order of motives may make it inexpedient to

fulfil the bargain. Bismarck set the fashion in this international opportunism. An alliance concluded by him with Austria against the possibility of French or Russian aggression, in no way prevented him from concluding with Russia a secret treaty of " reinsurance," by which he pledged himself to benevolent neutrality if Russia should be attacked by his ally Austria. Europe has been divided for a decade into two armed camps governed by alliances and understandings. In all European questions Britain, France and Russia on the one hand, Germany, Austria and Italy on the other, act as two groups of partisans pledged to give one another support up to a certain point. But the degree of intimacy and the amount of support vary from time to time within each group, and vacillate from crisis to crisis. It was only a moral support which Britain and France gave to Russia in the Bosnian affair, while Germany was ready to back Austria with arms. Britain stood behind France with her fleet in the Moroccan entanglement, but the attitude of Russia was often doubtful. There is usually less doubt about the ties which bind France to Russia and Germany to Austria, than about the mutual relations of the other Powers. Yet at the opening of the Bosnian crisis the *Temps*, which at that period was still the usual organ of the French Foreign Office, suggested that France would do well not to follow Russia and Great Britain too closely in their anti-Austrian policy, since a time might come when a renewal of the Moroccan crisis might make it expedient for France to have in Austria a grateful friend. The position of two of the Great Powers in these groups is normally equivocal.

While the influence of King Edward was at its height, Germans complained that Italy had been "debauched" from the Triple Alliance, and the French reckoned until quite lately on Italian neutrality in a Franco-German conflict. For some years before the advent of M. Poincaré to power in France, there were signs that her alliance with Russia was becoming loose and nearly obsolete. The *Temps* complained that it was no longer put in action (*pratiqué*), and it was claimed as the chief glory of M. Poincaré that he had restored it by his visit to St. Petersburg and the conclusion of a naval convention. While Anglo-German rivalry was at its height, Russia seemed to step outside the Triple Entente and concluded with Germany at the Potsdam meeting a separate bargain in regard to Turkish affairs, which entirely ignored the interests of her ally and her friend. Russia indeed seems to trade upon her notorious untrustworthiness as an ally. When she joins a combination, her friends must continually load her with favours in order that she may remain in it, while from its rivals she receives concessions that she may desert it. Her faithlessness is an inexhaustible asset. She is always in a position to make terms, and gathers from each side by turn a " refresher " or a bribe.

The adoption of the group system in Europe has, in short, brought diplomatists no nearer to the ideal of stability. It has changed the conditions of their problem, but they are still bound at every turn of the wheel to bargain for support and buy off opposition. Loyalty is a matter of expediency and shifting calculation. Usually it pays to support an ally and keep a bargain—if it were not so, there would be no bargains—but there is always a chance that any given crisis may bring the occasion for a weakening of the recognised ties, and a readjustment of the balance of power. Faced by an adverse combination, a restless Power at once sets to work to buy off one or more of its opponents, to take out a policy of " re-insurance," and to break through the diplomatic hedge which pens it in. Europe is in perpetual flux, and peace is preserved only by a constant readjustment of the strains and tensions which hold it together. Alliances, like armaments, are rather symptoms of a universal insecurity, than the means of building up a permanent peace. The group system stands condemned by its practice. The Budgets of all the Powers which are embraced in it betray their fears. The continual increase of armaments since the formation of the Triple Entente is the sufficient proof that it has done nothing for European security. Union ought to make strength. But in practice every alliance tends to stimulate each ally to the maximum of those preparations which are always supposed to be defensive. Each group aims at a preponderance in Europe, and each ally uses his influence to force his colleagues into costly sacrifices. Russian influence induced France to return to the Three Years' Service System. French influence is among ourselves a force making for conscription, and from time to time the *Temps* informs us that if ever we are to enjoy the full status of an ally of France, we must make ourselves valuable to her by creating a national army. Italy, seeking security in the Triple Alliance, presently found that she was expected to load her population with taxes in order to maintain the status of a first-class military Power. Our own experience at the moment teaches us how strangely a *quasi*-alliance may operate to increase armaments. Because we belong to the Triple Entente it is argued that we must build ships not merely against Germany, but against Germany's allies, Italy and Austria. But in reckoning our forces, the experts will never allow us to add the navies of France and Russia to our own. An alliance seems always to bring new commitments and dangers with it, but never to diminish perils or to enable its members to lessen their preparations for defence.

Ten years ago if we had invited statesmen and experts to define the tasks of the British army, they would have answered unanimously that we are obliged to maintain a large and costly land force primarily because we hold India and must prepare for its defence. By two treaties during this period our military position in India has been transformed. We have first of all concluded an alliance with Japan by which she is pledged, should India be invaded, to support us with an army of 300,000 men. Meanwhile with Russia, the only Power which could invade India, we have entered on an understanding by which she has become a *quasi*-ally. India has been insured and re-insured. We have made a friend of our only rival, and an ally of the most formidable military Power of the New East. But our army is no smaller for this favourable change in our position. The risks against which it insures us have been twice removed, yet we are unable to disband a regiment or dispense with a battery. The military budget of India have indeed actually increased since these two treaties made it morally impossible that an army should ever in our time be called upon to defend it against a foreign invader. The army is not diminished, partly because no one wholly trusts the Russian friend or the Japanese ally, but chiefly because our entry into the Continental system of alliances has imposed upon it a new military task. Its primary function is no longer to defend India, but to furnish an expeditionary corps for service in Europe. Alliances and understandings have had here also their normal results. Not for our own sakes, but to serve our friends and maintain the balance of power, we have been obliged to provide our Continental policy with a Continental arm. We require an army which can operate in Europe precisely as we did in the days of Marlborough and Wellington. The more deeply we commit ourselves to the policy of the balance, the more rapidly shall we be driven to the adoption of conscription. We are driven, by the very means which seem to conjure peril and make for safety, into a redoubling of precautions which betray our growing fears. Nowhere in Europe is this process of arming easy or uneventful. Everywhere it involves unpopular taxation, shaken credit, Cabinet crises, Parliamentary conflicts. A wanton enemy, a joyful aggressor, a primitive earth-shaking Imperialism there nowhere is in Europe to-day. Morally warfare is obsolete, and it is with conscious shame and unconcealed reluctance that statesmen and Parliaments face the assumed necessity of interrupting the industrial business of a modern State to provide for the constant possibility of war, on a scale which the barbarism of the Middle Ages at their darkest never rendered necessary. Ours is a mediævalism without its chivalry, stripped of the pride in arms and the delight in conflict which gave even to feudalism an ideal and not ignoble side. It is fear which goads Europe to-day into the extravagance of panic armaments. But the fear which causes the European Powers to form alliances and pile up armaments is not the simple fear of a nation which dreads aggression and invasion. It may so figure in the minds of the simple citizens who flocked to see " An Englishman's Home," and imagined that the Germans were already at our gates. It may so figure in the mind of the French peasant who remembers that the Prussians once occupied his farm, and forgets the dynastic ambitions of his rulers which provoked this invasion. In the minds of the governing caste it is rather a superb fear, an Imperial fear, a fear lest in the future some stronger Power may menace their acquisitions, recent or prospective, in various corners of the globe. There are nations, of which little Switzerland is the chief, which live secure without a professional or conscript army amid the rival camps of Europe. " To do justly and love mercy and walk humbly with thy God," is a rule of life which still preserves rare nations from the general fear. But these are the nations which covet nothing beyond their own borders.

To the humane onlooker who conceives the public life of nations as an effort, however slow and ill-directed, to realise the ideal of a co-operative commonwealth, the procedure of diplomacy and the growth of armaments is apt to seem a riot of waste and unreason. Yet it is at the worst a highly intelligent folly, which has its guiding thoughts, its principles of action, and above all, its economic motives. Let us attempt to study it a little more closely. Seen from a British standpoint the process has been influenced by three or four new departures which are in reality phases of a single policy—the conclusion of the French *Entente Cordiale* in 1904, the launching of the *Dreadnought* in 1906, the conclusion of the Russian agreement in the next year, and perhaps we should add the adaptation of the army by Lord Haldane to suit the new conception of its task as an auxiliary Continental force. " We ordinary mortals," said Lord Rosebery recently, " are not admitted behind the scenes . . . but one thing we do know about our foreign policy : for good or for evil we are embraced in the midst of the Continental system." The days of our " splendid isolation " are over. We have become in the full sense of the word a European Power closely involved with two partners in the rivalries of the Continent. The change in our position was probably inevitable, and it is likely to be permanent. Disastrous as some of its consequences have been, there are few who would wish to revive the conceptions of foreign policy which were taught by the " Manchester School." To make an ideal of " splendid isolation " would be to renounce our duties in the common life of nations, to check our sympathies, to deny the sense of solidarity which links us with identical interests and fellow-feelings to peoples beyond our shores. It is

better to go forward, however ill-guided the advance
may be, as a European nation aware of its share in
the common burdens, the common errors, and the
social duties of peoples which profess a common
civilisation, than to relapse into the insularity and
egoism of a narrow isolation.

To welcome our entry into the Continental system, is not to accept the fundamental principle
which has guided us   We have followed for nearly
a decade a policy defined as the preservation in
Europe of " a balance of power." It is a familiar
idea, and the words recall some of the most cherished
memories in our history. But like all traditional
phrases it illustrates the danger of adapting to
modern conditions a notion which bore for our ancestors a meaning which we cannot give it to-day. It
arrests thinking, confuses emotion, and covers
with its venerable mantle a policy which is in reality
entirely new. " To maintain a balance of power
in Europe " is the motive which inspired us to erect
the Triple Entente as a barrier against the Triple
Alliance, led us into a conscious and habitual rivalry
with Germany, made us the ally of France in a
quarrel not our own, and set us, after the Manchurian
campaign, to restore Russia by financial aid and
diplomatic backing to her place among the Great
Powers. All metaphors mislead, and this metaphor
is peculiarly fallacious. One may doubt whether
any statesman in his own inner mind ever desired a
balance, if the word means what it conveys—an
exact equipoise in force and influence among the
Powers of Europe. What every statesman desires
is that the scales of power shall be more heavily

weighted on his own side. He begins to talk of a
balance when the scales descend on the other side.
He piles a weight on his own side or snatches a weight
from the other, but he never stops at the crucial
moment when the scales are even. The balance is a
metaphor of venerable hypocrisy which serves only
to disguise the perennial struggle for power and predominance. When a statesman talks of a balance,
he means a balance favourable to himself. Equipoise between two rival groups, if ever it could be
attained, would mean a condition intolerable to the
normal human mind. It would mean stagnation
and stalemate, the throttling and handcuffing,
not of one nation, but of all. It is for liberty of
movement, for opportunity to carry out their
national purposes that all Powers strive. In a Concert that liberty is sought through the amicable
adjustment of interests round a Council-Board, and
just in so far as Powers form permanent groups
which support each other in issue after issue on the
principle of " my ally right or wrong " does any
Concert governed by the disinterested opinion of
neutrals become impossible. Without a Concert
the group system means that all negotiation, even
when it is outwardly courteous, is carried on with
the knowledge that arguments are weighed by the
number of army corps and guns and ships which each
combination can muster. The evil reaches its
climax when all the Great Powers are regimented,
as they are to-day, in one group or the other,
and none of them is free, without some measure
of disloyalty to partners, to approach any question
with an open mind or to consider any aspect of

it save its reaction upon the interests of these partners.

A Balance of Power is not a self-sufficing ideal. Power is sought for certain ends, and that is true whether it is at an equality or at a preponderance of power that one aims. It is here that the real difference emerges between the contemporary struggle to maintain a sort of balance in Europe and the epic wars of the eighteenth and early nineteenth centuries. When our ancestors talked of redressing the balance, and formed coalitions, subsidised allies and landed armies on the Continent, they had something to fear. They were fighting for hearths and homes. They knew that their own liberties, political and religious, were at issue, and if the struggle imposed on them inordinate burdens, the stake was worth the sacrifice. In the former of the two periods dominated by the notion of a balance, Louis XIV. had made himself the arbiter of Europe. He gave a king to Spain, a mistress and a pension to Charles II., stood behind a Catholic restoration under his successor, and menaced the Netherlands and the Rhine with unceasing and devastating warfare. When William of Orange taught our ancestors to think in terms of the balance of power, it was because our shores were threatened with an invasion which would have brought back a despotic king. His strategy was a league of the weaker Powers against a nation whose cohesion and superiority in culture and wealth overtopped the liberty of Western Europe. No less elementary, no less monstrous, were the perils which caused Pitt to revive the theory of the balance against Napoleon. Frontiers had become fluid under the tread of his armies, and his will moulded national institutions and made and unmade kings.   In both periods the things that were weighed in the balance were the home territories and the domestic liberties of the peoples which sought to adjust it.   The stake was their national existence, the fields and the cities which were their home.   Our fathers under William of Orange and Pitt did not aspire to a balance as a thing good and necessary in itself, or as a condition of the normal life of European societies.   They meant by the balance such a checking of the excessive power of France as would save Devonshire from her fleets, the Palatinate from her armies, their thrones from her nominees and their Parliaments from her dictation.   The balance, in short, was the condition of national self-government.

We must free ourselves from the obsession of this phrase, if we would judge contemporary diplomacy clearly.   There is no analogy, there is not even a plausible parallel between our own case and that of our forefathers who coined the phrase.   To pursue a balance for its own sake is not an axiom of British policy.   What is axiomatic is rather that we must adopt any policy necessary to the preservation of our national liberties.   The balance was always a means to that end ; it was never an end in itself. We shall not reason honestly about the modern problems of diplomacy, until we have first of all recognised that the dangers which forced our ancestors into European coalitions and Continental wars have gone never to return.   We need not argue that human character is absolutely better than it was in earlier centuries, nor even that the predatory instincts of mankind have grown appreciably weaker. Human character, for that matter, is not a fixed or self-subsistent thing ; it is the habit which human beings acquire of adjusting themselves to their environment. The environment changes and the character with it. What mainly differentiates our century from those which went before it is that the forms of wealth have changed. Wealth in the days of the wars for a balance of power meant primarily land. Wealth in our day is primarily the opportunity for peculiarly profitable investment. This economic evolution has modified most of our social institutions, and with them our diplomacy. Conquest in the old sense of the world has become obsolete. A predatory Power does not go out with drums and banners to seize estates for its feudal aristocracy. It applies pressure, and pressure which often involves the possession of fleets and armies, to secure concessions for its financiers. There is no advance in morality here, no conscious progress towards a Golden Age. The change cannot be described in phrases from Isaiah or in verses from Vergil. It is a non-moral development, but it has none the less a direct bearing upon our hopes of peace. The instinct to conquer is as sharp and insatiable as ever, but it has found a means of conquering beyond frontiers. Our modern *conquistadores* do not burn their ships when they alight on coveted soil, as though to anchor themselves for ever on its fertile acres. Our bankers will not do in China what Cortes and Pizarro did in the New World. They build a railway or sink a

mine.   Our Ahabs do not take Naboth's vineyard ;
they invest money in it.   The struggle for a balance
of power means to-day a struggle for liberty and
opportunity to use " places in the sun " across the
seas.   For the modern world a place in the sun is
not a smiling valley, or a rich plain in which a
victorious army will settle, and build homes and
found families.   It is a territory to " exploit," and
the active agents in the process are now the bankers
and investors who float loans, and secure concessions.   Even where conquest is incidentally
necessary, as in Morocco, there is no migration to
the new territory and the conquering Power rarely
troubles to annex it.   It " occupies " it, only because
without occupation it cannot safely employ its
capital in building railways or sinking mines.   Land-
hunger is not the malady of the modern world.   In
all this we shall not discover the faintest resemblance
to the perils and ambitions which roused the passions
and stimulated the sacrifices of the earlier struggles
for a balance of power.

What at the worst would have happened, if no
Triple Entente had been formed, or if it had been
broken by clever diplomacy or successful force?
What use over a long period of years would the
Powers of the Triple Alliance have made of their
predominance ?   Germany would no doubt have
continued her peaceful " penetration " of Turkey.
The Bagdad Railway would have been from terminus to terminus an all-German line, and the
German banker and the German mining engineer
would have followed its course, conferring some
incidental benefits on the Turkish population and

earning large dividends for Hamburg and Berlin. British trade would have shared in the increased demand for goods, but German political influence at the Porte would in the main have excluded our financiers from the large profits to be derived from concessions and monopolies. The French occupation of Morocco would probably not have been feasible, or if it had happened, would have formed a part of some comprehensive arrangement between France and Germany. The country might have been divided between them, or Germany might have been contented with economic facilities, if French capital had been put at her disposal for her industrial and colonial enterprises. It is not so much Morocco which the Germans have coveted, as the excellent iron ore which its mountains contain. Nor does France possess anything which Germany desires, save those endless stores of capital which French banks in concert with French diplomacy direct abroad to Russia, to Turkey, to South America— to every corner of the earth save Germany. By cajolery or by bullying or by that peculiarly German combination of both, German diplomacy, if no Triple Entente had existed, would somehow have found its way to the Moroccan mines and the Paris Bourse. What else would have happened ? Italy would doubtless have taken Tripoli, and with it perhaps some Turkish islands ; she might even have won some footing, half political, half economic in the Cilician region of Asiatic Turkey. Persia, if we had entered into no close association with Russia, would have continued to profit by Anglo-Russian jealousies, to maintain the reality of her independence,

and might with a free Parliament and the aid of such
foreigners as Mr. Shuster have advanced far towards
a national renaissance.   In the Balkans it is likely
enough that Austria, backed by the preponderant
influence of the Triple Alliance, would have availed
herself of one of the several crises which have followed
the young Turkish revolution, to force her way
to Salonica and to annex a part at least of Macedonia.   For my part, I do not doubt that the
Bulgarian population which she would have acquired
would have been happier under her rule than it is
now, or is ever likely to be under the Servians and
Greeks.   These are some of the consequences which
might have happened if no one had troubled to unite
Britain, France and Russia in a league to maintain
a balance of power against Germany and her allies.
The most probable consequence of all, however,
would have been the dissolution or at least the
weakening of the Triple Alliance itself.   Alliances
are held together more securely by the forces which
press against them, than by any internal cohesion.

It would be difficult to suggest any consequences more startling or sinister than these.
Europe had a long experience of German " hegemony " during the quarter of a century which elapsed
between the fall of the French Empire and the
creation of the Franco-Russian Alliance.   Nothing
disastrous happened.   No little states were over-run,
no neighbour's landmarks removed, no thrones over-
turned, no national or religious liberties menaced.
Not even if the Kaiser wielded a military power as
great as that of Louis XIV., can we conceive him
acting as the Grand Monarch acted.   High politics are

no more moral than they were, but predatory appetites have assumed a new form, and nations have acquired with Parliamentary government a cohesion and a personality which protects them more effectively than guarded frontiers and crowded barracks. In Europe the epoch of conquest is over, and save in the Balkans and perhaps on the fringes of the Austrian and Russian Empires, it is as certain as anything in politics can be, that the frontiers of our modern national states are finally drawn. If war should break out, it will be for some stake in the Near East or in China, and it will end without territorial changes in Europe—a geographical term from which the Balkans must always be excluded. The present territorial arrangement of Europe follows with few exceptions the lines of nationality. Even where it departs from them, trade and finance have united the conquered area so closely to the conqueror, that it would now reject independence as a free gift. That is certainly true of Russian Poland, which demands autonomy, but would regard separation as an economic disaster. It is probably true even of Alsace-Lorraine, which for all its hatred of Prussian bureaucratic rule and its preference for French culture, has entered irrevocably into the German network of commerce and finance.[1] If we are to continue in the twentieth century to inflate our patriotic rhetoric with sounding phrases about the balance of power, let us be clear at least about its modern meaning. No one will impose on us a

[1] P.S.—The experience of this war may have revived the wish for a return to France. German Poland, the Trentino, and Danish Schleswig are also exceptions to this generalisation. I question whether Germany aimed at the actual annexation of Belgium.

Catholic king, or remodel our institutions to fit the iron law of the Code Napoleon.   Shall the Germans dig for iron ore on the slopes of the Atlas, and carry it in the form of steel rails to Bagdad ?   That is the typical question of modern diplomacy, and sanely regarded, it is a good deal more important than the typical question of the old world, whether the King of Spain should be a Bourbon or a Hapsburg.   To settle this question, and similar questions which belong to the same order, the young men of Europe are drilled, the battleships are built and the taxes squandered.   Nothing is at stake which can affect the fortunes or ownership of a single acre of European soil.   Nothing would be changed in the politics or religion or public life of any European state if these questions were settled otherwise or were not settled at all.   When men were kidnapped by the press-gang in the streets of Plymouth to fight Napoleon, they had at least this consolation, that something which they valued as Englishmen would have been lost or jeopardised, if Napoleon had won.   But who in England would have cared if the iron-ore of Morocco had gone to cast German cannon at Essen, instead of French cannon at Creusot ?   There is no human reality in this modern struggle for the balance of power, no worthy end, no splendid purpose.   There is nothing real about it, unless it be the taxes levied to maintain it.

" But do you," the reader may ask with indignation and surprise, " do you really dismiss the tremendous Anglo-German rivalry of recent years, with all its war scares and its Dreadnoughts, as a dispute which turned on nothing larger than the

mines of Morocco and the railways of Mesopotamia ?
This is to trifle with patriotism and ignore national
ambitions." The normal human mind experiences
a certain revulsion at such an analysis. All the
abstract words, all the sounding phrases of politics
have hurtled about our ears during these years, and
we do not like to be told that the whole confusion
was caused by a matter of iron ore and steel rails.
There are two ways of testing such a diagnosis as
this, and we will apply them both. How did the
dispute originate, and how was it finally settled ?
The *Entente Cordiale* between Britain and France,
which marked the beginning of the tension with
Germany, was based, so far as the world knows, upon
a single document, which was nothing but a businesslike adjustment of French and British interests in
Egypt and Morocco. The French agreed to recognise our tenure of power in Egypt, and we in return
admitted their predominant interest in Morocco.
A secret clause, of which the Germans seem to have
had knowledge about a year after it was drafted,
went on to bind us to give diplomatic support to
France, if circumstances should render it expedient
for her to occupy Morocco, and in that event the
interests of Spain were safeguarded in any future
partition. Amid all the angers and contentions of
recent years there was never any concrete issue of
the first rank between Britain and Germany, save
this Moroccan question, and it was a question which
concerned the French more nearly than ourselves.
The German thesis was perfectly simple, and in
principle defensible. It was that France and
Britain had no right by an exclusive bargain to

settle the fate of Morocco without consulting other Powers. The answer of the French and British press was more plausible than convincing. It was our case that as what we call the " trade " of Morocco is mainly in French and British hands, Germany was not in any real sense an interested party. The " trade " of Morocco, if by that word is meant the exchange of European manufactured goods against the raw produce of its agriculture, is at the best inconsiderable. No one would risk the lives of soldiers and the money of taxpayers for the sake of the Moroccan market. What matters in Morocco is the wealth of its virgin mines. This was an open field, and here Germans had as good or as bad a claim as any one else. A German firm, the Mannesmann Brothers, could indeed boast that it had obtained an exclusive concession to work all the mines of Morocco in return for money which it had lent to an embarrassed Sultan during its civil wars. That this was the real issue is proved by the terms which were more than once discussed between Paris and Berlin for the settlement of the dispute. A " détente," or provisional settlement of the dispute was concluded in 1910, which had only one clause—that German finance should share with French finance in the various undertakings and companies which aimed at " opening up " Morocco by ports, railways, mines, and other public works. No effect was ever given to this undertaking, and German irritation at the delays of French diplomacy and French finance culminated in the dispatch of the gunboat *Panther* to Agadir as a prelude to further " conversations." Had M. Caillaux remained in power, we know from the subsequent investigations before the Senate's Committee, how those conversations would have ended. He would have effected not merely an adjustment of French and German colonial interests, but a general understanding which would have covered the whole field of Franco-German relations. The points on which he had begun to negotiate were all economic, and chief among them was a proposal to put an end to the boycott by French finance of the Bagdad railway, and to admit German securities to quotation on the Paris Exchange. The alarm which this bold step by M. Caillaux caused both to French patriots and to British Imperialists is not yet forgotten, and its echo was heard both in London and Paris, when, towards the close of 1913, M. Caillaux returned to office. In those informal negotiations he had made the beginnings of a readjustment in Franco-German relations which would have transformed not merely French but European politics, if he had been Premier for a few months longer. French patriots took alarm and feared that he was about to rob them of their dream of a revenge for 1870. British Imperialists in our Conservative press assailed him from a fear that if France composed her quarrel with Germany, this country would be left isolated. In a single sentence in the debate (27 November, 1911) which followed this Agadir crisis, Sir Edward Grey used a phrase which showed that our diplomacy had shared the fears of our Conservative press. There was a risk, as he put it, that France might be drawn into the orbit of German diplomacy. It was for that reason, and not because it really concerned us how much or how little compensation France paid to Germany in the Congo for her seizure of Morocco, that we were ready to back the less conciliatory diplomacy of M. Caillaux's successors, if need be, by force of arms. This was, perhaps, the most instructive incident in the recent history of European diplomacy. We need not pause to discuss the parts which the various actors played in it. What concerns us in this argument is the proof which it afforded that in the judgment of those who knew the facts, this feud between France and Germany, which for more than a generation has seemed to be a permanent factor in European politics, deeply seated in sentiment and entrenched behind powerful interests, might be ended by an economic arrangement. That clearly was the view both of those who desired and those who feared a reconciliation. Assuming that the Germans were wise enough at the same time to grant full self-government to Alsace-Lorraine, this view is probably sound. It means, if we accept it, that the importance of economic motives as the real spring of all the conflicts which centre in the balance of power could hardly be over-stated. The whole development of Anglo-German relations, since the Moroccan conflict ended in a compromise, has tended to confirm this opinion. Both Powers, after the crisis of September, 1911 had confronted them sharply with the real risk of war, acted with a new sobriety and cast about for the means of composing their differences. Lord Haldane made his famous visit to Berlin, and Baron Marschall von Bieberstein was sent to London. A comprehensive series of negotiations was opened, and some

brief account of it has been given by the German
Chancellor to the Reichstag. It turned on two sets
of questions—economic issues in Turkey which
centre in the Bagdad Railway, and colonial issues
which apparently concern future projects of expansion in tropical Africa. These negotiations were
nearly completed when the Chancellor last spoke of
them, and he implied that they had already sufficed
to make Anglo-German relations cordial and intimate.
Once more it appears that the questions which
divide rival Powers, and mobilise them in hostile
camps against each other, turn on no European controversies, and affect no question of honour, liberty
or nationality that touches our own homes. They
are all incidents in the effort of modern finance to
find openings in distant regions, to lay its rails in
Mesopotamia or to exploit the tropical produce of
Angola.

A doctor who explains the madness and death
of a man by a clot of blood in his brain, must seem
to a simple spectator to be assigning a ridiculously
inadequate cause for a tremendous effect. A student
who traces all the armaments and angers and heroics
of our seven years' struggle over the balance of
power, to the fact that German industry looks forward to the early exhaustion of its native supplies of
iron-ore, and hoped to replace them by obtaining
access to the mines of Morocco, may also seem to be
trifling. Was there really nothing else in all this
crisis ? Of course there was. There was the anger.
When the plain man sees the *Dreadnoughts* rising
on the stocks, and listens to the gossip about crises
and military preparations, his common-sense is

offended when he is told that the trouble is about nothing more serious than a few mines and railways and bankers' ventures. The plain man is right. The potent pressure of economic expansion is the motive force in an international struggle ; for a people like the Germans which has bent all its brains, and will bend them for a generation to the task of industrial organisation, mines and railways in the half-exploited regions of the earth are not a trivial matter. But the starting-point in such a rivalry is soon forgotten. Danger begins when a nation generalises, and declares that it is being " penned in," and threatened by a policy of " encir- clement." The difficulty between Britain and Ger- many was not so much Bagdad or even Morocco, as the general sense that a powerful diplomatic com- bination and a naval preponderance were being used to frustrate German purposes and to exclude her from " places in the sun." The moment that suspicion dawns, the origins of the rivalry are for- gotten. It becomes a general engagement, and all the channels of human folly pour into it their re- serves. The military instinct, with all the interests behind it, is aroused, and on its side fights the healthy national will not to be worsted in a trial of endurance. Subtler but not less potent is the scientific chauvin- ism peculiar to the German mind—the mood of self- complacency which dwells on German efficiency as opposed to British " slackness," our obsolete methods of education, the abundant leisures and pleasures of our propertied class, and all the phen- omena which suggest a crew resting on its oars and inviting a more strenuous people to pass it in the race.

It would be futile to attempt to dissect the froth of popular emotion, but there is little difficulty in explaining why secondary disputes like these of Morocco and Bagdad expanded into a world-shaking conflict. It was an offence that we should have joined the French in settling the fate of Morocco by a one-sided arrangement. Germany had been ignored, and the Kaiser quite naturally retorted that Germany must aim at becoming " so strong that nothing could happen in the world about which she was not consulted." The sequel suggested to German minds that the offence was deliberate, that we meant to erect it into a system. The Anglo-French Entente grew into the Triple Entente, and the Triple Entente presently seemed to be rallying minor partners to itself. First we excluded Germany from Morocco, and then we constructed a general league which hemmed her in on all sides. We " debauched " her ally, Italy, we brought Spain within our " orbit," gave British queens to Spain and Norway, and for a brief moment robbed Germany of her old influence in Turkey. The " balance of power " had been violently adjusted in our favour, and Germany, in Prince von Bülow's phrase, felt herself " penned in," and imagined that it was the purpose of the Triple Entente to confront her everywhere, to check her movements in every sea, and to shut her out from all " the places in the sun." The struggle which followed was really a colossal effort on her part to break down the " pen." She threatened France and Russia in turns, and against us she began to build a navy, which, though it could not hope to equal ours, might at least be strong enough to cause

us to pause before we attacked her. It can hardly
be doubted that for some years at least, the Triple
Entente was really inspired by the aims which
German alarm ascribed to it. Its real architects
were M. Delcassé and King Edward, and the former
at least made no secret of his ambitions. The ablest
defence of his work is to be found in the brilliant
pages of his friend, M. Victor Bérard. He illustrates
his idea by a striking metaphor. When the iconoclasts of the Reformation were minded to destroy a
Gothic cathedral, they did not trouble to storm in
upon it with mallet and crowbar. They simply cut
the flying buttresses which supported from outside
all the gallant tracery of its walls and the massive
strength of its towers. When that was done the
cathedral crumbled into ruins. The German Empire
was that Gothic cathedral. Its buttresses were the
Austrian and Italian alliances, its more than neigh-
bourly relations with Russia, its predominance over
Turkey, and its power of bringing other lesser states
like Roumania within the circuit of its influence.
M. Delcassé set to work with equal boldness and
skill to realise this masterly thought, and accident
favoured him when Lord Salisbury, who had always
been a friend of Germany, retired from office, and
King Edward, who had always been a friend of France,
came to the throne. For some years Germany was
very nearly isolated, and the Austrian alliance was
the only " flying buttress " which did not shake for
a moment beneath the hammers of the iconoclasts.
The cathedral in the end turned out to be more
solid than it had seemed at the first assault, and
experience cooled the ardour of the assailants.

These years of passionate unrest have left behind
them no permanent achievement. Neither group
is appreciably stronger than it was when the rivalry
began. Its only permanent monument is to be found
in the National Debts of the Powers which have
engaged in it, in their military and naval budgets,
and in their burden of taxation. For the rest, what
has been gained ? Our hold, indeed, is firmer on
Egypt. France has taken Morocco. Austria has
snatched a title to Bosnia. Russia with our connivance has destroyed the liberties of Persia, and
occupied apparently in permanence its more
advanced and populous provinces. There was talk
of a League of Peace and a coalition of the Liberal
Powers when we concluded our understanding with
France. What Liberal purpose has it furthered ;
what Liberal principle has it established ? We
soon discovered that what France wanted from us
was not our Liberal principles but our navy. When
Sir Henry Campbell-Bannerman talked of reducing
armaments, her press voiced a barely courteous disgust ; it is enthusiastic only when Mr. Churchill
undertakes (in his own phrase) to provide that
" shattering, blasting, overpowering force," which
helped France to seize Morocco. We soon discovered that if we would embrace Liberal France, we
must stretch our arms to include reactionary Russia.
We found Russia after the Manchurian War a stag-
gering chaos. We have helped to restore its solvency and revive its prestige, while it hanged its
Socialists, dissolved its Dumas, imprisoned its
deputies, flogged its noblest youth, oppressed its
Jews, defiled the free soil of Finland, and erected

its gallows in the cities of Persia. Nowhere has the Triple Entente served a Liberal thought, and at no time in the long rivalry has this battle over the balance of power turned on an intelligible principle, or a purpose which promised anything to the common good of Europe. Its angry career has only disclosed the futility and triviality of the ideas which have inspired it. In vain have we and our partners sought security in alliances. The mounting record of our armaments gives the measure of our growing fears. The rivalry is pursued on a greater scale. With each effort the standard of sacrifice is raised, and still no Power gains the sense of security or immunity from challenge. There is nothing to be won from all this uncompensated mischief, unless it be a clear vision of what is really involved. There is at stake nothing whatever in Europe, nothing at all that touches any vital interest of any European democracy. The angers and suspicions which the strife engenders, the megalomania on one side and the panic fears on the other—these are the psychological irrelevancies of the process. The tangible realities at stake are measurable, and they turn out on investigation to be nothing but certain opportunities for expansion valued by the restless finance of one Power or the other. It is an economic motive which underlies the struggle for a balance of power.[1]

[1] P.S.—The bearing of the war on the conclusions of this chapter are considered in a note on p. 337.

CHAPTER II

POLITICIANS tend to think in cant, as the masses and the aristocracy think in slang. For the secrecy of their foreign policy cant has provided them with a specious excuse. The suggestion is that democracy is incapable of a " scientific " handling of foreign questions. The ruling class invokes science to-day in defence of its privileges, as its fathers used to invoke revelation. This apology for a close and exclusive statesmanship involves several suppositions —that a science of foreign politics exists, that the bureaucrats of the diplomatic service are in possession of it, and further that they alone possess it, or are capable of acquiring it. To state these suppositions is to dispose of them. There is no science of foreign policy, and however much it may stand in need of careful and systematic thinking, no department of politics has received less theoretic attention. Certainly no book exists in our language which attempts in any systematic and constructive way to present a general view of foreign affairs, or of the principles which should guide their conduct. The consequence of leaving this department of public affairs to the uncontrolled conduct of a small caste, is not to promote their scientific handling, but rather

47

to give the rein to caprices, rivalries, and personal interests. The fewer the number of persons engaged in any given transaction, the less on the average will be the chance that it will be settled by any view of general interests, and the greater the probability that the issue will turn on purely personal factors. There has unquestionably been in the last century an immense improvement in the personal morals of diplomatists, a decay even in foreign affairs of the authority of monarchs, and a diminution of the risk that individual interest will deflect national policy. Save perhaps in the Balkan States, and there only in Belgrade under the late King Alexander, one may doubt, for example, whether anything is now effected in diplomacy by the Stuart-Bourbon method of subsidising the mistresses of foreign kings. Late in the eighteenth century our ambassadors in St. Petersburg used to bribe the ministers and courtiers of the Tsar. That method is obsolete even in Russia. But the personal factor is none the less still powerful and its motives are not always respectable or even patriotic. The memoirs which deal with the foreign affairs of the nineteenth century often suggest that the ultimate problem was frequently that of handling the caprices of the few individuals, the kings, statesmen and ambassadors, on whom the fortunes of European peace too often depended. Here, for example, is the picture which Lord Aberdeen, a weak but high-minded Prime Minister, drew of the diplomatic position which was to create the Crimean War (Stanmore, *Earl of Aberdeen*, pp. 270-1). Writing to a colleague (Graham) he describes how he and his Foreign Secretary are consciously but

miserably drifting into war, hurried along by the
ambitions of two men, the one an ally, and the other
a public servant, whose character they profoundly
distrusted :—

" I fear I must renounce the sanguine view
I have hitherto taken of the Eastern question ;
for nothing can be more alarming than the
present prospect. I thought that we should have
been able to conquer Stratford (Lord Stratford de
Redcliffe, the bellicose but capable British Ambassador in Constantinople), but I begin to fear that
the reverse will be the case, and that he will succeed in defeating us. Although at our wits' end,
Clarendon (the Foreign Secretary) and I are still
labouring in the course of peace ; but really to
contend at once with the pride of the Emperor
(Louis Napoleon, our ally), the fanaticism of the
Turks, and the dishonesty of Stratford, is almost a
hopeless attempt."

It was a " hopeless attempt." Lord Aberdeen
saw clearly that British interests could be safeguarded without war. What could not be appeased
without war was the resentment of Louis Napoleon
against the Tsar Nicholas, who had affronted him by
treating him as the thing he was—a *parvenu* and an
adventurer. War was declared, and the armies of
three nations starved and froze and bled before
Sevastopol for the pride of Louis Napoleon and the
" dishonesty " of a British ambassador. No venera-
tion for the inner ruling caste which has made the
wars of Europe, could survive a study of the memoirs
which deal with the life of Bismarck, and his suc-

cessor, Prince Hohenlohe. The Hohenlohe Memoirs, given to the world in 1906, expurgated though they were, remind the reader of the books in which our Puritan ancestors used to revel under such titles as *Satan's Invisible World Revealed*. The book is simply a dissection of the personal ambitions and intrigues of the courtiers, generals and ministers, who surrounded the German Emperor during the years when Germany exercised a species of supremacy on the Continent. One may take as typical of the mind of these persons an entry by Prince Hohenlohe regarding the policy of Germany towards France in 1889. There was at this time some serious question of provoking a war with France, and the main reason for hurrying it forward was apparently the eagerness of the German generalissimo, Count Waldersee, a most influential person at court, to reap the glory which is to be had only by leading armies in the field. There was unluckily no obvious pretext for war, but on the other hand Count Waldersee, who was growing old, was obsessed by the painful reflection, that if the inevitable war were postponed much longer he would be compelled, a superannuated veteran, to witness the triumphs of a younger rival. In the end it was found impossible to provide Count Waldersee with a European war, but to the astonishment of mankind, the Kaiser did, before he reached the age-limit, arrange a punitive expedition to China for his benefit. If he reaped no glory by it, the Chinese will not soon forget his prowess against non-combatants and movable property.

The inner history of the Russo-Japanese War is

an even more instructive revelation of the working of the personal factor in foreign affairs. The facts are fully stated in the translation from the first unexpurgated draft of General Kuropatkin's Memoirs which Mr. George Kennan contributed to *McClure's Magazine* for September, 1908. The causes of the war were the refusal of Russia to observe her pledge to evacuate southern Manchuria, and her stealthy encroachment on the Japanese sphere of influence in Northern Korea. These memoirs show that all the Ministers of the Tsar, Count Lamsdorf (Foreign Secretary), M. Witte (Minister of Finance), and General Kuropatkin (Minister of War) were sincerely disposed to evacuate Manchuria, and no less opposed to any advance towards the Yalu river and Korea. They failed, because the timber enterprise, which was the attraction of the Yalu district, was a court venture. These wealthy forests, made over to a Russian promoter in 1896, when the Emperor of Korea was a fugitive in the Russian Legation at Seoul, had passed into the hands of a courtier named Bezobrazoff, an intimate of the Grand Dukes, the Dowager-Empress and the Tsar. The company which he formed to work his concession had several of these people among its shareholders, and there is little doubt that the Tsar himself was interested to the extent of £200,000. Admiral Alexeieff, a creature of Bezobrazoff's, sent to the Far East as Viceroy, overruled the Ministers at home, and conducted the timber enterprise as an Imperial undertaking. It was neither the Russian people nor the Russian bureaucracy which had determined to keep the Yalu district and to fight

Japan for its possession. The resolution to possess it came from a little group of interested courtiers, who were using the national resources to further their private financial ends.

*　　*　　*　　*　　*

DIPLOMACY AND FINANCE

There can be no science of foreign politics so long as foreign affairs are in the hands of small cliques, among whom personal caprice is liable at any moment to upset calculations of national interest. What, moreover, are national interests ? There is no calculus by which their relative importance is assessed, nor is there any recognised standard by which even democratic states measure the point at which a vast private interest assumes the standing of a national stake. Certain assumptions become a tradition, which is handed on from one generation of diplomatists to another. Such traditions are always plausible. They are constantly repeated, rarely questioned, and their subtle transformation under changing circumstances is apt to go unmarked. Some of these axioms are beyond controversy. The first task of diplomacy is to preserve our national freedom and independence. Second in importance, for this country, comes the duty of preserving the freedom of the seas for our commerce, an interest which is national, not merely because our export trade is vital to us and half the world's carrying trade is in our hands, but also because our food supply depends upon it. Hardly less national is the obligation to further our trade in goods by main-

taining the " open door " for our exports in neutral
markets. Directly or indirectly that is the interest
of the whole community. The real difficulty of
distinguishing between a private and a national
interest begins when we consider the duty of our
diplomacy to " protect " our subjects abroad.
" Protect " is a vague word, which may mean anything from a determination to safeguard our subjects from physical outrage, up to a policy of promoting their efforts to secure concessions. The
word bore its simple meaning in the eighteenth
century, when we went to war with Spain because
Spanish officials in the West Indies had cut
off Captain Jenkins' ear. Modern Imperialism is
concerned with a Jenkins whose ears are seldom in
danger. It is for his investments that he demands
protection. The modern extension of the principle
was first enunciated by Palmerston in an historic
speech in 1850. It seems to hold that a subject
residing or trading abroad is entitled to call upon
the whole resources of diplomacy, backed if necessary by arms, to defend not only his personal safety
but his material interests, if these are threatened by
the people or government of the country in which
he resides or trades. Palmerston was censured by
the House of Lords, violently resisted by the Queen,
and opposed in the Commons by such wise Conservatives as Sir Robert Peel, but he carried popular opinion and party votes for his claim that

> " as the Roman in days of old held himself free
> from indignity when he could say *Civis Romanus
> sum*, so also a British subject, in whatever land
> he may be, shall feel confident that the watchful

eye and the strong arm of England will protect him against injustice and wrong."

The case which Palmerston had chosen for the establishment of this principle was painfully, even absurdly remote from any national British interest. Don Pacifico, a Portuguese Jew, resident in Athens, who in some obscure way had acquired British citizenship, had a fantastic claim for financial compensation against the Greek Government. He refused to sue in the Greek courts, called in British diplomatic aid, and so far succeeded, that a British fleet was sent to the Piraeus with a peremptory demand for a settlement. Palmerston's doctrine, looked at askance in his own day, has become the unchallenged dogma not only of our own, but of every other Great Power. In the heroic age Helen's was the face that launched a thousand ships. In our golden age the face wears more often the shrewd features of some Hebrew financier. To defend the interests of Lord Rothschild and his fellow bondholders, Egypt was first occupied, and then practically annexed by Great Britain. To avenge the murder of a missionary by a Chinese mob, the Germans annexed the town of Kiao-chau, and a district stretching one hundred miles inland—the town, it may be remarked, was noted not merely for its dislike of German missionaries, but also for the fact that it is a very valuable port. To protect investors who had speculated in its debt, a foreign financial control was imposed upon Greece. The claims of various financial adventurers, who had grievances against President Castro's Government, induced Britain and Germany to conduct a naval expedition against Venezuela.

When in Persia a civil war broke out between the Shah and his revolted subjects, Russia, with Sir Edward Grey's assent, claimed and exercised the right to send her troops into Persian territory to protect her subjects from the possible accidents that might befall them in these internal commotions. The comparatively recent history of Turkey tells of a naval expedition undertaken by France to the island of Mytilene to collect a usurious debt due by the Sultan to a pair of Levantine financiers with Italian names (MM. Lorando and Tubini). The extremest case of all is, perhaps, our own South African War. The quarrel between our subjects and Mr. Kruger's Government was extensive, but it turned mainly on two points, the objection of the mining industry to the dynamite monopoly, and the claim of the Outlander community that it should be allowed on easier terms to divest itself of its British citizenship in order to acquire a vote in the Burgher Republic. An odder application of Palmerston's doctrine could hardly be imagined. The *Civis Romanus* conceived it to be his interest to become a barbarian, to weaken the Empire by leaving it, and the Empire actually backed his claim. The law forbids a man to weaken the State by committing suicide, for it is supposed that the subtraction even of one broken life from the sum of its forces is somehow a loss. Here the State actually insisted that British subjects should be encouraged to withdraw their support from the Empire, and it backed its insistence by arms. What the mine-owners really at bottom desired, was cheaper labour, and their effort to acquire political power through the

franchise had no other object. "Good government,"
as one of them reckoned, would mean two and a
half millions a year in dividends. In one way or
another capital which expatriates itself will desire to
control the territory where it is employed. It is
often content with the informal good offices of
diplomacy. In graver cases it demands some form
of foreign control through foreign employees or a
foreign commission. In the Transvaal it thought
for a moment of securing its interests by means of the
votes of a foreign population composed mainly of its
own employees. The same proposal has been put
forward (see p. 123) by Lord Cromer as a method of
reconciling the claims of foreign finance with Egyptian self-government.

Palmerston's doctrine has, in short, become a
pretext which may excuse any and every act of
aggression and interference. The extent to which
it is carried in any given instance depends not so
much on the character of the interest involved and
the nature of the injury which it has suffered, as on
the mood of the Imperial Power, the weakness of
the State assailed, the tolerance of the other Great
Powers, and the amount of influence which the
interest affected can exert upon the diplomacy of the
Power which protects it. The applications of this
doctrine are apt to attract attention only when they
happen to lead to some catastrophe involving the
visible use of force. But for one overt and public
application of force, most modern Empires use
their strength a hundred times in less violent but
equally effectual ways. If a Power coerces once, it
may dictate for some years afterwards without re-

quiring to repeat the lesson. It is the first duty of
diplomacy abroad to protect the interests of its subjects, and these interests are now usually concentrated in the hands of great banks. The banks in
their turn work in concert with the groups of capitalists who are seeking concessions to construct
railways and ports, to instal electric plant, to open
factories, to work mines, to supply armaments or to
subscribe to loans. Palmerston's claim that a
State should protect its subjects from " injustice and
wrong," sounds plausible. But better than cure
is prevention, and the real business of diplomacy is
now rather to support these interests, so that no
" wrong " shall be done them, than to rescue them
by an angry intervention after the wrong has been
done. The methods by which support is given vary
indefinitely, and each Power has its own characteristic technique. Sometimes the financier is merely
introduced and recommended to the notice of a
foreign Government, and this process is clearly sim-
plified when the venture has at its head some noted
social or political figure. A British bank operating
in Egypt chooses Lord Milner as its Chairman. A
bank which aims at serving Turkey has at its head
Sir Ernest Cassel, who was often King Edward's
host. Lord Cowdray, battling in Latin America
against the Standard Oil Trust for concessions, sends
out as his ambassador the late Whip of the Liberal
Party. " Protection " in such cases means often
much more than support against the Government of
the weak and possibly unscrupulous State in which
our financiers are operating. It means also support
against European rivals, who in their turn have

diplomatic backing. In Turkey rival embassies compete like business houses for concessions, loans and orders, and mix inextricably their politics with their finance. The French and German ambassadors in Constantinople engage in an incessant conflict over the right to supply Turkey with armaments from the forges of Creusot or Essen. The banks take their share in the competition, and the usual procedure now is that Turkey is offered a loan by a French or German bank on condition that the proceeds are expended in buying cannon as the case may be from Schneider or Krupp. Austria has been known to make it a condition of concluding a tariff treaty with Servia that she should buy her cannon from the Austrian works at Skoda. Our recent *rapprochement* with Spain, which included a royal marriage, a treaty for the defence of the Spanish coasts, and some protection for Spanish interests in Morocco, was completed by the re-building of the Spanish navy by British firms.

To conduct these complicated negotiations with any prospect of success, the Great Powers are necessarily driven to take a hand in the internal politics of the country which they are assisting their financiers to exploit. We make partisans, for whose coming to power we hope and are occasionally supposed to scheme, and for whose fall we penalise the party which overthrew them. Kiamil Pasha in Turkey and Yuan-shi-kai in China were notoriously Anglophil. They were for the *Times* the only trustworthy reformers in their respective lands, and the disinterested opinion of the City, a nice judge in such matters, paid homage to their " Liberalism."

When they fell from power, the *Times* promptly despaired of the future of Turkey and China. It happened, for example, after Yuan-shi-kai's last fall from power, that a loan and railway concession in Canton, worth some £3,000,000, went to a German instead of a Franco-British syndicate. Our Ambassador at once protested against the signing of the contract, and when his protest failed, the correspondent of the *Times* in Peking predicted that the consequence would be to " alienate the sympathy of the British Government," on whose " support " in her various diplomatic troubles, China need no longer count. (April 9, 1909.) We expected, that is to say, to be paid in economic favours for our political support. In plain words, we sell it. How normal this official backing of the concession-hunter is now felt to be may be deduced from the quiet sentence in which the *Times* describes the present state of things.[1]   " The field," it writes, " is thrown open to private enterprise seeking to obtain railway, industrial or similar concessions, and the

---

[1] P.S.—Since this chapter was written, the whole system of diplomatic support for concession-hunters has been avowed by Sir Edward Grey. Speaking in the Foreign Office debate (July 10, 1914), he said : ' I regard it as our duty, wherever *bona fide* British capital is forthcoming in any part of the world, and is applying for concessions to which there are no valid political objections, that we should give it the utmost support we can, and endeavour to convince the foreign Government concerned that it is to its interest as well as to our own to give the concessions for railways, and so forth, to British firms, who carry them out at reasonable prices and in the best possible way."

Government of any country is free to support its
nationals in their application for such concessions
as are adjudged to have merit." There is apparently no lack of merit among British proposals, for
we learn that Messrs. Pauling (represented by Lord
Ffrench) have obtained a railway concession, while
Messrs. Lever, Brunner Mond & Crosfield have combined to found a vast factory which will supply all
China with soap. These concessions, as the *Times*
says of the railways, must be meritorious since our
Government supported them ; and it must have
supported them, for otherwise they could not have
been obtained. Such instances as these bring us
sharply back to the enquiry from which we started.
What is a national interest ? How in particular
are the interests of the people of these islands advanced when a group of Liberal capitalists succeeds
in manufacturing in China, with cheap native labour,
soap which used to be produced at Warrington at
Trade Union rates and exported to China in British
ships ? It is possible that the electors of Warrington and Port Sunlight might not feel that their
taxes were advantageously employed in " protect-
ing " such enterprises as this. But apart from this
curious instance, destined in all probability to
become increasingly common, the whole practice
of using diplomacy (with the fleet behind it) to pro-
cure concessions for British capitalists raises questions which have never been considered by Parliament or public opinion. It is a wholly modern
extension of the rights of the *Civis Romanus*, and
an extension which usually benefits no one but the
capitalist. But to what ideas of nationality have

we sunk, when the people of China may be told, that they, millions of human beings struggling towards self-government reaching blindly out towards Western ideals, menaced by the aggressions of predatory empires, and in need of every kind of brotherly aid, will forfeit the good will of a Government which in its turn represents millions of quite disinterested and moderately benevolent human beings in these islands, if it does not give a concession to a British bank or a British contractor ? The whole practice is a degradation of national intercourse and an offence as much to our own national self-respect as to the independence of the Chinese. It is moreover a perversion of the objects for which the State exists, that the power and prestige, for which all of us pay, should be used to win profits for private adventurers. The hunting of concessions abroad and the exploitation of the potential riches of weak states and dying empires is fast becoming an official enterprise, a national business. We are engaged in Imperial trading, with the flag as its indispensable asset, but the profits go exclusively into private pockets.

This Imperial trading has its questionable aspects from the standpoints of the British public and also of the nation with which our diplomacy deals. But it has another consequence which is no less serious. It brings us continually into conflict with the diplomacy of other Powers which are engaged in competing for the same concessions on behalf of their own financiers. It is not the rivalry of merchants engaged in selling goods which makes ill-feeling between nations. The merchant rarely invokes diplomatic aid to enable him to keep or secure a customer. The trouble arises only over concessions, loans and monopolies which bring the European financier into relations with a foreign Government. The rivalry is indeed felt to be so intolerable and so risky, that modern diplomacy now seeks wherever possible to avoid it, by mapping out exclusive areas of exploitation, " penetration," or " influence." When a claim to a national monopoly of this kind is once recognised by all the competing Powers, the result is of course to diminish the friction between them. The concord of Europe is saved at the expense of the independence of the exploited State—for a Power which holds such a monopoly is able at once to dictate to the local Government, and it usually manages to " control " its finances and to " organise " its police. The partition of Persia is the most notorious instance of this development. Our rather shadowy claim to exclusive " influence " in the Yangtse Valley, the richest area of China, has not yet been admitted by other Powers, and it may one day cost us a struggle to enforce it. In Asiatic Turkey the informal demarcation of spheres has gone further than in China. One may say vaguely that Syria is French, Anatolia German, Armenia Russian, and that Mesopotamia and Arabia are British, but there is much overlapping and no general agreement about boundaries ; and Italy, if the partition is long postponed, may be able to make good a claim to Cilicia. A new phase of this competition has just developed in Latin America, with an interpretation of the Monroe Doctrine put forward by President Wilson which seems to mean that no European capitalists may henceforward obtain concessions in the American Continent without encountering American opposition. President Wilson is an idealist, and what he personally meant was that the granting of any concessions to foreigners is a danger to the independence of the State which accords them. In practice, however, such a doctrine would probably mean opposition to European and support for American financiers. If it is to be strictly enforced, it would mean that the United States claims the whole of Latin America as its exclusive sphere of economic penetration. In that doctrine Europe is not likely to acquiesce, and America may soon be the field of a conflict as acute as any that Turkey and China have witnessed. Diplomacy in these rivalries becomes the tool of the vast aggregations of modern capital in oil trusts, steel trusts and money trusts, and wherever rival combinations of capital are competing, as British and American oil companies compete in Central America, the reaction will be felt in the relations of their Governments. The struggle for a balance of power is in effect a struggle to map out these exclusive areas of financial penetration. To this end are the working classes in all countries taxed and regimented in conscript armies ; for armies and fleets are the material arguments behind this financial diplomacy.

*   *   *   *   *

THE EXPORT OF CAPITAL

To a community like Russia, which is still in a primitive agricultural stage of development, actual

conquest is the aim with which armies are strengthened and diplomacy conducted. To the landed class,
which alone rules in these communities, broad
acres and numerous serfs are the most natural
expressions of wealth. It conquers and arms to
acquire estates. With the development of manufactures and oversea trade, these cruder views are
discarded. The landed class retains for a time its
hereditary bias to think in terms of actual possession.
But little by little the commercial standpoint
modifies the attitude even of the aristocracy. A
trading community like Early Victorian England,
which can still profitably employ all its capital in
its mills and ships, becomes indifferent to the
acquisition of territory, and even tends to regard
the colonies previously acquired as a useless encum-
brance. That was the normal state of mind of our
commercial classes during the middle years of last
century. They dealt in goods, and in order to sell
goods abroad, it was not necessary either to colonise
or to conquer. To this phase belongs the typical
foreign policy of Liberalism, with its watchwords
of peace, non-intervention, and free trade. The
third phase, the modern phase, begins when capital
has accumulated in large fortunes, when the rate
of interest at home begins to fall, and the discovery
is made that investments abroad in unsettled countries with populations more easily exploited than
our own, offer swifter and bigger returns. It is
the epoch of concession hunting, of coolie labour, of
chartered companies, of railway construction, of
loans to semi-civilised Powers, of the " opening up "
of " dying empires." At this phase the export of

capital has become to the ruling class more important and more attractive than the export of goods. The Manchester School disappears, and even the Liberals accept Imperialism. It is, however, no longer the simple and barbaric Imperialism of the agricultural stage. Its prime motive is not to acquire land, though in the end it often lapses into this elementary form of conquest. It aims rather at pegging out spheres of influence and at that sort of stealthy conquest which is called " pacific penetration." The old Imperialism levied tribute ; the new Imperialism lends money at interest.

The typical exponents of Liberal foreign policy, notably Cobden, were perfectly conscious of the connection between their economics and their international ideal. Their policy was primarily a statement of the relations which ought to subsist between Lancashire and its foreign markets. Lancashire had outgrown its purely predatory phase in earlier generations. It had destroyed its trade rivals in Ireland and India by means of tariffs. It could now afford to ignore the possibility of competition. It stood therefore for free trade and the open door the world over. It had nothing to gain from Imperialism or conquest. One can sell cotton to negroes or Chinamen without troubling to conquer them. To attempt to conquer, where one can trade without conquest, is a sheer squandering of national resources. Even the colonies were of no obvious use, and might, if they chose, follow the example of the United States amid the good-will and indifference of the mother country, which would still buy and sell in their ports if they became independent. Seeking no conquests for itself, this School objected to the conquests of other empires which were apt to disturb trade, to close " open doors," and to interfere with its clients.   Secure in its riches and its constitutional liberties and conscious of its virtues, the Manchester School desired to see the rest of the world reorganise itself on a British model.   Free Trade was a universal dogma ; Parliamentary rule a cure-all for every civil mischief, and the Protestant religion a faith to be inculcated the world over by Bible Societies and missionary organisations.   Its propaganda was, however, passive.   Liberal England was in the main content to watch the progress of Continental movements towards national and constitutional liberty with benevolent neutrality. It felt no such impulse to liberate the world as had animated revolutionary France.   Meetings were held for Garibaldi and Kossuth, but it was Louis Napoleon and not Free Trade England who used his armies to drive the Austrians out of Italy.   Palmerston would assuredly have gone much beyond benevolent neutrality, but the general feeling of the middle-classes was against active intervention in the affairs of the Continent.   Our fathers had their sympathies and their opinions, and it was their pride to express them boldly.   But even on behalf of a " small people rightly struggling to be free," crusading had no part in the policy of a mercantile community.

It was not a heroic creed, but it made for peace, it discreetly promoted liberty, and it held in check the spirit of conquest and militarism.   War it regarded as waste, and armaments as unproductive

expenditure. Exchange, fairly and honestly conducted, is a reciprocal benefit, and it was the best
aspect of this historic Liberalism that it cultivated
no spirit of grudging or envious rivalry. If other
nations prospered, the chances were that they would
be for that reason better customers for our exports,
and better producers of our raw material. On the
basis of this enlightened selfishness there grew up
a real spirit of benevolence. Interests were involved
in all these calculations, but they were much more
nearly national interests than those which Imperialism obeys. If a cotton-manufacturer exports his
wares to Egypt, the transaction is a gain in some
degree to large numbers of persons in both countries
—to the workers in Lancashire, to the seamen who
carry the wares, and to the peasants in Egypt.
But if a financier lends money to the Khedive of
Egypt, no direct share of the profits comes to the
English worker in wages, while the Egyptian peasant
is heavily taxed to find the interest. In producing
goods a mercantile community has constantly in
its mind the existence and well-being of its clients.
A bad harvest, a famine, an earthquake will have
an adverse effect upon trade, and, above all, political
troubles and misgovernment will in the end im-
poverish the foreign clients of the English mill. Such
considerations as this made indirectly for freedom
and for humanity. The concession-hunter who
obtained the right to invest his capital in Turkey
by lavishing bribes on the courtiers of 'Abdul Hamid,
was necessarily indifferent to the welfare of the
Turkish nation. Indeed it was simpler for him to
have a corrupt central despotism to deal with. It

cost him something in bribes, but on the other hand no free or national Government would have given its assent to the unconscionable bargains which European capitalists were able during some thirty years to drive at Constantinople. Lancashire, trading, as it does, mainly through Armenian merchants and agents, realised very clearly that bad government meant bad trade. German finance, mainly interested in banks and railways, preferred to have the despot's goodwill. English commerce objected very strongly to the massacre of its best salesmen and customers. That is possibly a somewhat crude way of representing the influence of interest on sentiment. It would perhaps be fairer to say that commerce in goods is no obstacle to the natural play of sentiments of humanity and goodwill in international politics. Free-trading England was firmly convinced that liberty was necessary to good government and good government to prosperity. Desiring the prosperity of its customers, it wished that its diplomacy should promote their freedom so far as prudence and safety allowed. Liberalism was at both ends a popular policy. The interest of a whole nation of producers and traders was its concern. On the interest of a whole nation of foreign consumers its thoughts were naturally bent. To it peoples rather than territories or governments were the reality. Peoples buy cotton, governments only want loans.

These economic considerations were no doubt seldom consciously present to the minds of statesmen. Still less were they often stated in speeches or leading articles. Oratory preferred, of course, to take higher ground, and to assume that politics are conducted on a basis of abstract right and disinterested sentiment. Nor need we suppose that the disinterested sentiments expounded by such idealistic Liberals as Gladstone were coloured by such calculations as these. But it was these calculations which gave the sentiments their opportunity and their vogue. A prophet of the religion of humanity would have preached in vain either to a feudal caste which thought of the world overseas as so much land to conquer, or to financial groups which thought of it simply as a field for their investments. An audience of manufacturers on the other hand was probably flattered to find that its own pedestrian habits of thoughts coincided so nearly with the dictates of an elevated altruism. It was quite ready to believe that the Armenians were its suffering brethren, because it already regarded them as its customers. Napoleon called us a nation of shopkeepers. Shopkeepers have this merit, that they are bound to desire the prosperity of their clients. The usurer on the other hand is often best served by the bankruptcy of his victim— provided of course that diplomacy will help him to foreclose.

The strength of the old free-trading, anti-Imperialist Liberalism lay in this fortunate duality. It combined philanthropy with business. It believed in freedom for other races and in opportunity for its own trade. These two things, so far from being incompatible, are usually found together, and may quite honestly be sought together. The Congo Reform Movement is perhaps the aptest illustration

of their consistency. The originators of this movement and its supporters in the churches and in
Parliament were of course, entirely disinterested.
They would undoubtedly have worked with
exactly the same self-sacrificing zeal if no
question of traders' rights had been involved.
They were thinking solely of the miseries of the
natives whom King Leopold and his financiers
exploit. The movement is a survival in an epoch
of Imperialism of the spirit which made an end of
the slave trade. But this movement would never
have attained the success which it has won, nor
would it have impressed itself to such a degree upon
the Foreign Office, had it confined itself to humanitarian arguments. Its devoted originator, Mr.
E. D. Morel, was wise enough to lay stress on the
commercial argument and to seek the support of
the Chambers of Commerce. It secured the attention
of the Foreign Office partly because its programme
included a demand for better facilities for British
trade.[1] The whole Congo affair is a perfect illustration
of the main thesis of Liberal foreign policy—that free
trade in goods is an interest consistent with humanity.
The beginning and end of Congo misrule consisted
in this—that a group of Belgian financiers, with
King Leopold at its head, carved out this vast territory into domains and concession-areas. In each
of these the King or the companies enjoyed a monopoly. They did not trade, for there was no exchange
of goods. They spent a certain capital upon

[1] See Mr. E. D. Morel's *King Leopold's Rule in Africa*
(Heinemann, 1904), pp. x., xi., and his *Red Rubber* (Unwin,
1906), p. 205.

river gunboats, the building of stations and railways and the arming of savage native levies. In
return they claimed as their own the land and its
produce (that is to say the rubber), and under the
guise of a labour tax, set the natives to collect it.
This was not trade. It was high Imperialist finance
in a peculiarly brutal form. Incidentally they
excluded from their monopoly areas all foreign
traders, and indeed there was no possibility of trade,
since nothing was left for the natives to sell. The
only thing which they could have sold was the
rubber, and this was appropriated by the financiers
in Belgium. The standpoint of the Liverpool
merchant was an entirely proper one. He is a trader
and a shipper. He wanted to do business with the
Congo natives as he does with the natives of the
Gold Coast. He would have exported cottons in
return for rubber. The Belgian monopoly stood in
his way, and he argued, fairly enough (1) that the
monopoly was a breach of treaty rights and (2) that
its consequences were hideous to the natives themselves. One need not enquire what was the relative
importance of the two issues to the Foreign Office
and to Liverpool. The point to note is that in
pursuing a traditional free trade policy, and in
backing British trading interests, the Foreign Office
was really serving the cause of the natives. They
could not become prosperous or free until they were
delivered from this monopoly ; incidentally their
prosperity and freedom would benefit our West
African trade. Here the essential antagonism
between the financier who uses his capital to exploit
native labour, and the trader who uses his capital

to develop a system of exchange between natives and Europeans, stands clearly revealed. Neither the trader nor the financier is disinterested. But the interests of the one are as consistent with those of the native, as the interests of the other are inimical to them. John Stuart Mill roundly denied that one nation can ever govern another ; a nation may, however, keep another people as a human cattle farm. The Congo was not even a well-managed farm. It was destined eventually to become a colony of the Belgian State. While it remained the property of King Leopold, his one concern was to extract from it as rapidly as possible the millions which he invested on real estate, squandered on showy palaces and triumphal arches, or spent on the pursuit of beauty in a frankly personal form. As for the companies their shares rose while the native population declined. Lord Cromer once declared that the unwavering pursuit of interests assumed to be national is the sole object of a foreign policy, and yet he assisted the Congo movement. There was no inconsistency here. The foreign policy of a trading nation may be consistent with freedom, so long as its main interest is export and exchange of goods. It is with the export of capital that Imperialism begins. There is no transition from disinterestedness to what the Germans call " real politics " in the passage from the Manchester School to modern Imperialism. Each alike rests on a calculation of interests. What has changed is the nature of the export

A critic belonging to the Manchester School might object that this antithesis between the export of goods and the export of capital is exaggerated and even false. The process of exporting capital, he would argue, cannot be isolated from the process of exporting goods. Lend money to the Argentine to build a railway, and what you really export is not gold but rails, while the interest comes back not as gold but as meat. This is of course as true as it is elementary, though the process is rarely so simple as this. What really takes place is a rather complicated series of transactions, carried out on an elaborate credit basis, at each stage of which the financier and the promoter makes his commissions and his additional profits. The French Périer Bank the other day lent a million pounds to the Turkish Government, which it used to pay the first instalment of the purchase price of a Dreadnought cruiser built in Newcastle. A few days later it was announced that the same bank, obviously as a part of its commission, had obtained a concession for a railway from Smyrna to the Dardanelles. While we must admit that the export of capital could not be carried out without some movement of goods, there is still a sharp distinction to be made between the financier's transaction and simple exchange of goods from the standpoint of the sociology of class. Commerce carried on upon an elaborate structure of credit is more profitable to the investing classes than the simpler exchanges which take place between nations on an equal level of economic development. If we send Welsh coal to France, and receive artificial flowers in exchange, capital makes two profits —the English colliery owner's profit, and the French sweater's profit. But if we lend money to the

Argentine, and with it she buys rails here, and afterwards sends out meat to be sold here so that the interest on the loan may be paid, then capital has made three profits—the English steel trade's profit, the Argentine meat trade's profit and the English banker's and investor's profit. It is this third profit which our leisured class chiefly values, and to develop the sort of commerce which requires this credit basis, that is to say commerce with weaker debtor nations, is the object of Imperialism.

There remains the question of how far or in what sense this constant acquisition of economic opportunity by political pressure which is called Imperialism can be justified by any kind of national bookkeeping, however sordid. Does the whole body of taxpayers profit by it to an extent commensurate with the sacrifices which they make to maintain the army and the fleet which are its ultimate sanctions ? Sir Robert Giffen, a Conservative statistician of unrivalled authority, has brought together the figures required for the study of this question, and Mr. J. A. Hobson has analysed them fully and clearly in his masterly work on " Imperialism," one of the most notable contributions of our time to the scientific study of contemporary politics. How far then does Imperialism promote trade, in the sense of the only kind of trade which can be considered a diffused and relatively national interest, the exchange of goods. The essential facts may be set out somewhat thus, for the period of expansion with which Sir Robert Giffen deals, the last quarter of last century:—

The area of our Empire in this period was increased by about one-third.

The national income rose during this period by about one-fifth, or 20 per cent. per head of the population.

This increase of income was not due to a corresponding increase of our external trade. Measured indeed in so many pounds per head of the population of these islands, the annual value of our external trade slightly dwindled (from £19 19s. 3d. during the five years 1870–4, to £19 7s. 10d. during the four years 1895–8).

In this external trade, the colonies occupy, relatively, a slightly less important place at the end of the period, than they did at the beginning.

The colonies themselves have become less exclusively dependent on us, than they were when the period of expansion began.

The progressive element in our trade has been our exchange with foreign countries and neutral markets.

Clearly, then, in so far as Imperialism means the acquisition of territory, it does not justify itself as a means of making or keeping " trade," if trade means the exchange of goods. Trade then supplies no explanation of Imperialism.

If trade fails as an explanation of modern Imperialistic expansion, emigration has even less to do with it. Of all the territory acquired or occupied by us during the most active period of expansion, only the Boer Republics are fitted to be a permanent habitation for a white race, but even in them English labour rarely makes a home. It is not a fact that Great Britain is over-populated: Its population is less dense than that of certain areas of Germany and the Netherlands, and we are all realising that a drastic policy of land reform would enable us to " colonise England." Statistics show that emigration during this period of active Imperialism has steadily diminished, and it is still true that half of it goes, not to colonies under our own flag, but to the United States. The same phenomena may be witnessed in Germany. There also the population is increasing both by natural growth and by immigration, but emigration has diminished, and no appreciable number of emigrants goes to the new German colonies, which are all unsuitable for settlement by a white race. But it is the recent history of France which shows with luminous clearness how factitious is the growth of modern Imperialism, how small is the group which promotes it or profits by it, how purely capitalistic it is in its origins and motives. No nation ever had more clearly marked out for it, as its destiny, the happy fate of " cultivating its own garden." France has no teeming population for which she must find colonies. To her case the metaphor of the beehive and the swarm has no application. Her population is stationary, and would actually dwindle were it not maintained by the influx of alien immigration. Her " garden " is fertile, her climate various. Nor does her national genius lead her to make gross produce for which uncultured peoples offer the natural market. Her speciality is to make ingenious and beautiful things for civilised men. These wares are not bulky, and therefore she needs neither a great mercantile marine nor a great navy to protect it. But her industry and her habits of thrift cause her to accumulate

capital with immense rapidity. Had she employed
that capital at home, the rate of interest must have
fallen to an almost nominal level. To the possessing classes foreign investment became therefore the
absorbing concern. Save in Russia, the struggle
to acquire land for purposes of genuine colonisation
came to an end with the Napoleonic wars which
gave us South Africa.

What then is the economic meaning of Imperialism?
It is only when we turn from the figures of trade to
the figures which measure the export of capital, that
statistics begin to correspond with our expansion,
and our book-keeping to bear some relation to our
aggressions. Mr. Mulhall calculated for the *Dictionary
of Political Economy* that our foreign and colonial
investments grew between 1882 and 1893 at the
prodigious rate of 74 per cent. per annum. Sir
Robert Giffen estimated our profit on foreign and
colonial investments in the year 1899 at between
90 and 100 millions sterling. The total is rising
rapidly.[1] Ten years later, as Sir George Paish
stated in a paper which he read to the Royal

[1] P.S.—Since this book was written, an elaborate technical study has appeared by Mr. C. K. Hobson (*The Export
of Capital*, Constable) which supplies invaluable statistical
and historical material. Taken over a wide stretch of
time, some part of this export may admit of a certain
economic defence (see p. 233), but this defence ignores its
reaction on international relations.

In his Budget speech (1915) Mr. Lloyd George estimated
the total of our capital invested outside these islands as
£4,000,000,000. The annual interest is about £200,000,000.
This amounts to about one-twelfth of our whole national
income (£2,400,000,000). It cannot be much less than a
fourth of the income of the middle and upper classes,
for the total income subject to tax is £900,000,000.

Statistical Society, our profits from foreign and colonial investments amounted to 140 millions. One no longer enquires why the unaggressive, anti-militarist, anti-Imperialist Liberalism of the free-trading England which was content to take Cobden as its guide, has given place to the expansionist, militarist, financially minded Imperialism of to-day. Regarded as a national undertaking Imperialism does not pay. Regarded as a means of assuring unearned incomes to the governing class, it emphatically does pay. It is not true that trade follows the flag. It is true that the flag follows investments. The trader is in a sense a nomad. If one market begins to fail him, he turns to another. If a country to which he used to export goods is torn by civil war or threatened with bankruptcy, he does not call for intervention. He goes elsewhere, or waits for better times. The investor on the other hand has acquired " a stake " in some foreign country, and anchored his fortunes irrevocably upon it. Unless he is prepared to lose his stake, he must, if the country in question goes bankrupt or is threatened by civil war or revolution, call in the Imperial arm to defend him. It is sometimes said that our navy is an " insurance " for our mercantile shipping, since it protects it from piracy or from capture in time of war. It would be more accurate to say that both our navy and our army overseas are an insurance, provided and maintained by the nation at large, for the capital owned abroad by our leisured class.

Here at length we have discovered the stake

which an armed Imperialism watches and seeks to
enlarge. The fear of war, the struggle for a balance
of power, the competition in armaments which in
Sir Edward Grey's phrase threatens to " submerge
civilisation," the universal nightmare amid which
we are " rattling into barbarism "—all this is seen to
be a characteristic product of modern finance and
modern capitalism. It makes the slum and it
makes the *Dreadnought*. One may go further. It
makes the *Dreadnought* because it made the slum.
Imperialism is simply the political manifestation of
the growing tendency of capital accumulated in
the more civilised industrial countries to export
itself to the less civilised and the less settled. To
secure itself, it seeks to subdue or to " civilise "
its new fields of investment—as it understands
" civilisation." In crossing the seas and entering
new lands, it must take with it the machinery
which renders the process of capitalist exploitation
profitable and secure—its laws of debtor and creditor, its police for the protection of property, its
armaments and its administrators.

Why, then, is it that capital seeks to export
itself ? There are many cogent reasons abroad.
At home the fundamental fact is the rapid accumulation of surplus capital. It grows in the hands of
trust magnates, bankers, and ground landlords more
rapidly than the demand for it at home. It tries
continually to get itself employed at home, and the
result is that periodic over-production, which shows
itself in a " slump " of trade and a crisis of unemployment. Capital, like. labour, has its periods of
unemployment, and its favourite method of meeting

them is emigration. When rates of interest fall at home, it begins to look abroad for something at once remunerative, and not too risky, and it is to diplomacy that it turns to protect it from risks. If, further, we go on to ask why capital cannot get itself profitably employed at home as fast as it is accumulated, the answer is briefly that its too rapid accumulation has stood in the way of a simultaneous development of the consumers who might have given it employment. Had a little more of the profits of a trade " boom " gone to labour, and a little less to capital, it is manifest that labour would have had more money to spend, and the new surplus capital —less considerable in amount—might have been employed in meeting this new demand. The share- holders of a Lancashire mill make their 35 per cent. in a good year—such cases occur. Had they and their fellows been content with something less than 35 per cent., and added to wages what they sub- tracted from dividends, the workers all over the country would have been spending more than before on the necessaries and the luxuries which these mills provide. There need then have been no slump, and the new capital might even have been used to make more cotton goods for the home market. But the shareholders insist on their 35 per cent., and the workers are foolish enough, or weak enough, to let them take it. What, then, is the too fortunate shareholder to do with his money ? He spends as much as he can on motor-cars and grouse-moors, town-houses and domestic display. But even to this, unless he is a mere spendthrift, there is a limit. He, therefore, invests what he is pleased

to call his " savings "—meaning by that term the
money which he has saved from other people's
wages, and failed to expend on his own pleasures.
The home market is " glutted "—which means that
the masses have nothing more to spend. He, therefore, looks abroad. An Egyptian Khedive wants
money to squander on ballet-girls and palaces and
operas. Japan wants money to build ironclads.
Russia wants money to pay for the repression of her
subjects. Or perhaps gold has been discovered in
Ashanti, or the niggers of West Africa have developed
a taste for gin. Into such enterprises goes the
capital that cannot find employment at home. The
reason for the too rapid export of capital abroad
is, in short, the bad division of wealth at home. For
there is " work " enough in these islands to " employ " more than all their surplus capital, if only the
consuming power of the masses could be increased.
Raise wages, raise with them the standard of comfort, and this restless capital need no longer wander
abroad. There ought to be enough for it to do at
home. It might build working-class dwellings in
reclaimed slums instead of palaces for an Egyptian
Khedive. It might " colonise England " instead of
speculating in tropical land. It might exert itself
in providing the English labourer with a more
frequent change of clean shirts for his back and clean
sheets for his bed, instead of enabling the Russian
Government to build in Russian dockyards at an
extravagant cost warships which it does not need,
to be navigated by sailors whose only hope is
mutiny and revolt. Capital conducts itself to-day
much as the primitive agriculturist behaves. It

must be for ever conquering fresh territory and bringing new fields under culture, simply because it does
not know how to make a good use of the fields it
already possesses.   The primitive farmer—in Russia,
for example—must become a conqueror, because he
has never learned to apply manure.   The capitalist
must rush abroad, because he will not fertilise the
demand for more commodities at home by the
simple expedient of raising wages.

The other reason which is most potent in inducing
capital to flow abroad is the elementary fact that
coloured labour can be more ruthlessly exploited
than white.   The supposed risks of a foreign investment, moreover, enable the capitalist to charge
usurious interest.   It follows that on both grounds
the profits to be made abroad are greater than the
profits to be made at home.

In one of the classics of the Imperialist muse, Mr.
Rudyard Kipling remarks that there are no ten
commandments east of Suez.   That may be an
attraction to Tommy Atkins.   The capitalist hears
the East 'a calling mainly because there are no
Factory Acts east of Suez.   That was literally true of
Egypt while Lord Cromer reigned.[1]   In India there
is a beginning of factory legislation, badly drafted
and ill-enforced.   The conditions which prevail were
recently investigated by a Factory Labour Commission.   From the evidence collected by it, I cite
the following facts : [2]

Operatives in ginning factories have on occasion

[1] See page 114.
[2] See especially the able report of the medical member,
Dr. T. M. Nair, dated Simla, May, 1908,

to work 17 and 18 hours a day, and in rice and flour mills 20 or even 22 hours.

In printing works men have had to work 22 hours a day for seven consecutive days.

In the cotton mills of Bombay the hours regularly worked are in some cases 13, in others 14, and others 14½ a day from one end of a month to the other.

In Agra the regular hours are 15¼ in summer, and in winter (because light costs money) 13¾.

The jute mills of Calcutta work, with few exceptions, 15 hours a day.

The wages of an adult male mill operative, working 13, 14 or 15 hours a day, vary from 15 to 20 rupees a month (*i.e.*, from £1 to £1 6s. 8d.). Labour, in other words (even if we admit that its low grade of skill balances the long hours), is therefore four or five times as cheap in Bombay and Calcutta as in Manchester and Dundee. That is one cogent reason why capital exports itself. If the labour were only more abundant and more skilled, there would be no limit to this exportation of capital.

Another great inducement is the ease with which in countries like Turkey or China a nation can, in plain words, be robbed. It was while travelling on a Turkish railway that this elementary fact came home to me. It seemed as though the line had laid itself across the countryside in the track of some writhing serpent. It curled in sinuous folds, it described enormous arcs, it bent and doubled so that a passing train resembled nothing so much as a kitten in pursuit of its own tail. Yet the country was a vast level plain. There were neither mountains nor rivers to avoid. Save for the obligation of

serving towns in its course, most engineers in planning such a railway would simply have taken a ruler
and drawn a straight line across the map. And oddly
enough this railway did not seem to serve any visible
town. Indeed, a plausible theory of its gyrations
and its undulations might have been that it was
desperately trying to dodge the towns. Stations,
indeed, there were, but they were at every conceivable
distance from the centres of population—one, two,
or even five miles away. The explanation was
simple enough when one heard it. The railway
had indeed been constructed by a private company,
and was owned by this company. But the concession included what is called a kilometric guarantee.
In order to induce the European financiers—who
all the while were bribing and competing to obtain
the favour—to perform the onerous work of " opening up Turkey," the Government agreed to guarantee
to the fortunate company an assured profit, reckoned
at so much on every mile or kilometre of rails which
it laid down. Hence the astounding performances of
the line in crossing the level plains, where rails can
be laid down cheaply. Every unnecessary curve
means so many miles added to the total length of
the line, and so many hundreds or thousands of
pounds to its annual guaranteed profits. It avoids the
towns because it has no interest in catering for traffic
or serving the general good. Whether it carries
one passenger or a hundred, whether it runs two
trains a week or several in a day, the financial result
is the same—a fixed profit on every mile. The concession, of course, cost something fairly considerable
in bribes, but for that modest outlay how rich is the

return ! Nor is this the end. In order to make certain that the Turkish Government will pay this annual tribute, the tithes of the luckless provinces through which it passes are mortgaged. Be the season good or bad, whether famine rages or massacre decimates, and whatever the deficit in Constantinople itself may be, so much of the tithes of grain are annually set aside, a first charge on the whole amount, to assure the punctual payment of this debt. And, further, since the financiers know only too well how corrupt Turkish officials are, the collection of this mortgaged revenue is placed in the hands of some European official responsible ultimately to the great Powers. Behind him are the embassies, and behind the embassies are the fleets of all Europe, which would steam at a few hours' notice to Turkish waters, if there were any delay or hesitation in paying over the revenues mortgaged to European railway companies or to the holders of Turkish bonds. Diplomacy and armaments are, in a word, employed to enforce the unconscionable and usurious bargains which Baron Hirsch and his imitators have struck, by means of bribery with Turkish Ministers whose hands no honourable man would condescend to shake. The Turkish peasant earns the tithe at one end of this international process of exploitation ; the European workman pays for the fleet which is its sanction at the other. The most ingenious aspect of the whole transaction is that the financiers extort a high rate of interest on the ground that Turkey is a disturbed and more or less insolvent country in which no investments are safe, and then contrive with the aid of diplomacy and the financial control to obtain for their enterprise a security which no investments possess in older countries. In China, in Egypt, and in Persia the same magic is repeated. Unaided capital and private enterprise could not achieve this magical transformation. It is private enterprise backed by diplomacy and armaments which works the miracle.

This is, in brief, the answer to the question why capital shows so marked a tendency to export itself abroad. On the one hand, capital accumulates in a civilised country so fast that the standard of living of the working classes, and their demands as consumers, do not keep pace with it. On the other hand it seeks abroad for labour which can be even more easily and ruthlessly exploited than that of Western lands. These are the two economic roots of Imperialism. To complete our survey of the motives of " real politics," it is necessary to glance at two powerful but secondary interests which Imperialism calls into action as it develops. There is first of all the social pressure due to the fact that Imperialism makes careers for " younger sons." Distant possessions have to be administered, and native levies must be officered. Even in James Mill's time—and few men knew India better—this was so obvious that he defined the empire as a system of out-door relief for the upper classes. A peer may hope for anything from a viceroy's almost regal glory to the decent splendours that attend the governor of some minor colony. The posts in the Army and the Civil Services have long been so numerous that they are opened to the sons of the prosperous middle classes. To these people India and Egypt have acquired at

last a real meaning—they are the places where a
son, a brother, or at the least a cousin, is " doing
well." Every demand for self-government in India
or Egypt is a blow at the vested interests of that comfortable family in Kensington or Yorkshire. Every
revolt threatens, it may be, the life of their nearest
and dearest. There must be tens of thousands of
families, all relatively wealthy, influential and well
educated, to whom the sudden ending of the Empire
would mean financial ruin and social extinction.
The larger the Empire grows, the more numerous
are the posts which it has to offer. The well-known
facts about India supply some measure of this
enormous force, half-social, half-economic, which
makes for Imperialism. The annual drain of wealth
from India, the indirect tribute which it pays to the
ruling class at home, is believed to amount to about
thirty millions sterling, consisting of the interest on
capital sunk in India or lent to India, of pensions
paid to ex-Anglo-Indians now resident at home,
and of remittances sent home by Anglo-Indians
resident in India. This sum is, of course, in great
part a payment for real services rendered by Englishmen to India, but the rate of remuneration is high,
and the services are sometimes such as Indians do
not desire and often such as natives could more
cheaply perform. It differs from similar payments
made to capitalists, officials and officers at home
chiefly in this, that it is spent not in India but in a
foreign country. In that sense it is a tribute, a
sum of wealth annually withdrawn from India and
spent for the advantage of Englishmen in England.
When Imperialists argue that our rule is providen-

tially necessary to India, it is well to remember that their judgment on such a point is biassed by the fact that our rule in India is profitable to ourselves. Enquire why it is that, despite the eulogies on the martial virtues and the proved loyalty of Sikhs and Moslems, native Indians are not allowed to hold commissions in the Indian army above subaltern rank, and the only candid answer will be that the closing of these posts to the young men of the English upper and middle classes would not be tolerated by public opinion at home.   The same influences have restricted the efforts made by reforming viceroys to admit a larger proportion of Indians to the Civil Service.   The real obstacle to their employment in its higher branches is not so much the supposed weakness of Indian character, as the interest of the educated class in England.

*   *   *   *

THE TRADE IN WAR

The influence of another powerful economic factor upon the growth of Imperialism has always been suspected, and it has lately been the subject of careful study, both in our own country and in Germany. If the pressure of the armament firms can hardly drive a nation into war, it may affect the scale of preparation, and set the fashion in costly methods and engines of warfare. A spirited or apprehensive foreign policy (the two words mean in this connection the same thing) involves an increase of armaments ; this increase creates a great industry, which naturally uses the whole of its influence, in the press, in society

and in Parliament, to stimulate the demand for
further armaments. The facts are now so well known,
thanks to debates in the Reichstag and to three
illuminating pamphlets [1] by capable writers which
have lately been published in this country, that it
may suffice to give here a brief summary of what is
generally known. The trade in armaments has
evolved along the familiar lines of capitalistic concentration. Competition has been nearly eliminated
among the British firms, and what is more curious
still, the relations of the chief armament firms the
world over betray a certain international solidarity
and some rudimentary organisation. There is not
yet an armament trust, as there is a steel trust and
an oil trust, but there is a measure of co-operation
which serves the same end. The British firms are
so closely interlocked by the common ownership of
minor firms, by common directorships, and by their
share in enterprises like the international Nobel
Dynamite Trust and the now defunct Harvey United
Steel Company, that they can be regarded only as
four allied combinations—Armstrongs, Vickers, John
Brown and Cammell Laird. It is a united industry
which confronts the Treasury, influences the
Admiralty, maintains prices, and works upon public

[1] *The War Trust Exposed*, by J. T. Walton Newbold, M.A.
(The National Labour Press, Manchester. 1d.), deals chiefly
with the inter-relation of the British armaments firms.
Armaments and Patriotism, by P. W. W. (The Daily News.
1d.) deals fully with Mr. Mulliner's share in creating the
naval scare of 1909. *The War Traders*, by G. H. Perris
(National Peace Council, 167, St. Stephen's House, West-
minster. 2d.), contains most of the facts given in the other
two pamphlets with some further matter. All of them are
based on material which is official and undeniable.

opinion. It is a prosperous concern. In the present century Armstrongs has never paid less than 10 per cent., and its dividend often rises to 15 per cent. The great French works at Creusot (Messrs. Schneider) have paid as much as 20 per cent. The building and equipment of a Dreadnought must mean at least a quarter of a million in profits to the firm which secures the contract. Such a stake is worth an effort, and these firms are well equipped for the exercise of political and social pressure. The share-list of Armstrongs alone includes the names of sixty noblemen or their wives, sons or daughters, fifteen baronets, twenty knights, eight Members of Parliaments, five bishops, twenty military and naval officers, and eight journalists. Among those interested in these firms there were last summer two Liberal Cabinet Ministers, a law officer of the Crown and two members of the Opposition Front Bench. There is an amusing correspondence between these share-lists and the membership rolls of the Navy League and the National Service League.

All this is natural in a capitalistic society, but one is not quite prepared for the simplicity which both the middle class parties have shown in their dealings with the firms. The naval scare of 1909 was a remarkable achievement in the manipulation of public opinion, and the whole credit of it seems to belong to Mr. Mulliner, the managing director of the Coventry Ordnance Company, of which John Brown & Co. and Cammell Laird & Co. hold between them seven-eighths of the shares. He was in close touch with the leading men of both parties. He was actually received in solemn audience by the Cabinet.

Either he or some fellow-contractor had been in consultation with Mr. Balfour and supplied him (as Mr. Balfour candidly stated) with " facts." His memoranda circulated freely in the House of Commons, but though the unique source of all the alarmist statements current about German preparations was well known, it occurred to no one to doubt the reliability of this interested witness. Mr. Mulliner claimed to have confidential knowledge of an immense secret acceleration in the German naval programme and of a vast extension in the resources and activities of Krupp's. The true facts were stated at the time by Admiral von Tirpitz in the Reichstag and also by the head of the Krupp firm. Parliament preferred to believe Mr. Mulliner. The result was that Mr. McKenna calculated that Germany would have seventeen Dreadnoughts at " the danger-point," March, 1912, and revised his own programme accordingly. Mr. Balfour even predicted for Germany twenty-one or twenty-five capital ships. The event showed that Admiral von Tirpitz had told the truth : when the time came Germany had nine. The scare cost us the price of the four " contingent " Dreadnoughts, a measurable quantity, while it added to Europe's stores of bitterness and mistrust what no figures can reckon. All this happened, largely because of that grotesque delicacy which in England forbids " respectable " newspapers and conventional politicians to say in plain words that a contractor's opinion is an interested opinion, and that a Minister who adopts it without corroboration is either a simpleton or a weakling who has allowed himself to be intimidated by newspapers which he could have routed by one straight sentence revealing the origin of the scare.

The international relations of the firms which trade in armaments offer a tempting field for satire. The inevitable comment lies on the surface of the facts, and they shall be baldly set down here. Capital has no patriotism. A leading German firm turns out to be conducted by French directors. German firms are rebuilding the rival Russian navy. British firms have branches in Italy which are building those Italian Dreadnoughts that are represented as rivals to our own. The Nobel Trust and till lately the Harvey Company were formed of all the leading armaments firms, British, French, German or American. At one time the French firm of Schneider and the German firm of Krupp united in a syndicate to develop the iron ore fields of Ouenza in Algeria. French public opinion in the end upset the partnership, but it was, while it lasted, an evidence of the ability of firms engaged in making cannon destined to destroy each other, to co-operate for their common good. If they can co-operate so far as this, there is plainly nothing to prevent them going further in joint efforts to manipulate public opinion across frontiers which do not really divide them. A German firm has been known to circulate in the French press the false news that the French Government was about to increase its purchases of machine-guns. Its object was, of course, to force the German Government to do in fact what the French Government had done only in fiction. It is unnecessary to labour this unsavoury topic further. It is enough to realise that in every country and

across every border there is a powerful group of
capitalists, closely allied to the fighting services,
firmly entrenched in society, and well served by
politicians and journalists, whose business it is to
exploit the rivalries and jealousies of nations and to
practice the alchemy which transmutes hatred
into gold. Against them are ranged the masses
with their more numerous but ill-organised votes.
The relationship is well illustrated by an arrangement which came into force in Germany during the
general election of 1906. The metallurgical cartels
(employers' syndicates) determined to support
Prince von Bülow's Liberal-Conservative Coalition
which was fighting Social Democracy on the Imperialist issue. Their employees for the most part
voted Socialist. The firms answered their votes by
contributing to the coalition's party funds one shil-
ling for every workman they employed. It would
be interesting to learn how much our own armament
contractors contribute to the secret funds of British
parties.

All over the world these forces, concentrated,
resolute and intelligent, are ceaselessly at work
to defeat the more diffused and less easily
directed forces which make for disarmament and
peace. The number of persons who have anything
to gain by armaments and war is relatively small,
when measured against the whole population of the
civilised world. But their individual stake is larger,
and they work in alliance with Society, which regards
Empire as a field for the careers of its sons, and with
finance which treats it as a field for investment.
Instinctively and by habit they support each others'

claims, and the governing class opposes to the half-conscious and badly-led democracy the solid phalanx of interest and ambition. The democracy, on its side, will still accept as its leaders men who cannot emancipate themselves from the social pressure of the class to which they belong. The idealists in modern politics are a volunteer band, without a trained staff, unpaid, and above all undisciplined, pitted against a regular army of mercenary troops which follows skilled generals and acknowledges the duty of solidarity and obedience.

CHAPTER III

THOSE who would test the theory that the movement of capital towards semi-civilised regions is
the disturbance which sets the European Balance of
Power oscillating, need be at no loss for a model
to observe. There is an episode in the modern
history of our foreign policy which in itself is the
perfect epitome of the tendencies which we have
sketched. Our occupation of Egypt had its origin
in finance. It marked the ruin of the old un-Imperial
Liberalism. In the interests of invested capital it
is avowedly continued. To most of the groupings
of the Great Powers over a period of thirty years,
and to most of the struggles to preserve the balance,
it is an indispensable clue. In its bearings on the
fortunes of the Egyptians themselves, it exhibits in
perfection the material benefits of Imperialism no
less than the moral losses which mark its triumph.

" The origin of the Egyptian question in its
present phase was financial." That is the opening
sentence of Lord Cromer's *Modern Egypt*, and
it spares us any historical controversy. Our
statesmen drifted, our agents schemed their way
into the occupation of Egypt, at the bidding of high
finance, and for no other reason. Capital had been

95

exported from France and England to the Nile Valley at an extravagant rate and with consummate imprudence. There came a moment when both countries perceived that the Khedive was injuring the security on which their capital reposed. They stepped in, precisely as a bank may foreclose on a mortgaged estate, first through the Dual Control, and then through the British occupation.

It was not Oriental stagnation which ruined Egypt, but the ferment of Western ideas. The Khedivial family, founded by that adventurer of genius, Mehemet Ali, was determined to defy geography, to reform the map and to make of Egypt a *quasi*-European state. French culture was acclimatised, European enterprise welcomed, the growing of cotton encouraged and the Suez canal dug. Egypt under this dynasty was tranquil and progressive, and it was no chronic or deep-seated disorder which led to the foreign occupation. The Khedive Ismail, who came to the throne in 1863, was a spendthrift of genius. But if he squandered large sums on palaces, operas and mistresses, he also did much on the lines laid down by his predecessors to develop Egyptian industries and culture. It is true that in the end he despoiled the peasantry, but the beginning of this spoliation was that the money-lenders and contractors robbed the Khedive. European contractors engaged in his great works of building and irrigation were known to have overcharged him anything from 80 to 400 per cent. For floating loans he had latterly to pay as much as 25 per cent. in interest. Of the 68 millions which was raised as a national debt, Egypt received only

44 millions, so that the nominal interest of 7 per cent. amounted in reality to 12 or 13 per cent. Of a loan of 32 millions which he raised in 1873 only 20 millions ever reached the exchequer.[1] Such were the transactions which British and French diplomacy covered with their support. Behind the bond-holders stood the great cosmopolitan firm of Rothschild, and in England their interests were in the hands of Mr., afterwards Lord, Goschen, who had been a Liberal, and was to become a Unionist Minister. Diplomacy is always ready to enforce a debt against a weak State. To it contracts are sacred, but it does not dream of interfering to insist that the contracts shall be equitable. Egypt, however, could have borne even this great load of debt had the interest been fixed at a reasonable figure. There were three obstacles to the re-establishment of Egyptian finances—the character of the Khedive Ismail, the absence of any native machinery which could control his despotism, and the rate of interest charged by the European bond-holders. The two former obstacles were removed long before the occupation took place. Ismail granted a constitution, and the Egyptian Parliament, with the national army behind it, became a real power which could be trusted to resist profligate expenditure. Midway in the crisis the spendthrift Ismail was deposed. Only the third obstacle, the usurious rate of interest,

[1] For these and many other facts in this chapter I am indebted to an acute and brilliant little study of the history of the Occupation based mainly on our blue books, *Egypt's Ruin*, by Theodore Rothstein.

remained. By delaying their consent to any satisfactory composition, the Powers kept their hold
upon Egypt. It was not until Lord Cromer was
firmly in the saddle that the debt was unified and
the interest lowered to an equitable rate. Had
Egypt been allowed to do what was permitted to
Lord Cromer, she might have restored her own
finances and avoided the need of foreign tutelage.

The history of the Dual Control shows with
painful clearness that the agents appointed by Great
Britain and France to manage Egyptian finances
in the interests of the bond-holders acted with no
more regard for the interests of the Egyptian people
than the bailiffs of a private usurer might have
shown. Ismail had been despotic, but it was under
the Dual Control that the lash was most ruthlessly
plied. In 1877, a year of famine, to pay the coupon
due to the clients of the Rothschilds, taxes were
actually collected in advance from the ruined
peasants.[1] Instead of reducing the usurious rate
of interest and debt, the Control cut down Egyptian
expenditure. The schools were starved, and from
motives of economy the control proposed at one
blow to dismiss with their eighteen months' arrears
of pay unpaid or only partially met, no less than
two thousand officers of the Egyptian army.
" Many officers and their families," Lord Cromer
admits, " were reduced, to a state of complete
destitution." [2] But foreign usury under a European
Control takes precedence of local debts. From
this act of folly and injustice dates the rise

[1] See Lord Cromer's *Modern Egypt*, p. 35.
[2] *Modern Egypt*, pp. 74 and 78.

of the Nationalist party under its gifted and popular leader, a Colonel of peasant origin, Achmet Arabi Pasha. Egypt had always been ruled by foreign conquerors from the days of the Macedonians down to those of the Turks. Arabi's movement meant for the first time the emergence of a conscious Egyptian nationality, which was opposed almost as much to the Khedives and the ruling Turkish landed and military caste as to the foreign financiers and the Dual Control. The movement, as Lord Cromer says (p. 226, *Modern Egypt*), was at once " liberal " and " nationalist," and was directed, as our Financial Commissioner, Sir Auckland Colvin, put it, mainly against " Turkish arbitrary rule." Mr. Gladstone unluckily chose to think that he had to deal with nothing more than a military mutiny, and his inveterate prejudice against Mohammedans forbade him to see that in Egypt, as in the Balkans, a down-trodden race was " rightly struggling to be free." The parallel is remarkably close between these Egyptian nationalists and the Young Turks of our own day. Both parties drew their force from the army, and relied upon it to put pressure on the local despotism. Both were Nationalist, in the sense that they aimed at throwing off the humiliating interference of Europe in their domestic affairs. Both were in theory constitutionalists, and aimed at creating a stable parliamentary government on a European model. The Egyptian officers acted in concert with a civilian party, and with a group of Liberal theologians which had just inaugurated a " modernist " movement in Islam. To all this the two Liberal Governments in Great Britain and France were blind. They had brought about the deposition of the Khedive Ismail. They supported his successor, Tewfik, against the Egyptian Parliament, because they had in him a pliable tool who was forced to lean on foreign aid. With the new Khedive and the Conservative pashas of the Turkish ruling caste the Control contracted a close alliance against the popular party. The unexpected vitality of the Parliament, and the fact that it could rely on the army in opposing the Court, placed unforeseen obstacles in the path of the Foreign Control.

There came a point when the Dual Control realised that nothing more was to be gained by supporting a weak sovereign against his people. It was necessary to make a crisis which would seem to justify an appeal to force. Its views, as Mr. Rothstein argues, were plainly confessed in the following despatch from Sir Edward Malet. (Egyptian Blue Book, No. 7 (1882), p. 107) :—

"It should be remembered that the present (Nationalist) Ministry is distinctly hitherto bent upon diminishing the Anglo-French *protection* (*sic*), and that as a matter of fact our influence is daily decreasing. It will not be possible for us to regain our ascendancy until the military supremacy which at present weighs upon the country is broken. . . . I believe that some complication of an acute nature must supervene before any satisfactory solution of the Egyptian question can be attained, and that it would be wiser to hasten it, than to endeavour to retard it."

In plain words, Sir Edward Malet was determined to make a catastrophe. Here was a nation, emerging at last at the menace of foreign intervention, from the lethargy and oppression of centuries, determining to govern itself, establishing a Parliament on European models, throwing off the personal rule of an autocrat, and appealing to the natural sympathies of the Liberal West. Had no question of money and " ascendancy " been at stake, Mr. Gladstone and Lord Granville would have followed its progress with the indulgence and encouragement which Mr. Asquith and Sir Edward Grey extended in our own day on the Young Turks. But the bondholders were strong enough to make public opinion in England and France. To them Egypt was only a debtor, and they preferred to perpetuate the rule of a Khedive whom they knew they could control, rather than encourage the growth of a nation which aspired to govern itself. In the balance hung in one scale the promise of a new national life, in the other a usurious debt which bore its interest at 12 per cent. The 12 per cent. carried the day. Lord Granville saw only one supreme necessity, the restoration of the Khedive's autocratic authority, and the crushing of Parliament, the army and Arabi. It was frivolous intervention which could destroy a living thing, a nation fired with ideals and hopes, for the sake of a money debt. It was, moreover, a superfluous profanity, for the Nationalists neither repudiated the debt, nor disputed the authority of the Control over the ample revenues assigned to its service.

For some time the same Mr. Gladstone who would

have driven the Turks " bag and baggage " out of Europe toyed with the idea of inducing Abdul Hamid to send a Turkish army to Egypt. But the extremer Imperialists had other views. We began in the conventional way by sending ships to Egypt. There was some nervousness about the safety of European lives during this critical period. But the ships were not sent to protect them. On the contrary, our agents on the spot reported to Lord Granville that the sending of ships might alarm and irritate the Egyptians, and so actually endanger Europeans. The ships were sent as a political menace, and for no other reason. " I have the honour to inform your Lordship," wrote Sir Edward Malet to Lord Granville, " that my French colleague and I think that the political advantage of the arrival of the combined squadron at Alexandria is so great as to override in consideration the danger which it might possibly cause to Europeans in Cairo." In plain words, to assert our " ascendancy," we knowingly risked the safety of the European colony in Egypt. The worse the situation became, the stronger would be the case for intervention. The ships arrived, and soon afterwards a massacre took place in Alexandria, in which some fifty Europeans, chiefly Greeks and Maltese, lost their lives. Its origin was obscure. It may have been a spontaneous outburst by the rabble; more probably, as Mr. Wilfrid Blunt argues in his invaluable *Secret History*, it was the work of the Khedive's agents, who wished to discredit the Nationalist Government. It is certain only that Arabi and his friends had no share in it, and regarded it with horror and dismay. But it was not this massacre which provoked intervention, and for three months after it the ships lay inactive at Alexandria. European opinion in Egypt revolted at the absurdity of regarding Arabi as a rebel, and knowing him to be honest, popular and tolerant, turned to him as the one man who could control a dangerous situation. So little was he regarded by disinterested Europeans as " fanatical " or lawless that the German, Austrian and French Consuls-General insisted that Sir Edward Malet's policy must be reversed, that the Khedive should consent to be reconciled with the Nationalist Ministry and that Arabi should be entrusted with the preservation of order. We were meanwhile negotiating at the Constantinople Conference for a Turkish occupation. It is doubtful whether we now desired that solution. We were quietly preparing an expeditionary army of our own, and at Alexandria our ships were getting ready for naval action. It was no disorder, but the exigencies of a financial policy which moved us, when our forces were ready, to act. So little was violence necessary in the judgment of our French partner, that when Admiral Seymour bombarded Alexandria, her ships weighed anchor as ours opened fire. We meant to be masters in Egypt, and it was because he had opposed the unmeasured pretensions of the financial control, that Arabi was declared a rebel, and crushed at Tel-el-Kebir.

The first consequence of Mr. Gladstone's policy in Egypt was to destroy or at least to maim the influence of Liberal ideas in foreign policy. Mr. Gladstone had come into power after the Midlothian campaign with a programme of resolute opposition to Imperialism. The chief act of his administration abroad was the occupation of Egypt. Henceforward Liberalism had a lie in its soul. For years to come it professed the intention of evacuating Egypt, when the task of restoring its order and solvency should be completed. It has never attempted to execute that pledge. From Egypt it was forced downwards to the Soudan, and the possession of the Soudan encouraged the grandiose scheme of the Cape to Cairo railway. The occupation had involved a flagrant breach of faith towards the Concert of Europe, which had (at our suggestion) decided that the occupation was to be the work not of a British but of a Turkish army. To retain our position, and to combat the enmities which it brought upon us, we had to abandon the traditional Liberal policy of non-intervention in the affairs of Europe, and to take our part in the incessant struggle to maintain such a balance of power as would allow us to continue our self-imposed mission. Legal title we had none. Our occupation ran two risks—from other Powers, and from the Radical wing of the Liberal party, which wished for many years to end it. It was more than anything else the difficulty of maintaining our hold on Egypt which brought the two historic parties together in their foreign policy, and established the now accepted watchword of continuity. There was now, when Liberal cabinets were being formed, a test question by which " impatient idealists " were tried. Finance continued to play its part. It is a matter of history that Mr. Cecil Rhodes offered to subscribe to Liberal party funds on the express condition that there should be no

nonsense about evacuating Egypt. Under such
influences Liberalism became an Imperialist party,
with Lord Rosebery, and, later, Sir Edward Grey
as the only possible directors of its foreign policy.
Lord Rosebery belonged by marriage to the Rothschild family, and it was the Rothschild influence
which brought about the occupation of Egypt. The
party as a whole accepted the new situation with
ease and grace. Save in the consistent columns of
the *Manchester Guardian*, it was rarely reminded
that we had gone to Egypt to assure the interest on a
usurious debt. The legend grew up that on the Nile
we were bearing the " white man's burden " and
fulfilling an unselfish mission, with the sole aim
of delivering Egypt from despotism. That we
had destroyed a Parliament and crushed a nation
struggling for that " self-government," which, in Sir
Henry Campbell-Bannerman's words, is better than
" good government," were facts which a complacent
Empire made haste to forget.

In the wider field of European politics, it would be
hardly an exaggeration to say that the maintenance
of our seizure of Egypt has been for a generation
the master-key of our foreign policy. Its first consequence was a breach with France which lasted a
full twenty years, from the bombardment of Alexandria in 1882 down to the conclusion of the *Entente
Cordiale* in 1903. France, recovering rapidly from
the consequences of the war with Prussia, was still
isolated in Europe. Self-interest and national sympathy alike made for intimate relations between the
two Liberal Powers. The first shock to their
mutual confidence came in 1875 with Lord Beacons-

field's secret and in some respects perfidious purchase of the Suez Canal shares.[1]   France felt herself
cheated, out-manœuvred and humiliated.   None
the less she agreed to act with us throughout the
period of the Dual Control.   Our diplomacy was
in the end the more aggressive and adventurous,
but up to the bombardment of Alexandria, France
acted with us, partly because she wished for our
friendship, and still more because she could not afford
to allow us to act in Egypt alone.   The central
fact of the situation was that French influence had
from the time of Mehemet Ali downwards been
dominant in Egypt.   It was French culture and
French institutions which the Khedives had tried
to adopt.   French teachers and French engineers
were rapidly Europeanising the country.   France
was proud of her work, and she enjoyed what we
have never won, the confidence and sympathy of the
Egyptian people.   The main reason why she refused
at the end to share in the risks of the occupation, was
that she dreaded the European entanglements to
which it might lead.   France is not an island, and
as M. de Freycinet put it, she could not afford to
challenge the hostility of a Continent.   For twenty
years she cherished the memory of our duplicity in
promoting Turkish intervention while in fact we
were preparing to intervene ourselves, our appeal to
force in bombarding Alexandria, our use of the
" cavalry of St. George " (the British sovereign) in
preparing the conquest of Egypt by the purchase of

---

[1] The full story is told in an admirable study by M.
Charles Lesage, *L'Achat des Actions de Suez*.   Paris.   Plon.
1906.

the Canal shares, and, above all, our failure to fulfil our continual promises that the occupation should be temporary.   Every traditional prejudice, every old doubt of our national honour, was revived by our conduct in this adventure and its sequel.   Moreover, as Egypt began to thrive under our rule, there was always present the bitter reflection that we were reaping where France had sowed.   At the International Conference which was sitting in Constantinople when we suddenly put an end to the negotiations by bombarding Alexandria, there was already discernible that grouping of the Powers which was to govern Europe for a generation.   Russia, like France, was furious, and proposed to break up the Conference as a protest.   It was in 1882 that the first suggestions of a Franco-Russian Alliance were made by Gambetta and Skobeleff, though some years were to pass before it was realised.[1]   That we were allowed a free hand in Egypt was mainly Bismarck's work.   His master-idea was to assure his own influence by dividing the European Powers. He had made bitter enmity between France and Italy by encouraging France to take Tunis.   He now perceived the possibility of embroiling France and Britain, by encouraging us to take Egypt. The plot succeeded, and for twenty years Germany exercised in consequence a species of supremacy in Europe.   The two Liberal Powers were estranged, and France in due time became the ally of our traditional rival Russia.   The French were slow to abandon the hope of one day forcing

[1] See Seignobos, *Political History of Contemporary Europe*, p. 827.

us to relax our hold on Egypt, and their diplomacy, though it could not defeat us, was able to hamper and annoy. The " policy of pin-pricks," as Lord Salisbury called it, culminated in 1898 with Major Marchand's daring march to Fashoda, an attempt to challenge our whole position by seizing the upper waters of the Nile on which Egypt depends. War was with difficulty averted, but the peaceful settlement of this crisis left nothing but bitter memories behind it. Twice at least during this period the country was convulsed by naval " scares," in which France or France and Russia together were supposed to be the enemy. The " Two-Power Standard," which until lately governed our shipbuilding, was a legacy from these rivalries. We have never had to fight for Egypt. But year after year we have paid in swollen armaments and increasing Budgets for the violence and ill-faith of our Egyptian policy in 1882. To measure its consequences we have only to ask ourselves what would in all probability have been the natural course of events had we maintained a modest co-operation with France, allowed the Egyptians to work out their own salvation, and contented ourselves with helping them by expert advice to restore their shaken credit. There would have been no breach with France, and the *Entente Cordiale* might have been established some twenty years earlier. European armaments would have been less crushing, and Bismarckian diplomacy less triumphant. Above all, the alliance would never have been concluded which filled the treasury of the Russian autocrat with French gold, and so perpetuated the cruellest of European despotisms.

No less disastrous were the consequences of our action in the Near East. France had a grievance, but Turkey, which was the Suzerain Power, had been still more seriously wronged by our occupation. From 1882 onwards Abdul Hamid became resolutely Anglophobe. Germany succeeded to the position of influence which we had hitherto held at Constantinople, and she used her power to encourage and exploit the tyranny of the Palace gang. The massacres of the Armenians, whom the Sultan always regarded as our particular *protégés*, were in some degree an expression of his fear of us. In 1882 he was not yet the insane tyrant that he afterwards became. The first generation of Young Turks was not yet exterminated, and the Press had still a certain liberty. Lord Beaconsfield's policy of leading Turkey gently towards reform by friendly aid and kindly pressure might conceivably have succeeded, had it been at all possible for Turkey to regard the conquerors of Egypt as friends. The result of our seizure of Egypt was that all our protests against the ill-treatment of Armenians, Cretans and Macedonians were regarded by official Turkey as the interested meddling of an enemy with Imperial ambitions to serve.

A new phase of the Egyptian question opened in 1903. France realised at last that she had nothing to hope from a policy of opposition. The Anglo-French Agreement consolidated our position on the Nile, while we in return gave her a free hand in Morocco. The result has only been to revive our troubles in a new form. We have now to reckon with the hostility of the Triple instead of the Dual

Alliance. Egypt, it is true, is not the ostensible cause of quarrel. But it was none the less the necessity which we experienced of strengthening our position in Egypt which caused us to approach France, and so to challenge the enmity of the German Powers. Egypt is still the clue to our diplomacy, and like some *perpetuum mobile* the series of consequences started by the bombardment of Alexandria continues to pursue us. We are still arming, still passing through naval scares, still watching the oscillations of the European balance of power. And if one asks why, the answer is still the same—because somehow or other we had to assure the fruits of an act of force, and to fortify our illegal tenure of the Nile Valley.

There remains the question whether, incidentally and as a by-product of our solicitude for the financial interests of our own investors, our stay in Egypt has none the less benefited the Egyptians. A critic who ventures to give a balanced answer to this question is at once overwhelmed by the weight of authority against him. Three books have been written to prove that the occupation has been an unmixed blessing to Egypt. Their authors have unquestionably an unrivalled knowledge of the facts. But the acceptance of books by Lord Cromer, Lord Milner and Sir Auckland Colvin as final authorities on the history of a period in which they were the principal actors, is an evidence of the superb assurance of our national pride. We should not accept even three works by high Russian officials as a convincing proof of the happy consequences of Russian rule in Poland. On such a point we rather incline to follow Polish opinion. But much of the merit which these writers claim for their own achievements may be fairly conceded. In nearly all material respects Egypt has marvellously progressed under British rule. There is no more opulent soil, no more generous climate, and no more industrious peasantry in the world. Egypt made astonishing material progress under the Khedives ; the advance in wealth, population, agriculture and trade, which was for a few brief years interrupted by Ismail Pasha's mad extravagance, was resumed and accelerated under Lord Cromer. French engineers did well under the Khedives ; English engineers, with a freer hand, have done better in utilising the Nile for irrigation. Corruption, though not extinct, has been immensely diminished. The liberty of meeting and until recently the liberty of the press have been respected. The extortionate collection of taxes and the sale of justice have gradually under English rule ceased to oppress the peasantry. On the material plane the directors of the Occupation are entitled to the favourable verdict which they have passed upon each other's work.

The success of the Occupation from the material and financial standpoint was what one might expect from a competent Imperialism which regards Egypt mainly as a field for investment. The Occupation has done what was necessary to make it a secure and valuable field, and on the whole it has done it well. But it must not be assumed that any large proportion of the increase in the wealth of Egypt has gone to the peasants. It has gone to great speculators in the newly-irrigated lands, who sometimes refuse even to lease their fields and let them out for tillage only for a crop at a time, to mortgage banks and investment companies, and also in great measure to the larger native landowners. Wages no doubt have risen, but so has the cost of food. The peasants are probably much happier and somewhat wealthier than they were in the later years of the Khedive Ismail. So indeed their old men have told me, with apparent sincerity. Yet the pictures which may be read of the poverty of the *fellaheen* in the graphic writings of Edmond About and Lady Duff Gordon, are still true in the main to-day. I shall never forget my first impression of their villages. As the train travelled slowly beside the endless canals from Alexandria to Cairo, I noticed near the line some quaint and untidy mud huts. I took them at first for temporary shelters, built, as I guessed, by gipsies, or by workmen engaged in repairing the line or the canals. But the whole landscape, which might, save for its palm trees and its buffaloes, have been lifted straight out of Holland, so green it was, so minutely and industriously cultivated, so intersected with canals, was dotted with these groups of tiny dilapidated mud huts and presently we reached a town of them. They are the permanent habitations of the peasants. The legend of the prosperity of the *fellaheen* which a study of Lord Cromer's reports had formed in my mind, had vanished ere I reached Cairo. Here indeed was wealth, order and industry, yet the villages exhibited a poverty such as I have never seen even in the mountains of anarchical Macedonia or among the bogs of Donegal. A nearer inspection

of the villages only confirmed this first impression.
I have heard it said that in this gentle climate no
one wants a solid house. Yet the native magnates
build solid and spacious and, according to Oriental
notions, luxurious houses. These exceptions only
emphasise the abysmal poverty of the masses.
The villages are crowded slums of mud hovels,
without a tree, a flower or a garden. The huts,
often without a window or a levelled floor, are minute
dungeons of baked mud, usually of two small rooms
neither whitewashed nor carpeted. Those which
I entered were bare of any visible property, save
a few cooking utensils, a mat to serve as a bed, and
a jar which held the staple food of maize. These
things, and the cotton gowns on their backs, were all
the peasants had to show as the result of their inordinate toil from dawn to sunset on every day of
the year, Fridays not excepted, in a climate which
has no winter, and on fields which yield three crops
in twelve months. The explanation is relatively
simple. There is no true system of tenancy. A
peasant may hire a field for one crop or one year,
or he may bargain for a share, sometimes only a
sixth, in the produce of the field which he tills.
But he is always at the mercy of an elaborate truck
system, always in the debt of his landlord, and
always in consequence tied to the land and unable
to sell his labour in the open market. To improve
this method of tenure, or to reform a truck system
which keeps the landless peasantry in a condition
of serfdom, the Occupation had done nothing nor
had it, so far as I could learn, even attempted to
study the question.

Worse still was the condition of the peasants who work in factories. There was then (1908) no Factory Act in Egypt. There are all over the country, ginning mills, which employ casual labour to prepare raw cotton for export, during four or five months of the year. The wages were low, from 7½d. to 10d. a day for an adult, and 6d. for a child. Children and adults alike worked sometimes for twelve, usually for fifteen, and on occasion even for sixteen or eighteen hours a day. In the height of the season even the children were put on night shifts of twelve hours. I have seen a foreman use a cane to chastise a child whose zeal flagged in this inordinate task. Fraud in some of the worst mills is so common, that the adult workers sometimes insist on receiving their day's wage in advance as they enter, pledging their outer garments in return. The atmosphere in which the children worked was so charged with cotton dust, that it resembled a November fog in London rather than the pure climate of Egypt. Lord Cromer used to say that legislation was legally impossible, because the capitulations stood in the way. His own *laissez faire* individualism was the more formidable obstacle. It is satisfactory to be able to add that, after a generation of neglect, a fairly satisfactory Factory Act was passed through the efforts of Sir Eldon Gorst and Mr. Harvey. This is not the only point on which Lord Cromer's successors have improved upon his work. I shall, however, continue to describe what I observed in 1908, when Egypt could still be seen as Lord Cromer left it. One ceased after a visit to an Egyptian ginnery to wonder why capital is exported to

Egypt. Without a Parliament, without trade unions, without a Factory Act, Lord Cromer's province was a paradise for the investor.

It is on its moral and intellectual side that Lord Cromer's work is open to the severest criticism. We remained in Egypt professedly with a single object— to train the Egyptians to govern themselves. In every Annual Report that object was avowed, in every year's work it was ignored. The system of government which Lord Cromer erected, incomparably superior though it was to that of the Khedive's in honesty and efficiency, was like theirs a system of despotic and personal rule. We went to crush the " military ascendancy " of a national army which had extorted a Parliament ; we suppressed the Parliament, and replaced it by a foreign bureaucracy, supported by a foreign army of occupation. Independence and initiative, even in English officials, were discouraged, and their words and acts were checked by an elaborate system of espionage. Natives indeed continued to be titular Ministers and titular governors of provinces, but at the side of every Minister there was an English " adviser," and above every governor an English " inspector." Ministers and governors alike were puppets, who were made to understand that they might draw their salaries so long as they treated every piece of advice as a command. Meanwhile, the importation of English officials became every year more considerable, and latterly, so little were we preparing to leave Egypt to govern herself, that Lord Cromer began to train young men at Cambridge for the Egyptian Civil Service on Indian lines.

Had we been sincere in our self-imposed task, it would have been on education rather than irrigation (if we had had to choose) that we should have concentrated our efforts. In twenty-five years we could have made a relatively well-educated nation. A young country, like Bulgaria, suddenly emancipated from Turkish rule, begins at any sacrifice by creating a system of compulsory education, and by establishing a University at which governing men may be formed. But neither in quality nor in quantity nor in kind, will our arrangements bear scrutiny. The expenditure of Prussia on Education represents one-eighth of the total Budget. Servia can spare one-fifteenth. At the close of Lord Cromer's reign education accounted for £1 in every £81 of the total national expenditure. With a population of over eleven millions she had only four governmental secondary schools for boys, and one higher primary school for girls. There was no University. Of the Mohammedan population only 4 per cent was literate. It was only in the latter years of Lord Cromer's reign that any attempt was made to create modern elementary schools for the illiterate peasantry, and even now the building and equipment of these schools is left to private benevolence. There was under the Khedive Ismail a system for subsidising Arabic literature and encouraging the translation of useful books from European languages. There was also an extensive system of bursaries and free scholarships, which enabled a poor lad to enter a primary school, and at the close of his secondary training to study at a French University. That system we entirely suppressed, partly

from the individualist tendency which coloured all
Lord Cromer's work, partly from mere economy.
Under such conditions it became difficult to obtain
competent native teachers. Poor men could not
study, and the salaries which we offered would
attract only poor men. We therefore imported
English teachers at considerable expense in annual
swarms, and the result was the complete denation-
alisation of the teaching. In the secondary schools
all instruction was given through the medium
of English, and even in the primary schools English
alone was used for certain subjects. There were
even for young boys no maps with Arabic lettering.
Some of these schools would be in every material
respect a credit to any European country, and the
English teachers are usually competent and con-
scientious. But to their boys they are mere aliens,
and nothing can compensate for the absence of
instruction in the mother tongue. Worst of all, the
education which is given under such grave difficulties by foreign teachers in a foreign tongue, is of
a severely utilitarian character. The object of
these schools is professedly to train officials, and
under the Occupation the Egyptian official was
expected to be a careful copyist, a docile subordinate,
a reliable clerk. He learns in these schools to speak
and write English and Arabic fairly well ; he acquires
a very little natural science and a smattering of
universal history—the latter, evidently, by rote.
But there are no liberal studies which might form
his mind or train him to think. English and Arabic
literature are almost equally neglected ; the predominant aim is to make a useful quill-driver who can

correspond in these languages correctly. Latin and Greek are wisely ignored, but no serious attempt has been made to put any humanising study, literary or scientific, in their place. The results of all these causes—the neglect of the mother tongue, the defects of the education itself, the absence of a University and the appointment of foreigners to every post the holding of which might encourage a capable man to study or write—may be traced in the utter death of all intellectual life in Egypt, and in the crudity of mind which prevails among the small " educated " class. The level of culture is incomparably lower and the educated class incomparably smaller than in any other country of the Near East with which I am acquainted. For that the responsibility lies with us. The Nationalists have agitated fiercely for better education and more of it.

On Lord Cromer's departure an emphatic change declared itself under the influence of Sir Eldon Gorst. Our control became less direct, our advice less imperious, our methods in education less antinational. We still however refused the demands of the Nationalists for a Parliament. They have become, more especially since the cruelty and injustice of the Denshawai affair, a numerous and uncompromising party—crude indeed, as all the beginnings of intellectual life in Egypt are crude, but resolute and determined to stand erect. The time for leading or influencing the Egyptians has gone by. The Egyptians are by nature singularly pliable and assimilative. Their admiration, amounting almost to hero-worship, for the few Englishmen who have cared to maintain with them kindly and human relationships, is an evidence that with tact and sympathy they might easily have been led. But with rare exceptions, there has been no teaching in any higher sense of the word. The Egyptians have learned our language, our technical skill, our orderly official routine. Interchange of ideas there has been none. The normal English attitude has been one of contempt and aloofness. Lord Cromer would not take the trouble to learn their language, and his book breathes on every page his dislike of their character, his hostility to their religion, his contempt for their history, their language and their institutions. The normal Egyptian attitude is now one of distrust. The English colony lives in absolute isolation. One never meets an Englishman in a native house. Our work is professedly one of inspection and advice. But an inspector who will not mix with the people cannot know what is going on. I heard in the country constant and detailed complaints of corruption among the irrigation officials. I even met two Egyptian landowners who admitted that they themselves habitually give bribes. These complaints were always followed by another—that the English officials are unapproachable, and consequently ignorant of the real condition of affairs. It is this ineradicable national failing, the result partly of temperament and partly of tradition, which seems to set a limit to our good work in Egypt. If we had possessed the gift of moral leadership, the magnetism that attracts and inspires, we should by now have trained up a generation competent to govern Egypt unaided. But the possibility of assuming that leadership has now irreparably gone. The Egyptians will learn nothing more from us. I ask myself whether the judges of Denshawai have anything to teach.

Why is it that we remain in Egypt? It can hardly be from any genuine love and goodwill to the Egyptians. If they cherish such a disinterested passion, our Imperialists are remarkably successful in dissembling it. One may admit at once that the Egyptians, if left to themselves, would make mistakes. But of these mistakes they chiefly would bear the brunt, and only by mistakes does a nation learn. It is probable that the mistakes of an Egyptian Parliament would be less irritating to the Egyptians themselves than were those of Lord Cromer. Capacity for government is a relative term. One may easily exaggerate the capacity even of Western races for self-government. Our armaments, our slums, our crises of unemployment would authorise some invading sage from a wiser planet to pronounce us as utterly incapable of government as we are pleased to think Oriental races. It may be said that there are too many European inhabitants in Egypt to be left to the uncontrolled caprices of a native administration. That argument ignores the fact that Europeans in Egypt are subject neither to native laws, nor to native courts nor to native taxes. It is also said that we remain in Egypt to protect the Suez Canal. Well, if that were so, the Egyptians would not refuse to surrender Port Said, if at that price they could obtain our withdrawal from the rest of the country. But our naval power and the possession

of Cyprus and Aden, ought to suffice to enable us to
control the Canal, which after all is not a British, but
an international institution.   It is well to remember
a terse parable of Lord Palmerston's in this connection.   " We do not want Egypt," he wrote in 1857,
" or wish for it ourselves, any more than a rational
man with an estate in the north of England and a
residence in the south would have wished to possess
the inns on the North road.   All he could want
would have been that the inns should be well-kept,
always accessible, and furnishing him, when he came,
with mutton-chops and post-horses."

The real reason why we refuse not merely to
evacuate Egypt, but even to concede to the Egyptians Parliamentary institutions, is not mysterious.
We conquered the country to assure the ninety
millions of money, English and French, which had
been sunk in its public debt.   Since the Occupation
the amount of capital added in one form or another
to this sum has become very considerable, and is
rapidly increasing.   The new capital invested in
limited companies created in Egypt between 1856-
1905 amounted to nearly 35 millions sterling, and
the new shares subscribed in 1905 alone reached a
total of over 10 millions.[1]   One has also to reckon
the older companies, numerous companies registered
abroad which operate in Egypt, the capital of individual investors, and the interests of the great
English contractors engaged in the colossal irrigation
works.   Some of the more recent enterprises are
under the guidance of persons who are in a position

[1] See Edmond Théry, *L'Egypte Nouvelle au point de vue
économique et financier*, pp. 164-6.

to exert considerable influence in the political world or at court. The new Bank has for its chairman Lord Milner, and among individual investors is Sir Ernest Cassel, whose name was often to be found in the *Court Circular* as the guest or host of King Edward. These foreign capitalists would regard the creation of a national government in Egypt as a disaster to their enterprises. If one enquires precisely why, the answer will require some sifting and interpretation. We should be told, of course, that a national government would be certainly inefficient, probably corrupt and possibly fanatical, all of which would be very bad for business. The real fear is, however, I think, that under a Parliamentary *régime* power would be entirely in the hands of the natives of Egypt, who are almost exclusively engaged in agriculture. Finance would be unrepresented, and in the inevitable clash of interests between those who own and till the land, and those who lend money on the land and handle its crops, the bias of a native government would certainly not be on the side of the foreign capitalist. The same fear which causes the City to dread and oppose a Liberal Government in Great Britain also ranges the same classes against a Nationalist *régime* in Egypt—not because the Egyptian Nationalists have radical tendencies (their leaders are large landowners), but because they would represent native as opposed to foreign interests. This standpoint is hardly concealed in some of Lord Cromer's recent polemics against the Nationalists. He contests in principle the claim of the natives of Egypt to any exclusive right to manage their own affairs. His demand is that if ever autonomy becomes possible, the Egyptian Government must somehow " represent the views and interests of all the inhabitants of the Nile Valley." If ever there is an Egyptian Parliament, he urges, " persons of foreign extraction should be represented on account of their intelligence and the stake they have in the country."[1]

In these sentences is outlined one of the most startling doctrines of Imperialism. It is the same claim which was put forward by the great mining houses on behalf of the Outlanders of the Transvaal. It amounts to this, that any country which is being developed by foreign capital, must be prepared to admit its foreign population to a share in its representative institutions, and this, apparently, even when the foreign population has no intention of acquiring the nationality of the country in question, or of taking up its permanent residence within it. No one who knows anything of Egypt can suppose that the Europeans resident there would ever dream of surrendering their favoured status as the privileged subjects of Great Powers. A European who did so would be regarded as a pariah by his fellows. Lord Cromer, however, proposes that men who will not become Egyptians should none the less have a vote in electing an Egyptian Parliament. Capital in such a claim mocks at the spirit of nationality, and degrades the conduct of a people's life to the level of a joint-stock company, in which every man who has bought

[1] See *The Situation in Egypt*, an address by Lord Cromer to the Eighty Club, published by Messrs. Macmillan in 1908, pp. 17 and 27.

a share is entitled to a vote. In one way or another, foreign capital which has once established itself in a weak country will insist on controlling its destinies —first by diplomacy, then by armies, and, finally, by the machinery of the ballot box. When Lord Cromer put forward this paradoxical proposal as an alternative to nationalism, and recommended it as an " ideal " to the Egyptians, he revealed the real reason why national self-government, in the view of the investing classes, is impossible for Egypt. Capital is opportunist. It has no rooted objection to representative institutions. It makes only one condition—that it shall somehow dominate them. It can have no illusions about Egypt. Against a solid native Moslem majority of 92 per cent., its agents could do nothing at the ballot-box. That is why it has steadily refused any real power to the rudimentary elective council which exists in Egypt. That also is why Lord Cromer, a subtle politician with a habit of forethought, looking forward to the indefinitely distant time when some kind of Parliament must at last be conceded, proposed to entrench the foreign residents, who stand on the whole for European finance, in a separate elective Upper House. Capital was strong enough to bring the occupation about. It is strong enough to maintain it. Despite all our pledges and promises, no Conservative Government will ever wish, no Liberal Government will ever dare to end it. It will last as long as our Indian Empire. When the time comes in India or in Egypt to recognise, against our will, the full maturity of the native races, we shall, in one form or another, be confronted with some proposal resembling Lord Cromer's scheme. Foreign capital has acquired a stake in these countries. It prefers to protect that stake through the strong arm of a foreign occupation. But if ever self-government becomes inevitable, it will urge that the millions which it has invested have somehow a personality which outweighs the humanity of the millions whom it exploits. Let every man, as Bentham used to say when he defined democracy, count for one, and no one for more than one. But capital must be balanced against their numbers. By arms or by diplomacy, by a commission of control or a plutocratic constitution, it will know how to acquire and to keep the effective mastery of any country which it enters.

We have traced in the recent history of Egypt the typical exploit of modern Imperialism. We have seen that the force which impelled our policy was not trade but finance. Confronted by the new power, Liberalism bent, broke, and in the end adapted itself. We have traced the influence of a single act of self-aggrandisement upon our relations through thirty years with other Powers. It made our enmities. It made our friendships. It dictated our behaviour in adjusting the balance of power. Once more and in detail, we have seen that the diplomatic rivalries and competing armaments which make the European fear, have their origin, not in the need of assuring our own homes and our own security, but only in the restless movements of capital to win fresh fields for investment. Behind the abstractions of high politics stand an indifferent democracy at home, which had in this adventure no interest to serve and no passion to sate, and in Egypt the passive figure of a subject nation, which our rule has kept ignorant amid left-handed gifts, and condemned to a paralysis of will, while it enjoyed the boons that are the by-products of our gains.

NOTE.

THE comparative neglect of Education under Lord Cromer in Egypt is far from being an isolated case in the records of Imperialism. It is indeed normal. In India, Mr. Gokhale and the more moderate Nationalists are still agitating with little prospect of early success for a system of compulsory elementary schooling. Our newer African colonies make an interesting study, both in what has been done and in what has been omitted. The record of good work stands beyond cavil or denial. Tribal wars and slave-raiding have been everywhere repressed. The making of railways and roads is gradually liberating the natives from the brutalising and dangerous occupation of carrying. Nomad tribes settle down to agriculture, and the agricultural tribes gradually improve their stupid and wasteful methods of cultivation. Most of these colonies have experimental botanical stations, and in the more advanced of them native instructors are going from village to village to teach the people how they may profitably grow the cocoa-palm, the rubber-vine and the cotton plant. The motive in all this is not primarily altruistic. It is being done because we in Europe require cheap and abundant tropical produce. It is none the less a civilising work of which no people need be ashamed. It is weaning the natives from rapine and war, developing in them a taste for work which is both educative and profitable, and raising their standard of living without subjecting them to servile conditions.

The ambition to make a colony profitable may achieve much, but it has its definite limitations. If the disinterested desire to civilise really played an appreciable part in the motives of colonising peoples, the work on which they would first concentrate their energies would be education. One may doubt whether a literary education is the best for negroes, and the system of attempting to Europeanise the natives which some of the older missionary organisations

adopted is open to grave criticism. But there can be little
intellectual advance until the natives read and write their
own language and acquire some habits of orderly thought.
Nature they know and observe, and they can be taught the
elementary facts of science—the first step towards the
destruction of superstition and the growth of the sense for
the causes of things. They have eyes and ears, and can
learn to draw and appreciate music. They are eager to
acquire the technique of weaving, carpentry and metal work,
and the practice of agriculture. The more the Imperialist
insists that they are children, the more obvious is it
that they ought to be taught. But the central fact which
emerges from a study of the Colonial Office reports, is that
teaching is the last duty which our Government dreams of
assuming. In some of these colonies, notably the Gold
Coast and Uganda, the Mission schools are numerous and
flourishing. But even in Uganda they receive no subsidy
or aid from the Government. In others, for example,
Ashanti, their work is as yet inconsiderable, and the report
for 1907 remarks (p. 28) that education will " progress
but slowly, because the chiefs regard the Mission Schools as a
means to an end, i.e. the proselytism of the children." If
that is true of the Ashantis, who are primitive pagans, it
must be still more applicable to Mahommedans. Yet nowhere has any attempt been made to help Islam under our
flag to fulfil a civilising mission in Africa. If one turns to
the records of a recent acquisition like Ashanti, one realises
what really are the essential and important things in our
colonial work. There are gold mines, and there is a railway
to serve them. There is also a prison, in which out of a
total of 691 prisoners there are 67 debtors, and 322 " political
prisoners awaiting trial or detained." Under the heading
of Public Works (p. 29), one finds this instructive information :—

" The following public works were commenced or completed during 1907 at Coomassie :—Post Office, female
prison, hospital and dispensary, European hospital,
laundry in which to wash Europeans' clothes, and several
buildings for the Gold Coast Regiment."

Turning the page, one learns that " a 13-hole golf course
has been completed." Gold mines, prisons, barracks, a
laundry for Europeans built with public money, and a golf
course, these are our works of civilisation. But there is no
school.

Here, clearly, is work for a critical group in Parliament to achieve. It is essential to protest against the occasional barbarism of military expeditions, the alienation of native lands, the imposition of ill-devised taxes, the stealthy introduction of servile labour conditions. But that is not enough. The first duty of an Imperial race which works itself into a passion of self-admiration over the " white man's burden " of civilising and teaching is to assume it. Niggers cannot be civilised by learning English oaths as caddies on the Coomassie golf course, nor even by washing European clothes in an Imperial laundry. The burden will be shouldered when we create in all these colonies a governmental system of education. There seems to be no real objection to subsidising Mission schools, under proper inspection, in places where (as in Uganda) large sections of the native population are quite pleased to be " proselytised." But a systematic effort should be made to raise the Mahomedans to the level of their own creed. That can be done only through Mahomedan teachers. A wise policy would begin by encouraging, in suitable centres, colleges (madrasseh) in which under qualified Moslem doctors, teachers, priests and judges would be trained, who would be missionaries of enlightenment as well as of Islam. The Arabic language and culture in an Arabic dress may penetrate where a purely Western civilisation would be a mere exotic.

CHAPTER IV

CLASS-DIPLOMACY

ONE heard constantly repeated during the period of our antagonism to Germany a statement as irrelevant as it is true. The two peoples, we are told, have no quarrel. There never yet was a war for which the masses of any nation were responsible. Yet wars occur. Over the march of foreign affairs, public opinion can exert only a rare and spasmodic control. It is interested in affairs abroad only when they are striking and spectacular. A revolution, a massacre, an ·earthquake, a general strike—such happenings excite its attention. ‚But the slow and tedious and often secret procedure by which the Powers conduct their diplomatic chess is rarely interesting, and never fully known. One may doubt whether more than a hundred persons in these islands made any sustained attempt to follow in close detail the elaborate intrigues of the Franco-German struggle for Morocco, though twice at least it came near involving‚ this country in war. Nor does the machinery exist by which public opinion, were it alert and decided, could bring to bear on the Foreign Office a degree of pressure which would seriously modify its attitude. In all European countries foreign affairs are in the hands of a close bureaucracy, which is rarely amenable to any pressure but that of the small governing class and the financial interests allied with it.

Public opinion under representative government has only one direct and effective means of expression, and that is at the polls. Twice only in our day and in that of our fathers have general elections turned even partially on a foreign or Imperial issue. Mr. Gladstone made his opposition to Disraeli's pro-Turkish and Imperialist policy prominent in the Midlothian campaign of 1880. Mr. Chamberlain's electoral strategy brought about an appeal to the country midway in the Boer War. These were broad and human issues, but in neither case was the contest so timed as to affect the conduct of affairs. The Eastern Question had been irrevocably settled for a generation at Berlin when Mr. Gladstone appealed to the verdict of Midlothian, and in spite of the verdict of the country against Imperialism, Mr. Gladstone at once proceeded to occupy Egypt. The " Khaki " election could hardly have modified the course of the war even had it resulted in a defeat for Mr. Chamberlain's policy. It would be hard to name a single bye-election in recent memory, save during the Boer War, in which a foreign question has been seriously raised even as a secondary issue. Nor is this surprising or unnatural. Save in moments of grave crisis, a foreign issue can never compete in the mind of the elector with such issues as tariff reform, industrial insurance, or even Home Rule. For the same reason parties need rarely fear the defection of their followers by reason of the aberrations of their foreign policy. The Denshawai hangings and the Russian understanding provoked much genuine indignation among Liberals. But did the party lose a dozen adherents because of them ?   It is, in short, in its domestic policy that a Government is judged in the country.   So far as any consequences go which can be measured in bye-elections and votes, its leaders in their foreign policy are virtually irresponsible.   This is, indeed, much more obviously the case with us than with the Germans, and that for a simple reason.   The German Reichstag is busied mainly with Imperial affairs— the army, the fleet and foreign policy—while the greater number of domestic issues are left to the diets of the several Federal States which compose the Empire.   With us the same Parliament is busied with the whole range of public policy, and the inevitable result is that parties are formed and Government judged primarily on the lines of domestic policy.

It has of late years been explicitly recognised that foreign affairs stand outside the sphere of party conflict.   There must be, it is said, " continuity " in foreign policy, and within certain limits, the doctrine is reasonable.   Our position in the world would suffer somewhat, if rival parties alternately denounced or amended each other's alliances and treaties, as they amend or end each other's laws. But in practice this doctrine has so operated as to destroy any possibility of a democratic impulse in foreign affairs.   When Lord Rosebery enunciated this principle of " continuity," Liberalism quietly renounced its special traditions in foreign policy, and proclaimed its readiness to follow with docility the lines which Conservatives had laid down. The first consequence of this doctrine was that in selecting his Foreign Secretary a Liberal Premier must choose a candidate who will be acceptable to the Opposition. In other words, whichever party is in power, the Foreign Secretary will always be an Imperialist, a personality whom the *Times*, the City and the Conservative Party can unreservedly trust. A Radical can no more become Foreign Secretary than a Roman Catholic can become Lord Chancellor. The doctrine of " continuity " means that foreign affairs have in effect been removed from the sphere of party government, and are now influenced only by the opinions of the governing class, of those, that is to say, who move at court and in society, who regard the army and the civil service as careers reserved for their families, and survey the world beyond these islands mainly as a field for the investment of their surplus wealth. The phase of middle-class sentiment expressed by such a newspaper as the *Daily News*, formidable in Gladstone's day, is now almost as powerless to affect foreign policy as is that of organised labour itself.

The purely bureaucratic character of our foreign policy is to some extent disguised by the existence of a certain number of unofficial leagues or committees which on minor issues do appear in different degrees to possess some influence in Downing Street. They fall into two groups. The Congo Reform Association, the Balkan Committee and the Anti-Slavery and Aborigines Protection Society do unquestionably exert a real influence. The various Peace Societies, the Friends of Russian Freedom, the Persian, Egyptian and Indian Committees can hardly be said to exert any influence whatever. The societies in the first group are wealthier and better organised than those of the second. That means primarily that the tendencies which they represent are well entrenched within the governing class. They can always secure peers and bishops for their platforms, and great capitalists sit on the inner executive committees of several of them. The Balkan Committee has no commercial connections, and it owed its measure of success to the unremitting devotion of Messrs. Noel and Charles Buxton, but it can reckon on the Archbishop of Canterbury when it has occasion to send a deputation to the Foreign Office. The Anti-Slavery movement has behind it the traditional support of many powerful families, mainly Quaker in origin, connected with banking and industry. It is, in short, rather the weight of the individuals which support these movements than the numbers behind them which ensures success. They are influential just in so far as they can persuade or delude the Foreign Office into the belief that they speak for society and for capital. An organisation which has large funds and imposing " names " behind it can always make an agitation if it secures a competent secretary. A society which has no funds and relies on unpaid services is seldom a real force. But it is doubtful whether any of these organisations could drive a Minister who had himself no sympathy with their aims, to modify his policy in accordance with their claims. Their function is rather to " strengthen his hands," and to create a public opinion in support of the policy to which he already stands committed. But none of these bodies is concerned with the more vital aspects of British policy. The decisive depart-ures of recent years—the Japanese Alliance, the French and the Russian *ententes*—lie wholly outside their scope. In the main lines of his policy a British Minister is quite beyond the reach of any organised opinion. It is indeed one of the most curious, and in a sense, creditable aspects of English national psychology that public opinion organises itself and seeks articulate and popular expression only in regions of foreign policy to which some humane instinct leads it. It really cares about negro slavery, Congo horrors and Turkish massacres, and on these questions asserts itself. It will, on the other hand, sit inert and dumb while a Foreign Minister concludes with an almost unknown and not exactly sympathetic Asiatic Power like Japan, a treaty of alliance which may at some distant date force us automati-cally to bear our share in a war in no way connected with our interests and quite beyond our control. One may admire the generosity of this curious concentration of attention on questions which do not directly concern us, but one cannot justify the neglect of other issues which are of vital moment.

These leagues rather make opinion than express the spontaneous movements of the mass mind. The same thing is roughly true of newspapers. On the broader issues of domestic policy newspapers are some guide to the trend of opinion, for the simple reason that if they took to expressing opinions repug-nant to their readers they would cease to " pay." If a newspaper prospers and is widely read, the

presumption is that its views about tariff reform or
Socialism or religious education are in the main
those of the tens or hundreds of thousands of persons
who buy it daily.   But no such inference can be
drawn from its views about the Japanese Alliance
or our policy in Persia.   Readers rarely have ready-
made opinions on such points, and if they have, do
not usually penalise a paper which takes the other
line.   The real importance of newspapers depends
less on their leading articles than on their power to
present or colour or suppress facts.   Here the masses
are absolutely at their mercy.   In this connection
one has to remember that their proprietors are
always capitalists, and are sometimes interested in
foreign investments or in armaments.   They sell news,
and it is usually the bureaucrat, the Minister, or the
financier who is able to supply news.   Occasionally
newspapers have been known to accept a service
of telegrams gratis or at reduced rates from some
individual or organisation which has an interest
to serve in forming public opinion.   The excitement
which produced the Boer War was largely fostered
by such methods.   A newspaper which takes an
anti-Imperialist attitude, even if it keeps its readers,
is often penalised by advertisers who withdraw their
advertisements to punish it for its " unpatriotic "
attitude.   Such withdrawals of valuable advertisements have happened, to my knowledge, because a
newspaper opposed an increase of the Navy Estimates.   A newspaper which opposes a loan to the
Russian Government will suffer in the same way.
Newspapers, in short, are one of the most powerful
means by which capital and the dominant interests

can create or suppress opinion. They are not in foreign affairs to any great extent a means by which spontaneous and disinterested opinion makes its power felt. The ability of the Liberal press to influence the Foreign Office has been tested during Sir Edward Grey's long term of office. The *Nation*, the *Manchester Guardian* and the *Daily News* have been steadily critical of the whole trend of his policy, and incidents have sometimes moved them to outspoken indignation. Yet it is only within modest limits, and then only when a section of Conservative opinion was with them, as it was in the later phases of the Persian question, that they have seemed to deflect his course of action.

The Constitution provides three checks by which a Foreign Minister can be restrained from the pursuit of an arbitrary or merely personal policy. They are usually, though not always, powerful enough to prevent a wilful Minister from following an eccentric or individual line of action. But neither any one of them, nor yet all three together, offer any guarantee that his attitude will be a deliberate expression of the national will. The checks in question are those exercised by the Crown, the Cabinet and the House of Commons.

The formal rights of control which the House of Commons enjoys are exceedingly limited. It may question the Foreign Secretary, debate his policy on motions or resolutions, and express dissatisfaction by reducing the estimates for his Department, but there its effective powers end. One has only to compare its rights with those of other Parliaments to realise how unusually meagre they are. In the

first place its assent is not required for a declaration
of war, which means that it cannot interfere effectually before the event to delay a rupture, to enforce
arbitration, or to overthrow a Minister who had
failed to exhaust on behalf of peace all the resources
of diplomacy.   In France the assent of the Chamber,
in the United States that of Congress, and in Germany
that of the Federal Council (Bundesrath) are required
for a formal declaration of war.   When once war is
declared and the reserves are called up, Parliament
must be summoned to vote supplies.   But the die
is already cast, and the friends of peace can then
register only an academic protest.   Perhaps the
worst consequence of this defect in our constitution
is that a Government may with ease drift or rush
into war during the long months between August
and February in which the House does not always sit.
If its assent were requisite, a Government would be
practically forced to summon it as soon as events
became critical, and to submit its conduct of the
negotiations to public criticism.   In the present
condition of party discipline a united Cabinet with a
large majority behind it, could usually count on
obtaining the assent of its drilled followers to a
declaration of war.   But the necessity of first submitting its policy to a detailed examination would
still tend to restrain it in any provocative course.
I have heard experienced politicians argue that the
South African War could not have broken out had
Parliament been sitting in October, 1899.

Still more important is the impotence of the
House of Commons in regard to Treaties.   Unless
they include financial provisions, there is no obliga-

tion to submit them to Parliament, and no discussion can take place upon them until they are already signed, ratified, and published to the world. One consequence of this is that a secret treaty is for us no less binding than a public instrument. A secret treaty duly signed and ratified by one British Government would bind its successors. In theory the King and his Foreign Minister, acting with the consent of his colleagues in the Cabinet,•can and do contract the most solemn and vital obligations in the name of the forty millions over whom they rule in these islands, without consulting their elected representatives. They can make war and peace, they can annex or alienate territory, they can assume obligations which may oblige not only us but our children to go to war in support of an ally in a quarrel not our own. Such unchecked authority belongs to few other civilised Governments. In France the consent of the Chamber, in Germany that of the Reichstag, in the United States that of a two-thirds majority of the Senate is required to render a Treaty valid. In practice the American Senate has often used its right to veto Treaties. In France and Germany the obligation is habitually evaded when Treaties of Alliance are contracted. The terms of the Dual and Triple Alliances are not fully known, though their general tenor may be guessed. It may be said that the right of revising or rejecting treaties is unimportant, because a Government can usually circumvent it by concluding secret arrangements. It could do so, however, only if Parliaments were servile and indifferent to their rights, and even so a secret arrangement unconstitutionally con-

cluded by one Minister could always be ignored or
modified by his successors. Two recent instances
serve to remind us of the immense power which this
right of concluding Treaties places in the hands of
the Foreign Minister—the Japanese Alliance which
compels us to support our ally with arms, if any other
Power should attack her, and the Anglo-Russian
Agreements which partitioned Persia into two
unequal spheres of influence, and so virtually sur-
rendered the destinies of the Persian nation, at a
moment when it was struggling to maintain its
constitution, to the discretion of the Russian
bureaucracy.

The extent to which Parliament may use its
general right of criticism and debate to influence
Foreign Policy has enormously diminished in recent
years.   Debates on foreign affairs in the generation
of Palmerston and Russell, and even in that of Gladstone and Disraeli, were more frequent, more animated, more influential. It is the doctrine of
" continuity," and the growing power of the Cabinet
which destroyed both the initiative and the control
of the House. It is now an established convention
that foreign affairs shall not be made a subject of
party controversy. Formerly the acknowledged
leaders of public opinion used all their resources of
argument and invective to criticise a Minister's
foreign policy. To-day the two Front Benches are
agreed to exempt all such questions from serious
debate. It is left to the Labour Party or to a few
incorrigible rebels on the Radical benches to introduce the only real element of criticism which survives. Their speeches are reported in a few lines,

and for the most part they speak to empty benches. The physiognomy of one of these discussions makes one despair of the introduction of any really democratic element into foreign affairs. The subject is, let us say, Turkey or Persia. The House empties at once, and a listless remnant of perhaps twenty members waits to encourage a friend or to seize the opportunity to speak. It fills again only when Sir Edward Grey rises to dismiss, with his musical voice and graceful address, criticisms to which few of his hearers had troubled to listen. One sometimes suspects that the House and the governing class generally regard it as an impertinence in any one outside the inner circle to meddle with foreign affairs at all. *Punch* recorded its opinion of one of these debates in a cartoon which deserves to be remembered. When Mr. Keir Hardie and Mr. John Dillon raised in the House the question of the Denshawai hangings, it depicted Sir Edward Grey, the defender of these panic-stricken methods of barbarism, as a mediæval knight in armour mounted on a splendid charger, at whose heels two ill-conditioned curs with the heads of the Labour and the Irish leaders barked and snapped in vain. " The Grey Knight rides on " was the legend beneath it.

The opportunities for these debates grow fewer every year. The House is busy with domestic affairs, and both Front Benches discourage these excursions into distant fields. There are only two or three regular opportunities during the session for formal debate, and even these are sometimes omitted and often curtailed. It is now rarely possible to raise an urgent question by a motion for the adjournment of the House, because the miserable stratagem of the " blocking motion " is freely used to prevent discussion. The subjects which do generally get discussed are those on which Ministers rather like to have their " hands strengthened " ; the Congo question, for example, was sometimes debated twice or thrice in a single session. On the other hand the really large and vital questions of public policy are rarely raised, or, if raised at all, raised too late. Thus it was quite impossible before the second Hague Conference to discuss the instructions given by the Foreign Office to our representative, Sir Edward Fry, and in particular to consider whether he should be empowered to support the obsolete barbarism of the capture of private property in wartime at sea. One all-important question has governed all our foreign policy since the Liberals came into office—the antagonism of the two European Groups, and the struggle to maintain a balance of power. Save for brief references in the naval censure debate of 1909, this subject has never been discussed in its general aspects, while the Moroccan crisis led to only one important debate (after the crisis of 1911) and even then it shared an evening with other topics. The practice of other Parliaments is more democratic and less secretive. The French Chamber and the German Reichstag have often in the same period discussed the larger aspects of European policy in debates which continued for two or three days. It is no compensation for the meagreness of our debates that our House of Commons has what other Parliaments lack, the right to " heckle " a Foreign Secretary by question and answer. Questions are invaluable for the clearing up of facts, but they are nearly useless for the discussion of policy.

One other point must be noted. Whatever moral influence the House of Commons may be able to exercise in a vague way by asking questions and making speeches, it is practically debarred from translating this influence into the imperative mood of a vote. A Foreign Secretary may if he pleases allow himself to be guided by the fact that the " tone " of the House was on a given occasion somewhat hostile or critical, or that respected members urged him to take up a certain line of policy. But he need never fear an adverse vote. It would nowadays be considered quite scandalous if the Opposition Whips were to tell against the Foreign Minister in a division. Be the Foreign Minister Liberal or Conservative, it is only the Labour Party and a handful of Radicals who ever do vote against him. The reasons are obvious. A vote against the Foreign Minister is a vote against the entire Government, and his defeat, in almost any conceivable circumstances, would entail a dissolution. Few members, if any, are prepared to jeopardise free trade for the sake of a scruple about Persia, or to risk the future of social reform at home to save the skins of a few Egyptian peasants from an unmerited death or a public flogging. As Lord John Russell once remarked when Palmerston obtained a majority for his highly provocative policy, " the fate of the Government had been staked upon it, and many people voted on that account who would not have supported the foreign policy." (*Queen Victoria's Letters*, ii. 313.)

In plain words members vote for or against a Government; they do not vote on the merits of any particular foreign issue. While that is so, it is evident that the House of Commons can exercise no serious control over foreign policy.

One is tempted to suppose that however weak the Commons may be as a board of control, the Cabinet is at least in a position to act as a serious check upon a Foreign Secretary. It consists of picked men; it sits in secret; it has all the facts and the documents before it, and it can intervene before an act is irreparably consummated. These are immense advantages, and though the Cabinet represents only one party, it usually contains enough diversity of temperament and opinions to make a real debate possible. It is difficult for an outsider to know how far any given Cabinet exerts its rights of corporate responsibility, but history furnishes some materials for an answer, and they are not reassuring. Much depends on the personality of the Minister. A headstrong and obstinate man will have his way in a Cabinet, as in less august committees, if he is also able and a power in the country. Queen Victoria's letters are a mine of information on this point. It is clear from them that Lord Palmerston, one of the ablest but one of the most reckless Foreign Ministers that this country has ever produced, was on most occasions a law unto himself. No Minister stood more in need of constant control, yet he was usually successful in evading it. It is frankly admitted in these letters that Lord John Russell, the Prime Minister, was quite unable to control Palmerston, who constantly acted in large

issues without the authority either of the whole
Cabinet or even of his chief. He even went so far
as to recognise Louis Napoleon after the *coup d'état*
entirely on his own responsibility, and against the
wishes, not only of public opinion, but of the Queen
and his own colleagues. To the suggestion that he
should be dismissed, Lord John Russell always
answered that if he were dismissed, he would avenge
himself by going into Opposition and overthrowing
the Government. How just this fear was, events
showed. He was eventually forced to resign at the
end of December, 1851. By February, 1852, he had
unseated his late colleagues. A Cabinet which
cannot dispense with a Minister must be prepared
to give him a free hand.

There is a further difficulty in exerting any real
control. A Cabinet is not a simple committee. It
is a Committee in which each Minister is the head
of a department. His main concern must always
be to further the interests of that department. His
reputation depends less on the general policy of the
Ministry than on the success of his own Bills. If he
on his side has to meet some opposition in the Cabinet, he will be the less disposed to rouse further
antagonism by interfering with a colleague. A
Minister has, let us suppose, concentrated all his
dreams on passing a certain Bill. He becomes
meanwhile uneasy about the trend of foreign policy.
He makes a protest, which passes unheeded. Is he
to insist, knowing that insistance may involve his own
resignation, and the loss of the Bill on which he has set
his heart ? The chances are that in such a dilemma
he will usually elect to go on doing his own duty

in his own department, and to leave the Foreign Secretary to bear the responsibility for his own omissions or mistakes. The tendency will always be to leave a Foreign Secretary alone, if he on his side is equally considerate to others. Thus Lord John Russell, attempting to explain to Queen Victoria why it was so difficult to control Palmerston's vagaries, remarked rather naïvely that he was " a good colleague," a term which he proceeded to define as a Minister who does not interfere with other departments, and demands in return a free hand for himself.

The Foreign Secretary is indeed, as a rule, much more his own master than any other member of the Cabinet. He makes virtually no demands for money, and therefore the Chancellor of the Exchequer is not called upon to exercise over him the constant vigilance which he is authorised to use towards the great spending departments. But the main reason for his freedom is the simple fact that in most Cabinets, and more particularly in Liberal Cabinets, few Ministers have the requisite knowledge to enable them to check his proceedings. Thus, in 1860, at a time when foreign affairs were intensely interesting, and all England was moved by the resurrection of Italy, Palmerston put it on record, in speaking of his colleagues, that " Mr. Gladstone is almost the only one on the Treasury Bench who follows up foreign questions close enough to take an active part." In a Cabinet so constituted, the Foreign Secretary will certainly have his way, simply because he is the recognised expert. His colleagues may feel a vague disquiet about his doings, but they lack the detailed knowledge to meet him in debate. In the Liberal Cabinet, as it was formed in 1906, Mr. Bryce was the only member who had studied foreign affairs closely enough " to take an active part," and he left it early to become Ambassador in Washington.

But one is not left to conjecture in estimating the small part which Cabinet control plays in the conduct of foreign affairs. There are instances in modern history which show how slack and nerveless is this control, even when the issue of peace and war is at stake. It may be enough to cite two of them in order to illustrate this point. The history of the negotiations which led up to the Crimean War goes to show that four men and four only were responsible for British policy,—Lord Clarendon, the Foreign Secretary; Lord Aberdeen, the Prime Minister; and Lords John Russell and Palmerston, whose experience made their advice worth seeking. The war was made by these typical representatives of the governing class, and it is especially significant that none of the commoners in the Cabinet seem to have claimed a voice in the negotiations. Lord Morley, in his *Life of Gladstone*, who was one of the silent members in this Cabinet which allowed itself to drift under its aristocratic leaders into this most unnecessary war, adds this comment (Vol. I. p. 357, popular edition) :—

> The Cabinet as a body was a machine incapable of being worked by anything like daily and some times hourly consultations of this kind, the upshot of which would only become known on the more important occasions to the Ministers at

large, especially to those among them charged with the most laborious departments.

In other words the Cabinet as a whole had no real responsibility for the war, and some at least of its members were even content to remain in ignorance of the detailed steps by which war became inevitable. Moreover, Mr. Gladstone and Lord Morley are apparently of opinion that the Cabinet is a machine which cannot be used with effect to control delicate negotiations. Another even more startling illustration is to be found in Lord Morley's *Life of Gladstone* (Vol. II. p. 4). In August, 1865, the *Alabama* affair entered on a critical phase, when the American Ambassador presented a demand for compensation for the damage done by this privateer during the civil war ; should compensation be refused, he suggested that the affair be referred to arbitration. Lord Russell flatly refused all compensation ; what was much more serious, he refused no less categorically to submit the question to arbitration—a refusal which was reversed three years later by a Conservative Government. This despatch was written and presented on Lord Russell's sole responsibility. The Cabinet had not so much as discussed the question. If a Foreign Secretary may refuse arbitration without consulting his colleagues, it is hardly too much to say that he may by his own individual act render war inevitable. The modern practice seems to be to leave even the gravest questions to inner circles or sub-committees of the Cabinet. It was admitted, for example, that Mr. Lloyd George's Mansion House speech during the crisis of 1911, in which Germany was publicly warned that we were prepared to go to war over the Moroccan question in support of France, was made without the authority of the Cabinet.   It was delivered after a consultation between Mr. Asquith, Sir Edward Grey and Mr. Lloyd George.   That speech came near provoking war, and left a heavy legacy of bitterness behind it. If the Cabinet need not be summoned to consider even such crucial acts of foreign policy as this, it is clear that it cannot be regarded as a trustworthy check upon a Foreign Minister.

There remains a third check, which, unlike the others, is really operative, but it is a check which rather enforces than bridles the normal tendencies of the governing class.   The Crown under Queen Victoria succeeded after a long and bitter struggle with Whig Ministers in establishing its right of control over the minutest details of foreign policy, and under King Edward its privileges were more than maintained.   Queen Victoria's letters are in the main a record of the immense part which she and the Prince Consort played in determining foreign policy. Her point of view was logical and consistent, and it was almost invariably anti-national and anti-democratic.

The Queen's attitude towards the resurrection of Italy is peculiarly interesting, because it is typical of the mode of thinking which even the most enlightened Monarch would almost always assume in similar circumstances.   She was very far from being reactionary, and she uses on occasion very critical phrases about Metternich and the Tsar Nicholas.   On the other hand, the world in which she moved was a world of monarchs and governments.   Nations she

neither knew nor recognised.   In the tremendous
upheaval between 1848 and 1860, which was creating
an Italian people, she saw nothing but a series of
aggressions by Sardinia against Austria.   All governments, in her eyes, were alike entitled to the same
respect and the same fair treatment.   She based
herself exclusively on treaties and the *status quo*,
and to her the fundamental fact was that Austria
had certain " rights " in Italy.   Her personal sense
of honour was keen and sensitive, and towards other
monarchs and other governments she never forgot
the golden rule, but her interpretation of history
was tinged by an almost legal bias, and she would
argue over the fate of an Italian province exactly as
a lawyer might argue over the ownership of a free-
hold.   When Palmerston and Louis Napoleon were
talking in 1848 of a plébiscite to decide the fate of
Lombardy, she declared that " it will be a calamity
for ages to come " if peoples are allowed to transfer
their allegiance by universal suffrage.   Garibaldi's
expedition to Sicily filled her with something much
deeper than political disapproval, and she tried
hard to induce Russell to express " moral reproba-
tion."   She had a fellow-feeling with Austria, and
it was quite in vain that Russell and Palmerston
used to remind her that the King of Sardinia was
doing in Lombardy exactly what William of Orange
had done in England.   Never through this whole
period does she seem to have caught a glimpse of
an Italian nation.   She saw only an Austrian
Emperor and a Sardinian King.   In the main she
failed to deflect Whig policy, but she did impose
hesitations and delays, and it is just possible that

if she had supported Palmerston in 1848, Italy might not have had to wait eleven years for liberation. Sometimes, indeed, she based her caution on a love of peace. But while she loathed the idea of any policy which might conceivably end in armed Anglo-French intervention to free Italy, she wholly approved armed Anglo-French co-operation in 1854 to maintain the integrity of Turkey. Her point of view was not personal. It would be that of any monarch for whom kings and governments are the central realities of politics.

The control exercised by the Crown is in short open to all the objections that may be raised against the control of the House of Lords over legislation. It is almost certain to be anti-popular, and it will almost certainly be one-sided. The Crown throughout the period covered by Queen Victoria's letters used its influence with remarkable steadiness, and always in one sense. There is nothing in these letters to suggest any attempt to hold up the other scale of the balance while the Tories were in office. A constitutional monarch, who regarded himself as a trustee for his people and a permanent force making for continuity, moderation, and peace, would be compelled to argue on occasion for the Whig against the Tories, and for the Tories against the Whigs. But that would imply an almost impossible agility of mind. Nor did the Queen's intervention satisfy the other ideal requirement of a constitutional check—that it should be so far as possible an impersonal *vox populi*, uttering in secret affairs the unspoken, and perhaps unconscious, opinion of the nation. In all the debates between the Queen and the Whigs, the one argument which she never used was that British opinion was on her side. She argued from prudence, from justice, from legality, but never from public opinion. Indeed it was rather for the monarchs of Europe that she seemed to speak, as Lord John Russell hinted, when he defended Palmerston's policy from her criticisms ;

> Somewhat of the good opinion of the Emperor of Russia and other foreign Governments may be lost, but the good will and affection of the people of England are retained.

The most determined of several attempts which the Crown made to remove Palmerston from the Foreign Office took place immediately after the great debate on foreign policy, in which his memorable "*Civis Romanus Sum*," won for him an ovation and an overwhelming vote of confidence. Parliament was more than satisfied, but the Crown still demanded his dismissal. The Crown is certainly a powerful check upon the Foreign Office, but it is necessarily an incalculable and purely personal check. Above all it is a check which tends to make our policy even less democratic and more conservative than it otherwise would be. There is little or nothing in her letters to suggest that Queen Victoria allowed any personal dislike which she might entertain for a foreign monarch to deflect her attitude in politics But rumours, too numerous and too consistent to be quite disregarded, suggest that the personal antipathy between her successor and the German Emperor played a considerable part in estranging their two Governments. A dangerous constitutional precedent was created when he was allowed to pay what clearly were political visits to foreign monarchs, unaccompanied by the Foreign Secretary.

A survey of the machinery of our foreign relations would be incomplete, which was content to demonstrate the absence of any guarantee that it will broadly interpret national interests and public opinion. The character of the machine itself is at least as important. From Downing Street to Pekin, the diplomatic service is based on the assumption that the relations of States mean in practice the relations of their upper classes. Commerce and finance enter into its calculations as they rarely did in earlier centuries, yet diplomacy continues to be the game of courts. The Foreign Secretary is almost invariably a peer, or if not a peer at least a member of some historic governing family. Entry to the diplomatic service is still by nomination, though nearly every other branch of the Civil Service has been thrown open to competition. No young man can enter it unless he is possessed of private means. By such methods its permeation by democratic sympathies is carefully guarded against. Once within its ranks a young man readily learns that alike at home and abroad he is expected to move in " good society," and in " good society " alone. He becomes familiar only with that aspect of the life of a foreign nation which is normally frivolous and reactionary. He will meet the Ministers and the leaders of fashion of the country to which he is accredited ; he will not meet the people. In such a country as Russia it would be fatal to his prospects, if he were even to consort with middle-class Liberals. It happened on one occasion that Professor Miliukoff, the Russian Liberal leader, visited the United States on a lecturing tour. President Roosevelt proposed to receive him. The Russian Ambassador successfully protested, and the visit did not take place. One may infer how little probability there is that our Embassy or any Embassy in St. Petersburg will meet persons who are in bad odour at the Tsar's court. It follows that the views formed by an Ambassador and embodied in his despatches, are views matured in the atmosphere of courts, by a man isolated from popular influences in the country where he lives. It sometimes happens, moreover, that the Ambassador does not know, and does not take the trouble to learn the language of the country in which he lives. He does his work in French. In such a country as Turkey the consuls are commonly better equipped as linguists, more closely in touch with the people, and much more popular in their sympathies than the staff of the Embassy. But it is the Ambassador's opinion in policy and not that of the consular corps which reaches the Foreign Secretary. Diplomacy is in all countries the acknowledged preserve of wealth and birth. The German Emperor actually objected to a man of some eminence and distinction, whom the United States proposed to send as Ambassador to Berlin, on the ground that his private fortune was not large enough to permit him to entertain on a scale as lavish as fashion in the Prussian capital exacts.

The words of an Ambassador or a Foreign Secretary carry weight only because behind them is the force of docile and ignorant masses. To arm him with the prestige which he wields, to back his threats and to execute his promises, they drill, they labour, they are taxed. He is the trustee of their wealth, the director of their strength. For good or for evil, by their acquiescence he moulds the fate of distant nations, makes for them enemies and friends, fosters or thwarts the fortunes of popular movements in remote continents, adjusts frontiers, drafts treaties and plays with the issues of peace and war. That power the people place in his hands unchecked and uncontrolled. Nations aspire in vain to fraternity and peace, while the ambitions, the prejudices and the interests of their governing caste dictate their movements and govern their intercourse.[1]

[1] P.S.—The disclosures in Sir Edward Grey's speech on the eve of the war have a bearing on this chapter. He stated that in 1906 he conveyed both to France and Germany an intimation, which was something less than a promise or threat, that we should support France in a war over Morocco. This action was taken after consultation with Sir Henry Campbell-Bannerman, Mr. Asquith and Lord Haldane, and the practice of regular military conversations with France was thereupon adopted. The Cabinet was not consulted, because an election was in progress. Owing to this accident, the fundamental basis of our foreign policy was not reviewed by the Cabinet, until " much later on " (November, 1912). That so long a delay could have occurred in reviewing our military relations with France, is a proof that the Cabinet was not the body which controlled our external policy. This work has passed to its inner ring. The most serious result of these secret " conversations " was that the French fleet was concentrated in the Mediterranean, since our fleet was expected to defend the northern coasts of France. That arrangement in itself forbade our neutrality in the present war. An open alliance would have been less dangerous than this incalculable commitment.

PART II

CONSTRUCTIVE

CHAPTER V

THE earlier chapters of this book have essayed the
task of analysing the economic tendencies which
explain the armed peace in Europe. As a study of
the forces opposed to any humane ideal of the relations which should obtain between peoples, it is
incomplete : as an estimate of the real forces at
work it is still less adequate. The financial motives
which make for Imperialism and underlie the struggle for a balance of power have been isolated and
emphasised in this sketch. Behind these influences
there are potent causes, intellectual rather than
material, which are still at work in the world,
attenuated indeed, disguised and shamefaced, but
still active as they have been since the dawn of history. The charity, the sympathy that pass beyond
frontiers, the sense of a common brotherhood amid
the problems of life, the perception of a common
interest in opposing predatory and anti-social forces
—these have been of slow growth, and even to-day
they are a formed habit and a conscious ideal only
among the more enlightened individuals of civilised
peoples. They seem to have little relation to culture, and are sometimes more highly developed
in the proletariat than among the " intellectuals."

157

The pride of race, the insolence of colour, the megalomania which swells as it contemplates great possessions and vast territories, the theatrical instinct
which hails even war as a relief from the drab mono-
tony of modern industrial life, the ignorant distrust
of the " foreigner," the inability to seize the standpoint of a rival—all of these reinforce the financial
pressure towards expansion. It is not necessary to
assume that the interests which profit by Imperialism consciously and deliberately play upon these
primitive passions, this vulgarity of mind. They
need rarely take that trouble. This emotional
crudity, basing itself, as it does, upon a whole series
of fallacious axioms and half-truths, requires little
prompting. It is always ready to spring into activity
at the first hint that British interests are in conflict
with those of a rival people. As little need we
suppose that the bankers and bondholders and contractors, whose private enterprises are the origin of
an international complication, are aware of what
they do when they exploit patriotism to secure their
dividends. The human mind has an infinite capacity
for illusion, and abstract words were made to assist
the process. The average selfish employer who
withstands a demand for a living wage, convinces
himself with ease that he is a pillar of society, and
that he is resisting anarchy and fighting against an
agitation which would be " the end of all things."
We have all learnt to think in a fog of words and to
clothe ourselves in abstractions, lest haply we should
know that we are naked, and learn to discern evil
from good. With the same mellow, habitual hypocrisy, the financier who embroils a nation over his

distant ventures, persuades himself that his own cause is that of the Empire. He reads of himself every day in leading articles. He is one of the " pioneers." He is concerned in " trade," and our trade has " made us what we are." By general consent, it is the business of the Empire to foster and protect our " trade." There is nothing personally sinister in all this, because the financier is acting in accordance with the accepted moral standards of his class, and these are still the dominant standards of every industrial State. The financier who prompts the press to appeal to the lower passions of the mob is not engaging in a cold and calculated wickedness. Subject himself to these passions, he appeals instinctively to those who share them.

The mass of the voters in any civilised country are the prey to interested promptings, when a foreign crisis arises, partly because their knowledge of the actual facts is limited, and still more because their perception of the real causes which govern international rivalries is hazy. They can be stirred by any eloquent emotional appeal. Two tendencies lie latent in their minds in a semi-conscious confusion. Let a group of Labour leaders, English and German, address a mass meeting of British working-men. It can be roused to a real sense of the solidarity between the two proletariats ; it can be induced to vote a contribution from its own trade union funds to assist German miners on strike ; it will leave the meeting with a real desire for peace and fraternity between the two nations. But it has little power to transform this energy of goodwill into political pressure, and in the existing condition of Parliament there is

comparatively little which a Labour Party can do
to further the wishes of their electors in this direction. The good will is unluckily rather fleeting.
The same crowd, prepared by the press and artfully
stimulated by skilful orators, could also be induced to
applaud the speeches of naval scaremongers, and
to go away shouting for more Dreadnoughts, and
looking for German airships in the sky. The two
sets of instincts co-exist in the popular mind, and
either can be roused by an emotional appeal. There
must be a more educative propaganda, a more
conscious effort to fix principles, before any democracy can be trusted to stand firm in moments of
national crisis. It is not enough to make the masses
feel, as they always can be made to feel while a
good orator is speaking, that war is horrible and
barbarous, armaments wasteful, and a peace based
on arbitration desirable. That feeling is not an
adequate intellectual defence against the special
pleadings which can always be used to show that
each case as it arises is the exception to the general
rule. There is no security until the mass-mind has
come to understand the working of the capitalistic
pressure which tends towards Imperialism and makes
great armaments in order to achieve a balance of
power favourable to expansion. It is necessary
to implant a general and rooted scepticism, which
will instinctively ask, when the glowing words and
the specious abstractions are deployed, " About
what loan or concession or sphere of economic
interest are you really talking ? " Such a task is
beyond the scope, it is sometimes beyond the
insight, of the special propagandists of peace. There

are limits to the vision and even more to the action of a propagandist whose outlook is what is rather vaguely termed Liberal. Sincere, disinterested and well-informed though he may be, he cannot always dissociate himself from the very forces that maintain the armed peace of the " Balance." Talking to-day of disarmament and arbitration, he will work to-morrow for a party which is hardly less dependent than its rival on the great contractors and bankers who maintain the modern connection of diplomacy and finance. The work of education and organisation on behalf of peace is carried on adequately only by the Socialist parties, and they alone represent a force whose undivided vote will always be cast against militarism and Imperialism.

The permeation of public opinion by " pacifist " thinking goes on apace, in spite of these difficulties. It has lately received a powerful intellectual stimulus from the work of Mr. Norman Angell. He is probably the ablest pamphleteer who has used the English language since Thomas Paine, and he brings to his task a knowledge of affairs and an insight into the detailed working of the world's machinery which few of the early Radicals possessed. With this he has kept that faith in the power of reason which was the great gift to mankind of the pioneers of Paine's generation. He does not doubt that if he could convince mankind that war is irrational, war would forthwith cease. To bring back such a faith as this into our daily life would be an even greater achievement than the banishment of war. For want of it all our progressive agitations are nerveless and timid. We have reacted so far against the eighteenth century conviction that man is a reasonable animal, that we have almost ceased to hope anything from fundamental argument. The main thesis of " The Great Illusion " is already so well known and so widely accepted, that we need not pause here to demonstrate it. From a national standpoint war is a mistake and conquest an illusion. A nation does not own its colonies, and by taking provinces from a rival it would acquire nothing for itself. Conquest indeed in this barbaric sense of the word is obsolete, and belongs to the agricultural stage of civilisation. If a civilised State annexes a fully occupied country inhabited by another civilised race, it will neither expropriate land nor lay hands on any of its realised or potential wealth. The conquerors will be no richer, and the conquered no poorer for the change. Where then is the gain of conquest ? It is also manifestly true that a war between two elaborately organised industrial States like Britain and Germany would so shake the whole fabric of credit in both, that the conqueror, for all his triumphs, might emerge from the struggle weakened and impoverished. Once more war is unreason. The gain is an illusion ; the losses are a certainty. It ought to follow, if this reasoning is sound, that armaments are useless and will be abolished when nations have grasped the fact that war is an anachronism, indeed, well-nigh an impossibility in a society based on a respect for private property, and accustomed to conduct its business by a system of cosmopolitan credit.

This summary does some injustice by reason of its

brevity and simplicity to Mr. Norman Angell's doctrine, but it is too well known to need a full re-statement. Its main positions are unassailable. It is a sound logical fabric, and the world will be a more habitable planet when it is generally accepted. One may, however, subscribe to its general truth, and yet feel that it fails in some vital particulars to grasp the whole subtlety of the dry warfare, the armed peace of modern Europe. At the risk of seeming to trifle with a paradox, one may sum up a criticism of this doctrine in a sentence. The purpose of armaments is not necessarily war; with a great army one may bully profitably for a generation, keeping a risky peace. If the view taken in the preceding chapters of the meaning of the struggle for the balance of power is even partially and approximately true, then this pacifist argument against armaments is an elaborate missing of our opponents' point. Let us admit at once that war is a folly from the standpoint of national self-interest; it may none the less be perfectly rational from the standpoint of a small but powerful governing class. Further, if war is a folly, it does not follow that the typical forms of modern expansion, which are commonly achieved with the aid of armaments but without war, are follies from this same capitalist standpoint. We share with Mr. Norman Angell the belief that war between European Powers for the possession of European soil or of old-established colonies has become an anachronism, as an economic venture. The reason is perfectly obvious. Between two States which are approximately on the same level of industrial development, conquest promises no gain, even to the financier. If the Germans could annex Lancashire they would alter nothing in its economic life. It is self-subsisting. It has capital enough for its own needs, and more than enough. It is, so to speak, saturated with capital, and could absorb no more from German stores. It is being as fully " exploited " (to use a convenient if controversial word) as it possibly can be by its own native capitalists. The same thing is true of the Rhineland, and what is true of Lancashire and the Rhineland is true in some degree of all civilised countries, including not only our " white " colonies, but our older tropical possessions. They are not the " places in the sun " to which the modern Imperialist turns his gaze. He seeks new countries to " exploit," promising regions with virgin mines, untilled fields, cities without banks, routes without rails. These are the opportunities he covets. He is pleased to have them without conquest, and he does not desire war. His ideal is to fence them in as an economic sphere of interest, within which he may dump his capital as a national monopoly.

This is the process which we must visualise if we would understand the survival of armaments, and it is a process of which Mr. Norman Angell's doctrine takes too little account. We are all accustomed to repeat the axiom that capital is cosmopolitan. So, indeed, in many senses it is. But it is also national in its workings ; the flag, as Mr. Cecil Rhodes used to say, is an asset. Explain the connection as one may, it is the fact that the capital invested in any new country which has come into the possession of a given Power, or has been recognised as its sphere of influence, tends to belong to subjects of that power. An English company will not receive a concession to build a railway in a German colony, nor in spite of our devotion to the maxims of Free Trade and to the principle of the open door, does one find German railways in British colonies. A curious phrase was employed in the Anglo-Russian convention relating to the recognition of separate spheres in Persia. It was stipulated that neither Power should seek " political concessions " in the sphere of the other, and the term was defined by enumeration to include railways, telegraphs, roads, harbours, and the like. Such public works as these, if they are in private hands, will usually, for reasons of policy, belong to subjects of the dominant Power. The great engineering works in Egypt were executed before our occupation by French contractors and engineers. They have now become an enormously valuable opportunity for British firms. Capital moves with the flag—sometimes before it and sometimes after it. The Balkan conquests supplied an interesting illustration. One of the first acts of the Servian Government in the portion of Macedonia which it had annexed, was to expropriate the privately-owned railway, which belonged chiefly to Austrian subjects. This order of facts has been passed over too lightly by Mr. Norman Angell in his controversy with the brilliant German Socialist writer Kautsky. To adopt Kautsky's illustration, it is surely impossible to deny that the German governing and financial class (if not the German nation) would derive considerable profit from the conquest, let us say, of India. The actual investments of British capitalists would, of course, be respected. But the privately-owned railways would tend to pass by purchase into German hands. German banks, assured of official patronage, would compete on favoured terms with the existing British banks, and would soon control the credit system of India. The profits of all the new loans required for public works ánd military works would fall to German financiers, and the immense gains from contracting would go exclusively to Germans. To Germans also would fall the large sum that now flows in pensions and salaries to England. To recognise this fact is not to question the central doctrine of *The Great Illusion*, that conquest does not benefit a nation. But the small class which in every country maintains Imperialism is not deficient in intelligence, and there is no fallacy in its egoistic calculations. But let us add, however, that this class would readily find adventures more attractive and more profitable than the conquest of India. It would prefer an untilled and unappropriated field, like Turkey and China, not merely because it may with luck be had without fighting, but even more because the capitalists of the favoured Power could operate there without competition. It would be " bad business " to attempt to conquer a thoroughly capitalised European country, and for the same reason it would be relatively foolish business to attempt to take for choice an old and established dependency like Egypt or India.

It follows that we must seek the reason for the survival of armaments in some cause more rationaĺ and more permanent than the prevalence of falla-

cious thinking and the persistence of barbaric sentiments. If the world at large has failed to embrace
the cogent logic of Mr. Norman Angell's doctrine,
the explanation is that powerful private interests
have their motives for resisting it. Armaments are
not necessarily required for war at all. They serve
a purpose first of all in giving prestige to the diplomacy of the Great Power which is seeking from
an undeveloped State concessions for its subjects.
They are valuable in the second place when rival
Powers are competing for some sphere of influence.
The " balance of power " is a balance of armaments,
and modern States appear to desire a balance favourable to themselves, primarily because it will assure
them freedom of movement in the competition
to secure " places in the sun." When the Triple
Entente is dominant, it takes Morocco and divides
Persia. When the Triple Alliance recovers its
lead, it takes Tripoli, assures its hold in Bosnia, and
makes progress in the economic penetration of
Asiatic Turkey. The oscillations of the balance are
registered moreover in the gains or losses of each
group in the open competition for economic opportunities in China. These summary sentences convey,
perhaps, a provokingly simple account of a process
which is in reality extremely complex. Certainly
when our representatives in China try to obtain a
concession for a British syndicate, they do not
threaten Chinese statesmen with the instant bombardment of a Chinese port. Diplomacy is neither
so brutal nor so predatory as that. But Chinese
statesmen in dealing with us must none the less
remember that we have sometimes bombarded their

ports and sacked their palaces. They must calculate that if they annoy us beyond a certain point, they must reckon in some one of the future crises which are sure to confront them with our hostility, and if they satisfy us, they may count in some measure on our support. Our hostility is dangerous, and our support valuable in the last resort, because we are a great naval Power. So, too, in our dealings with Germany over the Bagdad Railway or our " sphere of influence " in the Yangtse Valley, it is true that we are unlikely to go to war for either of these objects. But continual friction is risky because on the appropriate occasion we have the ability to assert ourselves in a manner disagreeable to Germany —in the midst of her Moroccan negotiations with France for example. For years in succession Powers may bicker over their economic interests without moving a cruiser or uttering a threat, but their bickerings are affected and even governed by the knowledge that sooner or later, on one issue or another, decks may be cleared and armies mobilised. It is characteristic of our civilisation to disguise the connection of diplomacy with armaments on the one hand and finance on the other under an elaborate code of courtesies and hypocrisies. Pacifists risk the misdirection of their movement if they allow themselves to be deceived by it. The possession of armaments influences all the dealings of nations, and more especially it influences their rivalries to secure financial advantage in countries unable to protect themselves. When British and German bankers and contractors compete in Peking, they do not meet as rivals of the same nation meet at

home.   There is a clash of armour-plate when they
jostle.   The problem of pacificism has not been
faced as a whole so long as it confines its argument
to a demonstration of the folly of war.   Few modern
Europeans want war, and of those few, fewer still
have the sinister strength to declare it, when the
moment of decision arrives.   But large and powerful
strata of European society desire armaments and
the bloodless warfare of the contemporary struggle
for a " balance."   They desire armaments, because
armaments have become indispensable for the
pursuit under actual conditions of the gains of economic " penetration."   Our problem is much larger
than the abolition of war or the reduction of armaments.   If all the Great Powers were to resolve
to-morrow by a sudden inspiration of good sense
to reduce their armaments by half, that would not
free us from the moral consequences of the elusive
conflict to adjust the balance of prestige and force.
On the lower scale these reduced armaments would
still be used to exert pressure on undeveloped
States, and to win monopolies for the financiers of
the dominant Power or Group.   The taxpayers'
burdens would indeed be lightened, but the shadow
of a financially-minded diplomacy would still darken
the liberties of struggling nations, and on bourses
and in Foreign Offices those who profit by expansion
would still assess the relative power of these
halved navies and diminished armies.

The problem for men who have reached a
humane vision of international relations is to bring
about some organic change in the machinery which
governs the action of the Powers abroad.   It is a

problem with two aspects. We must first consider how the will of a democracy can be brought to bear upon the processes of diplomacy, how the small governing class which everywhere promotes its own economic ends and imposes them on public opinion as national interests, can be combated and dispossessed. We must devise a mechanism by which public opinion, as it becomes enlightened, may check and guide the working of diplomacy. The second half of the problem is even more complicated. We must consider whether the restless export to undeveloped countries of capital accumulated at home can in any degree be regulated, and in what measure and by what means it can be controlled. Is it possible or desirable to divorce diplomacy from finance, or by any expedient to denationalise exported capital so that its dangers, ambitions and rivalries shall no longer engage the action and imperil the relations of the nations whose ruling classes own it ? Finally, is it possible to conceive an organisation of Europe by which some process less risky, less wasteful and more civilised shall supersede the struggle for a balance of power ?

Before we attempt to answer these questions in detail, there are two developments of the modern opposition to war and armaments which deserve consideration. With the " anti-militarism " of Continental Socialism we will deal in the next chapter. It is an elaborate doctrine with a completed theory and a carefully thought out strategy, and it demands full consideration. Slighter and simpler but none the less interesting is a phase of opposition which is to be found in the writings of some Christian thinkers. A man of clear insight and unflinching logic might urge, as Tolstoy did, and as a few English writers, notably Dr. Horton and the late Dr. MacKinnel, have done, an ideal of mere retirement from the armed rivalries of Europe. The prophetic vision of a "martyr nation" has long haunted the imagination of the Society of Friends. Let some one people set the brave example of total disarmament, beat its cannon into plough-shares and turn its ironclads into floating sanatoria, and await, unprepared and unresisting, the effect of its splendid example. It is an alluring suggestion, and on one condition it would probably not involve any considerable risk. If we attempted to retain our colonies and dependencies, while we disarmed at home, we should at once be dismembered and overrun by stronger Powers. The millionaire who left his door ajar would certainly be robbed. The cottager may sleep secure by the high road without locks and bars. If we chose to be simply an unarmed and unaggressive island on the confines of Europe, we should have nothing to fear. We should be as safe as are neutral Switzerland and Holland. They owe their immunity from invasion not to their small and doubtfully efficient armies, but to the conscience of Europe and the rivalries of military Powers, any one of which could crush them without an effort. If we became an island Switzer-land, we should not be a "martyr nation." We should, however, be a parasitic nation. For we should owe our safety to the fact that the armaments of France and Russia neutralised the armaments of Central Europe. We should indeed have retired from the competition, but we should continue to profit by it. Safe ourselves, we should none the less have ceased to play a part, or to exert an influence in the general progress of the civilised world. We could not intervene to check even the grossest inhumanity, and such an accident as the rise of some conquering Napoleonic despotism might end our experiment and with it the hope of any European advance towards an assured and permanent peace. To devote ourselves to the preaching of such an ideal as this is, moreover, to sacrifice the present to a remote and perhaps impossible future. This ideal could triumph in our country only if it become sincerely Christian or completely Socialist. Before the coming of that Utopia whole races might have been sacrificed, and civilisation itself destroyed by the unchecked working of capitalistic forces.

It is a much harder and a much more complicated problem which confronts those who aspire to a permanent peace. We are citizens as well as idealists ; we have our share in the responsibility for all that our rulers do in Egypt or in India. We have a duty not merely to posterity, but to the men who are being drilled for slaughter to-day with the money which we as taxpayers provide. While we state and defend our distant ideal, we must also find some strategy which will even now check the worst consequences of a capitalistic foreign policy, and, if possible, turn it to some partial good. The thinking of Socialist idealists has imposed a constructive policy of domestic reform upon the present generation of Liberals. The same task must be faced in

the less familiar field of foreign policy. Nor can
the two fields be isolated. Imperialism, with its
spendthrift and wasteful expenditure, its positive
encouragement to the rapid accumulation of capital
for investment abroad, and the distractions which
it invents to divert the attention of the masses
from their more intimate preoccupations at home, is
to-day a more formidable enemy to social recon-
struction than the nearly obsolete individualism of
the Manchester School. Our first task will be to win
the bare possibility of influencing the foreign policy
of the governing class. Our first battle must be
to secure the effective control of the democracy over
the external policy of its rulers.

CHAPTER VI

SOCIALISM AND ANTI-MILITARISM

WE have spent time enough in analysing the obscure causes, hidden in counting-houses and embassies, that go to the making of wars. We have found little of the old joyous patriotism and chivalry among them. Can we discover in the modern world an idealism which will stir masses of men among the forces that combat war ? The Anti-Militarism of the Socialist parties on the Continent is based on a faith as great and precarious as Mr. Norman Angell's pacifism. He is convinced that mankind is guided by reason. The Socialist is sure that humanity survives under a uniform. On that belief he has based a strategy which shall abolish war between modern peoples. It is a great hope. Let us start from experience in our examination of it, and read its proposals in relation to the peculiar psychology of war.

In what temper does the soldier achieve the miracle of disciplined murder ? When I attempt to answer that question, my memory goes back to a battlefield in Thessaly. It was the last engagement in that futile Græco-Turkish war of 1897. In the centre at Domokos the Greek army was preparing to retreat. But of that we in the legion of foreign volunteers knew nothing. On the far left we had more than held our own, though with heavy losses. We had kept our positions, and in our little corner of the field had checked the Turkish advance.

Suddenly our Italian comrades, with a Garibaldi at their head, swing into view, marching at the double round a hill on the plain below us. They ran rather than walked, upright in full view of the enemy's marksmen, disdaining cover, and challenging death in the conspicuous red shirts which carried on Greek soil the great tradition of Italy's wars of liberation. It was one of the bravest sights which life has to offer, the sight of men, commonplace perhaps and timid in quiet moments, rising in an hour of exaltation to a joyous and defiant heroism. We ran down from our positions to reinforce them. A few scattered volleys, a few rushes, and the line of red fezes, which was for us the Turkish army, had wavered and retreated. We sheathed our bayonets, shook the hands of comrades, and slowly returned to our own lines. After the shame and disillusion of this disastrous war, this first success filled us with elation. We were pleased with ourselves, not over-anxious about our wounded comrades, and ready to reckon the joy of battle as the crown of life. It was in this mood that I stumbled across a thing in the grass. It was a dead Turk, prone on his back, his rifle still held in his clenched hand. A clean bullet wound in the temples showed how sudden the end must have been. I am ashamed to think that my first thought was one of satisfaction. The dead man lay in the line of fire of our company. One of us must have sent that bullet. And then I looked

at his face.   He was an oldish man, and his scanty
hair was almost grey.   He wore the uniform of the
last class of the reserve, called up only in grave
emergencies.   It was a simple peasant face, round,
and good-natured, clean and healthy.   He was
short and rather slight, and the hand which held the
rifle seemed childishly small.   The dead face smiled
up from the ground, and the simple gentleness of
this old man, so little formidable, so clearly a stranger
to the lusts and passions which we on the " Christian"
side liked to associate with the name of Turk, made
its direct appeal to the normal human instincts
which war can silence only in the rushing hours of
animal excitement.   It flashed upon me that this
was the first Turk whom I had yet seen near enough
to touch—save indeed a miserable spy whom some
soldiers hanged head downwards from a tree over
a fire of straw until the officers rescued him.   And I
thought I could tell what manner of man it was that
we had killed—a kindly old farmer, who had lived
his quiet life up to this war among his children and
his neighbours, pruning his fruit trees and gathering
his harvests, good to man and beast, and totally
ignorant of the eddies of world politics which had
caught him in their whirl.   A fellow-volunteer came
up at that moment and began roughly to rifle the
corpse in quest of trophies.   He even proposed to
scalp the old man—that was, he said, what was
usually done during the native wars in Rhodesia,
where he had served before.   I found myself
defending from outrage the enemy whom an hour
before I was trying to kill.   In the misery of the
retreat which followed our transient victory I under-

stood what this experience meant. I had not known that I was firing at simple peasants. I had been firing at " the enemy," " the Turks," " the Sultan's brutal soldiery," " the forces of Oriental barbarism," and other names, phrases and abstractions. I had seen only a line of red caps which made in the distance a serviceable target.

As we neared our own lines we overtook our wounded. An Italian, whom I helped to limp along, told me that another volunteer had just robbed him of his blanket. I took him, calling loudly for water, into the barn which served as a field hospital. When I had found water, a sentry at the door roughly forbade me to enter—it was the order of his superior officer. I remember still the anger with which I pushed past him, and then the sudden horror of the great room filled with moaning men, some dying, some only frightened by pain, some waiting patiently to lose a leg or an arm. There was more to think of on the retreat. I understood at length that that military discipline which I had been proud to obey myself, and to impose on others, was the necessary condition of this criminal stupidity called war. Men can be got to shoot at other men with whom they have no quarrel, only because they have first been taught to lay aside their own personality, their own judgment, their free choice between good and evil. They become automata which shoot at other automata as little conscious of what they do as the rifles in their hands. And that brave scene of the charging Garibaldians, I knew now that it had no more to do with ideals or heroisms than a rush of horned cattle or a stampede of wild horses. It is the physical impetus which makes a fine charge, and not the idea behind it. Men will show the same forgetfulness of self and the same disregard of others in a sham charge on a field day at Aldershot. English cavalry regiments have been known to ride into one another with all the fury of battle, and to continue their rush in spite of broken limbs and injured horses. " It was a good thing that we had not our sabres out," said a trooper on the casualty list to a newspaper correspondent after a recent incident of this kind on manœuvres. Prince Kropotkin tells in his memoirs of a famous charge of a Russian cadet battalion at manœuvres. They bore down on the Tsar himself, and would have trampled him to death if he had not avoided them at the last moment. A uniform will serve as well as an idea to inspire soldiers with solidarity, and the animal exhilaration of swift movement will produce all the phenomena of heroism. I saw now to what bestial degradation war had reduced these same Garibaldians. One would steal a blanket from a wounded comrade ; another would threaten to stick his bayonet into me because I was bringing water to a wounded comrade against the orders of some worried or stupid officer. War is the suspense and annihilation of the individual conscience. It blots out for the soldier the humanity of the men whom he opposes, and blurs them together in one unrealised and unimagined horde which he calls the enemy. It destroys, while it does this, the duties and the sympathies which bind man to man. The whole process meanwhile is rendered respectable by a veneer of illusions. In adopting

the attitude of passive obedience the soldier convinces himself that he is submitting to a patriotic
obligation. He throws the responsibility of what
he does upon his officers. They in turn obey the
statesmen, and the statesmen themselves are as little
able to judge of what they do, because they also are
never in contact with the visible fact of war, and the
human reality of their enemies. War is vicarious
crime. The statesman does through the soldier what
he would not do in his own person. The soldier
does at the bidding of the statesman what he would
shrink from doing if the whole decision lay with
himself.

I had to learn after this war that the diplomacy
which provoked it had in all probability no aim more
serious than to save the throne of the King of Greece.
I had also to learn, through meeting them in time
of peace, that the Turkish officers against whom
I fought, so far from being, as I had supposed, the
willing tools of the late Sultan's despotism, were even
then beginning to organise for revolution. The process of disillusionment left me doubting whether
there ever was in history a just and necessary war of
aggression. Certain it is that in any war which we
can conceive in Europe, two armies mainly composed of working-men would face each other in the
service of some capitalist intrigue, and in the defence
of interests whose chief concern is their exploitation.
These men lead in all modern countries the same
life. The essential question for them is what percentage of their harvest will be left to them after the
landlord has levied his rent, what food will cost them
after the manipulators of the tariff have taken their

toll, or what proportion the wages bill of their factory will bear to the total profit. Yet, thanks to the mystifications of a false patriotism, to the influence of a benumbing discipline and a drill expressly designed to turn men into machines, they may, in ignorance or fear, proceed to slay each other in order to decide whether it shall be French or German. financiers who shall export the surplus capital (saved from their own wages bill) destined to subdue and exploit the peasants of Morocco.

Such reflections as these are made by thoughtful men before, and by experienced men after every war. They have been the common property of Radical and Socialist thinkers since the days of the French Revolution. One may find them, limpid and forcible, in the pages of Thomas Paine, who himself had fought in America against King George's red-coats. They are familiar to-day to millions of working-men throughout Europe, the men who will form the conscript armies of the next great war— if, indeed, another great war is possible in Europe. To popularise them, to make them among the workers as familiar, as axiomatic, as much a part of their class-morality as the ideas which inspire them with loyalty to their Trade Unions—that is among the first duties of Continental Socialism. Can it carry this task further ? It is something to detach the workers from the crowds which shout for war. Can they be induced to refuse to carry a rifle in an unjust cause ?

The idea of a fundamental opposition to all war is no new thing in the history of civilisation. It has usually taken root among men whose outlook on life was ethical and individualistic. The Quakers in Australia and the Doukhobors in Russia have refused under any circumstances to serve in armies, because their consciences were bound by the law of Christ. The teaching of Tolstoy has placed this position on a reasonable and undogmatic basis, which makes a powerful appeal even to minds which cannot embrace the doctrine of non-resistance to evil. A man's readiness to adopt that doctrine depends ultimately on the degree in which he is concerned for his own personal righteousness. If one's ruling passion is to deserve the approval of one's own conscience, one may find it possible to stand inactive while a child is maltreated or a horse beaten before one's eyes. If, on the other hand, a man's chief concern is to check suffering, if he thinks rather of the pain of the child and the horse than of himself, then at the risk of any loss of personal saintliness he will, if remonstrance fails, resist evil by using his fists. The right of rebellion in extreme cases and of resistance to aggressive wars rests on the same basis. Tolstoy could never have made a mass movement against war. The pacifist movement is weak for other reasons. Men and women divided on other issues, and acting in concert only to hold meetings and listen to lectures against war, will rarely be formidable to any government. Governments have more to fear from a party which is united on all issues and votes when it has talked. Tolstoy and the pacifists created a favourable intellectual atmosphere. It remained for Socialism to create the party of peace.

Two contemporary reasons combined to make the

French the leaders in this practical anti-militarism. The revelations which attended the Dreyfus case aroused a profound uneasiness in all democratic minds. For some years under a clique of officers, secretly Royalist, openly clericalist, the army had become the tool of a well-organised reaction. Anatole France has satirised the situation in his inimitable *Ile des Pingouins*. For the moment the danger was averted, but it lurks in some degree in all professional military castes, and even under conscription the officers must be professionals. In the second place the French Radicals, and more especially M. Clemenceau, had made a ruthless use of the army to repress strikes, which properly roused the fury of the working-class. These two contemporary conditions combined to aid the work of Gustave Hervé. No " extremist " has been more persistently maligned. Those who know him describe him as a personality of great charm. His published speeches, despite some regrettable crudities and violences of language, are powerful compositions, closely reasoned and admirably phrased. His courage has been tested by numerous prosecutions and imprisonments. His position, stripped of subtleties—and in controversy he can be extremely subtle—has a simplicity which appeals to men of every grade of intelligence.

Patriotism, in Hervé's view, is an illusion sedulously cultivated by the capitalist class in order that it may the more easily enslave the workers, and shear the sheep without their even perceiving that they are being shorn. It unites in one community the exploiters and the exploited, until they begin to believe that they have some interests in common. It is a conservative emotion, which brings the classes together, and helps to keep them tranquilly one under the other within the bosom of the same country. It is an intelligible sentiment only for the class for whom the motherland is a milch-cow. For the workers she is rather a step-mother. The motto of Socialism must be, " Workers of all countries, unite across your frontiers." The motto of Patriotism is, " If your country commands it, workers of all countries, massacre one another." To be sure, nationality is a fact. But it is not an eternal or necessary fact. Nations came into being by a slow historic progress. They may be dissolved or amalgated by a contrary process. There is nothing sacred in the chance of war which has made most modern nations. For the worker there is nothing to choose between them. Go from one country to another, and you will find everywhere the same prisons, the same barracks, the same police, the same brothels, the same Ministers of the Interior. Cross what frontier you please, and you are still only a living tool, which is worth only its current price in the labour market. If one is to be exploited one might as well be exploited by a foreign as by a native capitalist. It follows, then, that the workers can have no interest in the issue of any war, even when his own country wages it. His country is not in fact his own. Let him then refuse to risk one square-inch of his own skin in any war, and keep his courage for the revolution. When war breaks out he will neither ask who is in the right and who in the wrong, nor fly to the aid of his country under the spur of patriotism. In any event, since diplomacy is secret and the press mendacious, he never can judge which of two warring nations is the aggressor. The proper strategy to follow on declaration of war is to desert the flag, to proclaim a general strike, to follow that up by insurrection, and in the confusion to carry out a social revolution. In no circumstances ought any Socialist conscript to assist any capitalist government, even in a purely defensive war.

A thinker who defends so extreme a thesis as this performs a great service. He forces us all to think, to go back upon our premises, to make it clear to ourselves why our judgment revolts against his conclusions. There is a valuable half-truth in every one of Hervé's vehement statements. But in the first place it is untrue to say that the worker has no share in the heritage of nationality. Its ideal riches even now are open to him. His language is a mother-tongue. The treasures of literature enshrined in that language are open to him. He feels a thrill in the knowledge of his history, its heroisms, its revolutions, its struggles towards liberty. He imbibes whatever is distinctive and original in the national spirit. It is true that the man of leisure and wealth shares more fully in all these benefits. But the worker commits a folly who despises and scorns them. Instead of vilifying his motherland, he should determine to possess her. It is, if possible, still more false to make light of the evils of conquest and foreign domination. An alien exploiter is, in spite of Hervé, incomparably worse than a native. Every difference of race, language or religion aggravates the miseries which a subject people has to suffer from its ruling class. An Irishman, a Pole or an Armenian would never have fallen into this flagrant error. Indeed, as Bebel (thinking mainly of the Poles) and Bernard Shaw (thinking mainly of the Irish) have said, each in his own way, the chief mischief of racial domination is that under it the proletariat is so obsessed by its national wrongs that it has no leisure to think of its economic subjection. It is so busy fighting for its autonomy, its language or its Church, that it has no ears for social questions. Nationality is not in itself an evil. On the contrary it is only by the collaboration of many nations, each with its own temperament, its own history, its own language, that civilisation can hope to attain its full development through diversity. The right of every nationality to defend its liberty and its identity against conquest, is a right which Socialism has always been the first to respect, and will be the last to abandon. The general adoption of Hervé's theories by the more advanced nations would be merely an invitation to the less advanced to conquer and enslave them. If his doctrine were Socialism, this inevitable consequence would follow —that the country which had the most Socialists would be the first to be devoured and exploited by its neighbours.

Hervé luckily has been followed only by a small though very active minority of French Socialists. The real importance of his campaign is that it has induced Jaurès, supported by the majority, to define a policy of anti-militarism, which is at once better in theory and sounder in statesmanship.

Jaurès starts from two premises ; that nations have the right and duty to maintain their independence, and that the opposition of labour to war must be something more effective than an academic or sentimental abhorrence. It must be a will to prevent wars by acts. It is obvious that the most effective way in which a proletariat united across frontiers can prevent war is not to stand aloof from all wars, but to use its joint forces to check aggression and assist defence. If, let us say, Germany were to meditate a wanton attack on France, the best way to deter her is to announce in advance that by common accord, and in full agreement, German Socialists will impede the attacking force within its ranks and in its rear, while French Socialists will aid the defending force with all their ardour and courage. Could this be realised, the German attack would certainly fail, and were it anticipated, no sane Government in Germany would dare to take the risk of aggression. Were this formula generally adopted, could the whole force of labour in civilised States be used for the defence and against the aggressor, it is certain that war, in Europe at least, would have become unthinkable. If Hervé objects that it is difficult to determine who is the aggressor in a war between two capitalist States, Jaurès has a ready answer. The aggressor in any international dispute is the Power which refuses to submit its case to some form of impartial arbitration. One may doubt the sincerity of some of the Powers which have played at arbitration at Hague Conferences. But the clever policy for the workers is to take the diplomatists at their word. Labour, drilled, conscripted, regimented, has the power to enforce a real respect for arbitration, by giving its numbers and its courage as a premium to that side in a quarrel which will appeal to reason. The duty of a Socialist party in a country which meditates an aggressive war is to resist the Government by " every means in its power, from parliamentary action and public agitation, up to the general strike and insurrection."

The French Socialists carried this doctrine, concentrated in resolutions passed at Limoges and Nancy in 1906 and 1907, to the International Conference held at Stuttgart (1907). The debates both in committee and in the full conference were of unusual interest. In the end the following resolution (with a long preamble), framed by Vandervelde on the basis of a draft by Jaurès was unanimously carried :—

If war threatens to break out, it is the duty of the working class in the countries concerned and of their Parliamentary representatives, with the help of the International Bureau as the means of co-ordinating their action, to use every effort to prevent the war by all the means which seem to them the most appropriate, having regard to the sharpness of the class-war and to the general political situation.

Should war none the less break out, their duty is to intervene to bring it promptly to an end, and with all their energies to use the economic and political crisis created by the war to rouse the populace from its slumbers, and to hasten the fall of capitalist domination.

In its practical effect this resolution hardly differs from the French proposition. It is to be noted, however, that it does not specify the means by which war may be prevented. All practicable means are to be adopted, and in paraphrasing the resolution some of the German orators expressly added the

words " without excluding any." Among the precedents held up for imitation is the action of the
Swedish Socialist party, which threatened to declare
a general strike if Sweden should make war on
Norway. The Germans very frankly explained that
they could not publicly pledge themselves in advance
to action so extreme as the general strike in case of
war, without at once exposing themselves as a party
to wholesale repression. When the crisis arrived,
they would know how to act. The discussion
between the French and German leaders revealed
some interesting points of theory. Germans were
not prepared to say in advance that it would always
be the duty of a proletariat to assist its Government
if it were attacked. Kautsky, a very acute thinker,
remarked for example, that it certainly was not the
duty of Russian Socialists to defend the Tsar's
Government in the late war, though technically
Japan was the aggressor. He also denied that in
any war over Morocco it would be the duty of
German Socialists to defend Germany, even if she
were attacked. Bebel went so far as to say in the
heat of the debate that if Germany attacked Russia
he for one would be the first to shoulder a rifle,
because the event of such a war would be to liberate
the working classes in Russia and to weaken the
reaction even in Germany itself—a most hazardous
calculation. These interesting debates on nice
points of theory led to wonderful misunderstandings
in the capitalist press. The French papers held up
the German Socialists as a model of patriotism to the
French. The Prussian official gazette on the other
hand announced " that the German Socialists are

the least patriotic in the universe." The plain truth is, of course, that the whole congress unanimously rejected " patriotism " in the conventional sense of that word. No Socialist party will say, " My country, right or wrong." No Socialist party will allow its duty in case of war to be prescribed for it by a ruling class. The French leaders will enquire which side is the aggressor, and will unhesitatingly oppose it, even if it is their own country. The German leaders put the criterion somewhat differently. They will be guided, not by national interests, but by the interests of labour the world over. Some difference in theory there is. There can be none in action. For French and Germans are equally resolved to be guided in any definite case by the decision of the whole Socialist world, to act in concert, and to act through the International Bureau. That is the real significance of the Stuttgart decision.

In practice the growth of this conscious anti-militarism within the Socialist movement has introduced a new factor of enormous importance into European politics. Henceforward every European Government which meditates war has to reckon with the certainty that it will be opposed, certainly morally, and perhaps physically, by a powerful and organised party at home. It may even have to pay at the polls for its adventure. What happened in Bulgaria after the avoidable second war against Servia and Greece is a warning to all Governments which meditate aggression. The party of MM. Daneff and Gueshoff, whose arrogant diplomacy made that disastrous war, possessed an overwhelming majority in the Chamber when they began it. In

the general election which followed the war, their
party was annihilated, and secured only six seats in
a total of over two hundred. Even more significant
is the fact that the Socialist and Peasant Parties
between them, feeble before the war, secured nearly
a third of the representation after it. But far more
serious than the risk of disaster at the polls, is the
danger that Socialist opposition within an army
may sap the spirit which alone wins victories.
General Kuropatkin, in his able report on the causes
of the defeat of the armies which he led in Manchuria, emphasised among them the indifference and
hostility of the Russian soldiery. They had already
begun to hate the autocracy and to desire revolution ;
they were totally indifferent to the Imperialist
ambitions which made the war. The same moral
factor goes far to explain the defeat of Bulgaria in
the second of the Balkan wars. Her armies entered
on the first war with spirit and enthusiasm. It was
a war of liberation, undertaken on behalf of the
oppressed peasant of Macedonia, and every Bulgarian
soldier knew from the tales of his elders or from his
own experience the misery and degradation of the
Turkish yoke which he fought to overthrow. The
first war was protracted by the grasping diplomacy
of the Bulgarian Government. The spirit of the
men flagged under inaction, privation, and disease.
They had liberated Macedonia, and cared nothing
for the further objects which kept them in the field.
As the time of harvest approached, no discipline
could avail to keep them with the colours. They
deserted during the long months of inaction in such
numbers that General Savoff abandoned all attempts

to coerce them, and when a man disappeared he was written down in the lists as " on leave." The second war against Bulgaria's allies stirred no such enthusiasm as the first, and when it opened the strength of her armies was diminished by the 80,000 men who had indulged in this tolerated desertion.

This experience conveys a moral of importance. It means in the first place that even without deliberate Socialist propaganda, the moral factor must be reckoned with in modern wars. A conscript army is not a mere machine which can be set in motion against an enemy with equal prospect of success, whatever the cause of the war may be. The ardour and endurance of the men will have some relation to their opinions about the justice and necessity of the war. In the second place it means that there are limits to the sacrifices which a conscript army will willingly make. It cannot be kept in the field indefinitely without losing something of its spirit, even in a war which it approved at the start. This means that there is on moral grounds a time-limit to a modern war, even if the finances of the belligerent Power are equal to its prolongation. A modern war is necessarily brief, and this means that permanent conquest has become nearly impossible. The conqueror, after his first successes in the early months of the war, will find it increasingly difficult to prolong the campaign. He will be less able than he was in the days of small professional armies to meet a determined enemy defending his home-territory by guerilla tactics. One may doubt, for example, whether any conscript army could have done what our professional army did during the three tedious years of the South African War. The action of Roumania is another object-lesson, which would probably be repeated in any modern European war. When the conqueror is exhausted by costly successes, a neutral Power, a *tertius gaudens*, is almost certain to intervene to limit the struggle and rob him of the fruit of his victories. A generous mind revolts against the meanness of this predatory policy, but, undoubtedly, it handicaps the conqueror, diminishes the gains of conquest, and thereby strengthens the motives which may induce even a strong State to refrain from making war. Nor was it only in the Balkans that this Balkan crisis illustrated the extent to which a military Power must take the sentiments of its conscript soldiers into account. Austria mobilised a part of her army when the crisis began, in order to check any attempt at intervention on the part of Russia. She abstained, however, as far as possible, from calling reservists of the Slav races to the colours, because she knew that their sympathies would be with her Russian adversary.

The experiences of Bulgaria are full of encouragement to those who hope that the opinions and interests of conscript armies, consisting as they do largely of reservists summoned from their homes and their fields, may in the future deter aggressive Governments from aggressive and unnecessary wars. The Bulgarian soldier is by temperament singularly patient and enduring, he submits readily to discipline, he is patriotic as the soldier of older nations rarely is, and he has only just begun to feel the influence of Socialistic thought. If he grew " stale " as the

campaign dragged on, a French or German army
would reach the same condition much earlier.
When once a spirit of reluctance and criticism
invades an army, it becomes incapable of meeting
even an inferior enemy inspired by a belief in the
justice of his cause. Commands are obeyed stupidly
and slowly. There is an end of self-sacrifice, of
promptitude, of spontaneous intelligence. Regiments will not do their best in forced marches, nor
stand firm under a murderous fire. The consequences
may be even worse than this. It would take some
heroism to desert or revolt, or make a general strike.
But any average man can do less than his best in
handling the big guns or aiming his rifle. It is
doubtful whether the indifference of an army which
disapproved of the war in which it was engaged
would ever be shown fully in the first excitement of
a battle. When once a soldier is under fire his
instincts bid him fight in self-defence. It is a good
deal safer to be on the victorious side than to be
engaged in a disastrous retreat. But, undoubtedly,
this spirit of opposition would check the ardour
of an attack, and put a limit to the endurance which
men will display under difficulties. It would be
shown most easily of all during the mobilisation,
where everything depends on the promptitude and
goodwill of each unit, and men are not yet heated
into unreason by contact with the enemy. In a
German army in time of war one man in three would
be a Socialist voter. Some of these at the best of
times are only superficially under the influence of
Socialism, and others would be carried away by the
excitement of the national crisis. But it is hard to

believe that if in a war of aggression this army were to be hurled against France to-day, German Socialists would show any ardour in shooting down French workmen. The spirit which marched through Sedan to Paris could not be revived in our generation.

How far the general strike could be used with success to prevent the outbreak of war is a more difficult question. The Italian Socialists, ill-organised at the best, and sharply divided when the trial came, made no use of it to stop the adventure in Tripoli. They were taken by surprise, for this war was both secret and sudden in its origin, and it was conducted mainly by the young troops of the active army. European soldiers will never feel the same reluctance to shoot down an uncivilised enemy which one hopes they would feel if they met white troops. It is fairly certain that French Socialists would make an attempt to stop an aggressive war by a resort to the general strike. It would require superb heroism and perfect organisation if it were to succeed. Martial law would at once be proclaimed. The press would be silenced, and the leaders would be arrested and shot. It is unlikely that the mobilisation could be stopped, or that any appreciable proportion of the reservists would refuse obedience. But even a slight delay might embarrass the plan of campaign, and large numbers of men would join the colours in a mood which wins no victory. The question is not, after all, whether a Government could manage, in spite of the hostility of the organised working-class, to stumble somehow into war, and get its armies up to the front. Its aim is something more than that. The question is not whether an aggressive Government can still contrive to make war, but whether it can reckon on victory. To crush Socialist resistance is one thing ; to embody the working-classes in the fighting line embued with the fighting spirit, is a wholly different matter. If any modern Government knew that it had to deal with a powerful Socialist party, courageous, united, well-organised, and firmly opposed to war, a strike would be superfluous. The experiment of a strike against war will never be made under favourable conditions ; it will be made only if Socialism is so weak that the Government can safely despise it. In no country with a conscript army in which Socialism deserves to be respected, will a Government dare to-day to make an unnecessary war. It is always a mistake to invent heroic methods, where simple facts will suffice. The simple fact that the working-class hated the idea of war, and the knowledge that it would fight half-heartedly, would in themselves suffice to keep the peace, at all events between nearly equal antagonists. In France and Germany, if not as yet in Austria and Italy, Socialism has already attained this degree of strength. It is even now perhaps the most formidable factor in the preservation of the peace of Europe, and its pressure is none the less real because Governments will never willingly admit that it has influenced them.

The Socialist opposition to war is effective, because under modern conditions on the Continent a war must be the effort of the whole nation. A minority makes its influence felt here even when it is impotent in Parliament. The Socialist deputies in Reichstag or Chamber may always be voted down, and their resistance has counted for little. But the Socialist soldiers in the army are indispensable to it. It will win no victories while they are an element of active or even passive discontent. In its opposition, on the other hand, to the accumulation of armaments, to colonial expansion, to the armed peace of the Balance of Power, Socialism, even where it is strongest, is as yet unable to prevent middle-class States from " rattling into barbarism," or even greatly to retard the pace. Lord Rosebery in the same speech in which he coined that memorable phrase, invited the masses to rise up and say, " Enough of this folly." The dependence of those who have learning and leisure and wealth on the insight of working-men, with whom it is a rare event to read a book, is one of the oddest ironies of modern civilisation. No Socialist party is strong enough to make this dramatic gesture of disgust effectively, without the aid from middle-class Liberals, which as yet they hesitate to give. The arming, the export of capital, the rivalry to win fields of exploitation, and the consequent division of Europe into two hostile camps, go on in spite of Socialism. It is possible that the long discussion of the rather theatrical revolutionary device of a strike against war did harm by directing attention exclusively to the risk of war, and in diverting it from our modern dry warfare. But if that was a mistake, it is being corrected to-day. The aphorism of Jaurès that the preparation for war is an evil hardly less than war itself, expresses the general trend of Socialist thought not only in France but also in Germany. The

Socialist appeal to a general strike, like the pacifist appeal to reason, falls far short of solving our problem and for the same reason. It leaves untouched that ceaseless play of rivalries, that incessant competition to accumulate force, which devastates even when it lights no torch of war, and divides mankind though it orders no battle.

[1] P.S.—The failure of international Socialism to affect the outbreak of this war is only less depressing than the failure of the Christian Churches. The moral is that diplomacy is much more astute in concealing aggression than are the masses in detecting it. The German Socialists had agitated on the eve of war for peace, and when war came they officially condemned the diplomacy which had made it, as, later on, they condemned the violation of Belgian neutrality. But they allowed themselves to be obsessed by the fact that Germany had to defend herself against Russia. Here the action of Russia in ordering a general mobilisation before any other Great Power had done so, undoubtedly made it easy to argue in Berlin that whatever may have been the merits of' the war, the immediate duty was defence. Had the war arisen over Morocco, its Imperialist bearings could not been have concealed, and the reluctance of the German Socialists to engage in a war with France on such an issue may have been one of the reasons why the universal war came not in 1911 over Morocco, but in 1914 with Russia as Germany's enemy. The moral is that democratic forces must dismiss the illusion that they can circumvent diplomacy by a sudden rally in the hour of crisis.

CHAPTER VII

THE CONTROL OF POLICY

A WRITER who advocates the effective extension of democratic control to foreign affairs must expect to meet a series of familiar objections. Where will you find among the masses of any modern State the knowledge and experience which are required for the conduct of a nation's external policy? How shall the Lancashire weaver or the Durham miner, who know no language but their own, who do not travel and have little leisure to read, judge of the designs of Germany, the ambitions of Russia or the needs of Egypt? They can judge shrewdly enough of an Insurance Act or an Eight Hours Act. These things, complicated though they are, come within the round of their daily experience. They are the persons concerned, and whether they judge ill or well, you cannot refuse them the right to judge without disputing every principle of self-government and freedom. But foreign questions, it will be said, do not touch them so nearly. They lack the means to form a judgment, and in any event their interests are only slightly and remotely affected. The conclusion from this objection, however it is phrased, will be that foreign policy is best managed by some moderate statesman, guided by an expert profes-

sional service, and subject to the promptings, the
encouragements and the criticisms of the governing
class and the higher world of finance and commerce,
which has the experience to judge of these recondite
matters, and undoubtedly has a great interest at
stake. This is the system under which we live,
and probably it reflects fairly enough the general
trend of middle-class thinking in England. There
is only one context in which Imperialists of either
party affect to think that the general body of electors
does or should control foreign policy, and that is
when they are telling women that they are quite
unfit to possess the vote, because they are unfit to
judge Imperial issues. In nine cases out of ten the
speaker who flatters himself on this male prerogative
is as reluctant to trust the mass of men as he is to
enfranchise women. The plain fact is that the
average man has no more control over foreign policy
than the voteless women.

The democratic answer to this objection is simple
and direct. We do not desire the rule of the
majority because we cherish any illusion about the
intelligence or the virtues of the masses. Like
average men in all classes, they are content to have
their thinking done for them by their leaders and
their newspapers. We do not count brains in a
modern State ; we count interests. The ballot is
a rough method of deciding the greatest good of the
greatest number. If the greatest number is muddle-
headed in perceiving its greatest good, it must learn
its lesson by hard experience. The anti-democratic
attitude in foreign affairs involves a naked claim that
certain interests shall rule. We have analysed these

interests in a previous chapter. At their head are the great bankers and contractors. Their rank and file is composed of the comfortable class which invests abroad, and of those families which see in the services of Empire a career for their sons. We have traced the effect of their pressure in the gradual identification of the investor's interest with the national interest, the promotion of the export of capital as a quasi-official national undertaking, the use of diplomacy to support concession-hunters' claims, the marking off of spheres of interest as the preserve of our financiers, and, finally, as a result of the rivalry which these processes engender, the struggle for a balance of power, and the consequent inflation of armaments. The various links in the chain hang together in a perfect sequence, and manifestly the chain has been formed by a national policy dictated by the interest of the possessing classes. It is not inevitable ; it is not axiomatic, it is not a necessary deduction from the idea of the State. The whole chain would be cut, and the fatal consequences of its last links would fall from us, if one point of policy were decided otherwise. If we could but say that an investor, a contractor, a money-lender, when he trades beyond these islands, trades at his own risk and must ask the mother-country neither for backing to reach success, nor for protection to avoid loss, the whole fatal chain of consequences might be stayed and the impulse checked which has led us into this desolating rivalry with all that it involves of waste and folly and fear. Such questions are not to be decided by pure reason. Ought the contractor and the banker to be backed in

their private ventures abroad ? The answer will
depend on the nature of the audience to which you
address your question. All England would have
answered with a No before the days of Palmerston.
The Tory Party would have said No while it was
still mainly the party of landlords and country
gentlemen. Carry your question to the Carlton Club
to-day and the answer will certainly be Yes. Take it
to the Stock Exchange, and members will be amazed
that you should dare to ask such a question at all,
and stare at you as though you were a bomb-
thrower or an Early Christian. At the National
Liberal Club the answer would be doubtful, compromising, and far from unanimous. Carry your
question to a Trade Union Congress or a Labour
Conference, and the answer will be as unhesitating
and as united as it was at Capel Court. But it
will be No. Move away from all these crowds,
collate their answers, and then enquire whether
it really and obviously is a national interest that
diplomacy should support finance. It is so, if the
nation wills it. But the nation as a whole is never
consulted, has never considered the question, is
barely aware that such a question exists as a possible
subject of debate. Yet it underlies our whole
external policy ; it is the stocks on which our Dreadnoughts are built. The Lancashire weaver and the
Durham miner ought to consider it. It concerns
them as closely as the gentlemen in the Carlton Club.
It would indeed reduce the total income of the club
by a heavy ratio if it were answered otherwise.
But at the same time it would release a portion of
the national income sufficient to transform the

Insurance Act, and to remove the defects of which the weaver and the miner complain. The voteless woman from this standpoint is no less directly affected. For a real judgment of national interests we must go to the nation at large. While we evade this judgment we are allowing a single class, deeply interested in the issue, to conduct our national affairs unchecked. It conducts them, as all history would teach us to expect, for its own profit. The real problem of the balance of power is the problem of the adjustment of the interests of the few and the many which co-exist within each national State. Let us not be deterred by the ignorance of the masses or the complication of the problem. Democracy has its invention to meet that difficulty. The system of representative government exists to solve it. The mischief in our case is that our representatives have all but ceased to concern themselves with foreign affairs.

In an earlier chapter we have traced the impotence of the House of Commons to control the foreign policy of the Empire. It is preoccupied with domestic questions. It lacks both the time and the knowledge to check our diplomacy. It has fewer constitutional rights in this field than any other Parliament of Europe. Its action is limited by the party system, which makes it practically impossible to dissent from the external policy of the Government without undoing its domestic work. It has accepted the doctrine of " continuity " which excludes foreign affairs from the conflict of parties, and thereby hands them over to the unchallenged influence of a governing class, which in society, in the press, and in the diplomatic service is always, so to speak, " in office," despite the fluctuations of national opinion. It is, finally, frustrated by a practice which withholds from it all official knowledge of policies, treaties and negotiations, until they are already accomplished facts which Parliament may regret but cannot alter.

To bring about a complete change, and to invest democracy with a real control over foreign affairs, would require little less than a revolution in our habits of thought and our constitutional practice. Let us cherish no illusions about the difficulties of the task which we are setting ourselves. It would be easier to overthrow the monarchy than to depose the inner governing class from the authority which it has usurped over the external policy of the Empire. The worst obstacle of all is that the House of Commons has in great measure lost its earlier instincts of independence and its habits of self-assertion. It is grotesquely sensitive about its dignity, when some young woman affronts it by disturbing its debates. But to the overgrown authority of the Cabinet and to the coercion of the party " whips " it is placidly resigned. These are moral and intellectual weaknesses which no agitation can remedy. They will continue while our rigid party system endures, and while they continue we shall enjoy only a simulacrum of representative government. One may, however, note certain changes of a general character which would tend to strengthen the House of Commons, and therefore in some measure to exert a favourable influence upon the control of foreign affairs. Proportional representation would assure each member that he had behind him a real constituency of opinions. The entry of a third party into politics ought to have done more than it has yet done to break up the traditional party system, but Independent Labour struggles helplessly against the original sin of its birth. It cannot be independent while nearly all its members depend for their election on Liberal votes, and this dependence will continue so long as we retain the single-member constituency. Nor will it ever be possible to secure a sincere vote in the House of Commons on foreign questions, so long as parties worship the fetish of collective Cabinet responsibility, which Cabinets have themselves set up in the interest of discipline. It ought to be possible to vote against a Minister's opinion without thereby demanding either his resignation or that of the Government. It ought to be possible for the House to dismiss a Minister without evicting all his colleagues. The House should be free in short, at its own pleasure, to distinguish between a vote which expresses an opinion to which it expects a Minister to bow, and a vote which expresses its want of confidence either in a single Minister or a whole Cabinet. Until these reforms are carried, we can have nothing but a fettered House of Commons. Our whole political life suffers by the delay, but perhaps the conduct of foreign affairs suffers the most seriously. On most of the broad issues of domestic policy a majority in the House, if it has the country behind it, will in the long run have its way. Foreign questions are the exception, because they are not the grounds on which the average elector casts his vote.

There can, however, be little hope of securing due attention for external questions, without some fundamental change in our constitutional machinery. The chief obstacle is the inordinate complexity of modern politics. To say that Parliament has no time to deal at once with English, Irish and Imperial affairs is to state only half the difficulty. It is obliged to range itself, and to form its parties in accordance with the most vital issue of the moment, and that issue is almost always a domestic question. It is partly the imperative necessity of simplifying issues that has led to the growth of the doctrine of " continuity " in foreign policy. The real verdict of the country must be obtained on the vital questions of home policy. It is hard enough even so to detach one issue, and to say that the electors have had or ever can have a chance of pronouncing on one definite home subject, even when it is of the first importance. But the complication would be intolerable if foreign issues were also presented for judgment. This consideration has reinforced some others, to induce both sides to remove external questions from the area of party controversy. This instinctive simplification was probably inevitable, but it has had from the democratic standpoint the most disastrous consequences. In removing external questions from the field of party controversy, it has withdrawn them for all practical purposes from the decision of public opinion. The sections of society which make their influence felt outside the mechanism of parties are those which have wealth and social standing behind them. The average man is formidable only by his vote, and of this weapon the convention of " continuity " has disarmed him.

There is no real remedy for this breakdown in our constitutional machinery, save by the separation of external from domestic issues in some scheme of federal " devolution." Towards this solution we are moving inevitably and rapidly. In one form or another we are bound within the next few years to evolve some scheme of " Home Rule All-Round." The problem has been approached too exclusively from the Irish standpoint. Realising that we must give autonomy to Ireland, we see that this concession will hardly be workable unless we go on to do the like for Scotland and Wales. An Imperial Parliament will be left when the process is completed, which will be free to concern itself primarily with the whole range of Imperial questions, from foreign policy to the fighting services, from tariffs to the government of India and the Crown Colonies. It would lie far beyond the scope of this book to dwell in any detail on this inevitable change. But it seems relevant to urge that in the consideration of this constitutional reform, we should give due weight to the positive need of creating a Chamber whose duty it will be to deal, as the German Reichstag does, primarily with Imperial questions. To think of this Imperial Parliament merely as the shell which will be left when the subordinate national Parliaments have been created, would be a laughable short-sightedness. We need this Parliament. We who are democrats ought to create it with enthu-

siasm and eagerness, because it offers us for the
first time in our history the chance of subjecting our external policy to the real judgment of
public opinion. The voter will acquire his share in
the control of the Empire, only when he has the
chance of electing a Parliament which will deal
mainly with Imperial affairs.

When the time comes for the remodelling of the
Constitution, the democratic parties, if they are
alert, will insist on removing some of the obvious
defects which distinguish our Parliament unfavour-
ably in comparison with the Chambers of other
European peoples. Some of these defects have been
considered in a previous chapter (pp. 128-154). It is
hardly necessary to argue that treaties ought
to be submitted in draft to Parliament before they
are ratified and become binding. No one who pro-
fesses any ideal of self-government, however Conservative, could defend the conclusion of such an
instrument of alliance as the Japanese treaty by a
Cabinet which represents one party alone, and may
be nearing the end of its term of office. A solemn
obligation, by which the nation contracts to fight,
in circumstances unknown, in the dim future, ought
to be undertaken, if at all, by the representatives
of the whole nation. One would indeed wish to
prescribe that treaties of alliance must be sanctioned
by something larger than a bare majority of the
House. It is true that if it is attempted, as the
United States Senate often does, to amend a Treaty,
Parliament would expose the Foreign Office to grave
embarrassments. But an adroit Secretary will
learn how to provide against that inconvenience

by ascertaining, before he completes his negotiations, what the trend of Parliamentary opinion is. It is hardly less axiomatic that declarations of war ought to be made only with the sanction of Parliament. Accustomed as we are to our party-ridden Commons, it is difficult to imagine circumstances in which the House would refuse, amid the excitement of a warlike crisis, to sanction a war to which the Government was already committed. But even as things are to-day such a provision would impose some check upon a headstrong Ministry. It would be compelled to measure public opinion carefully. It would not dare to move faster than the Opposition allowed. It would be obliged, finally, to meet with some show of reason a motion that the dispute be referred to arbitration or to the mediation of neutral Powers. The Labour Party, one hopes, would know how to improve that opportunity.

A House which really meant to control foreign affairs would not be content to assert its control over treaties and declarations of war. It is the conduct of affairs between one great crisis and another which ends in the treaty or the war. What has to be controlled is precisely what is least known —our policy in pressing for concessions or in drawing the boundaries of spheres of influence. What is wanted is some mechanism of control which can operate steadily and quietly, while an affair is still in the stage of confidential negotiation. This mechanism must admit of secrecy ; it must also impose control without involving at every turn the fate of the Government and the continuance in office of the Foreign Secretary. We ought not, of course, to commit ourselves to the principle that foreign affairs ought to be conducted secretly.   From that assumption spring half the evils of diplomacy. The veil of secrecy means too often a claim to do beneath it what no man who respected his own honour, or cared for the good opinion of his fellows, would dare to do in public.   If international controversies were conducted by the public exchange of despatches, wars and aggressions would be almost unthinkable.   The fear of causing a panic on the Stock Exchange, the dread of alienating opinion both abroad and at home, and the necessity of being accurate in statement and cogent in argument, would soon impose a restraint upon diplomatists that would transform international morals.   It would be necessary to argue questions solely on their merits, instead of conducting a mere conflict of wills. There is, moreover, another argument against the present secrecy of diplomacy.   It is that the secrecy is only partial.   The enterprise of the press, and the desire of some diplomatists to win for them-. selves partisans and supporters, has gone far to make the intercourse of nations public.   But the mischief of this system of illicit revelation is that it is rarely honest.   Diplomatists divulge secrets with a pur-pose, and newspapers publish the facts with a bias. Documents are edited, and conversations distorted. One usually knows within a few hours when one Power has delivered something resembling an ulti-matum to another.   But the course of events is always represented in each country from a stand-point favourable to the diplomacy of that country. An exaggeration or distortion published in Paris or London is of course at once officially denied in Berlin. But as the denial almost invariably denies too much, we do not by this process arrive at truth. The mischief of a dishonest and partial publicity is only to be cured by an abandonment of the fiction of secrecy. That must be the aim of any sincerely democratic party. But clearly it is not quite at every stage or in every detail that diplomacy can as yet, if ever, achieve complete publicity. The early phases of a negotiation, whether between individuals or societies or nations, may gain something by being confidential. Much may be effected in conversation by a tactful Ambassador which could with difficulty be achieved through an exchange of despatches, particularly if every sentence were penned with a view to publication. But even over the preliminary steps of a confidential negotiation Parliament ought to have some check. For it is precisely in these preliminaries that a Minister lays down the lines on which the subsequent fate of the transaction will depend.

The mechanism by which secrecy can at certain stages be preserved, and control none the less secured, has already been discovered in one form or another by several foreign Parliaments. In France a Sub-Committee chosen through the Bureaux from the whole Chamber examines the Budget of the Ministry of Foreign Affairs, and contrives by this means to exercise in private a certain check upon the Minister. The Sub-Committee of the Senate conducts on occasion elaborate retrospective enquiries into past transactions—as for example after the Morocco crisis of 1911. In Austro-Hungary

" delegations " from the two Parliaments discuss
Foreign Policy with the Minister.   In Germany a
Federal Council representing the Governments
of the federated States of the Empire has certain
rights of control, and its sanction is required for a
declaration of war.   But the most powerful of all
these bodies is the Foreign Affairs Committee of
the United States Senate.   Sitting in private it
discusses with the Secretary of State even the details
of his policy, and studies his treaties line by line
before they can be ratified.   Its record is unfor-
tunately by no means encouraging, for it has prevented the conclusion of many treaties which would
assuredly have made for peace.   But a Committee
can be no better than the House from which it is
chosen.   The Senate stands for organised commercial
interests and for the sectional selfishness of the
individual States.   It would not be reasonable to
argue that effects which manifest themselves under
the peculiar conditions which prevail at Washington,
would be reproduced by a similar institution in our
country.

The proposal which arises from these preliminary
considerations shapes itself somewhat. thus :   There
might be elected from the House of Commons by
ballot on a proportional basis, either annually or
for the duration of a Parliament, a small standing
Committee for the special consideration of foreign
affairs.   It should be large enough to represent
fairly every phase of opinion—seven or eight
members would be a minimum—but not so large as
to make businesslike procedure difficult.   It would
meet periodically at frequent intervals both during

the session of Parliament and in the recess. It should be summoned if any new situation demanded a decision which involved a departure from a policy previously sanctioned. It should have the right to demand the production, under the seal of confidence, of all essential documents and despatches. The Foreign Secretary would naturally be present at its deliberations. It would also be useful that it should have the power to request the attendance, on occasion, of experts in special questions, both official and unofficial. It should be consulted in the negotiations which precede the drafting of treaties, as well as in the later phases when the bargain is embodied in a final form of words. It would be unwise and unnecessary formally to require the Foreign Secretary to abide by the decision of the majority of this Committee. That would involve too wide a departure from our present traditions, But it should be provided that in the event of a capital disagreement, either the Minister or the Committee should have the right at any time to refer their differences to the House of Commons. Over certain acts, such as the issue of an ultimatum, a declaration of war or the conclusion of a treaty, the Committee might be armed with a right of veto, pending the decision of Parliament The general idea of such a Committee would be that it should exercise over the Foreign Office the control which the Cabinet so rarely exercises to any purpose. Its members would give to foreign affairs, as the members of a Cabinet cannot, a close attention. Most of them would be well-informed in some degree before they were elected, and all, with these new opportunities and new responsibilities, would tend to become expert. They would not in their debates be thinking of the fate of their own measures and the independence of their own departments as Cabinet Ministers often do. Nor would they, in the privacy of a committee room, be fettered by the party ties which oppress the private member in the division lobby. Three claims may be made for the adoption of such a system as this. It would give some guarantee, if the Committee was well selected, that the policy of the Foreign Office really reflected the will of the nation. It would place a check upon rash actions and Machiavellian designs. It would also help to secure, by the wisdom of several heads, a higher level of efficiency than the Foreign Office at present attains. There would still remain to a strong and capable Minister a considerable range of unfettered action. He would have to face the test of frequent and intimate debate. He would not be free to conclude treaties binding on his country for years to come, or to send despatches which might provoke immediate war, save with the sanction of the Committee. But over the general conduct of foreign affairs he would remain the responsible Minister, subject only to the risk that if in vital matters he ignored its opinion, the Committee would appeal against him to the House of Commons. In practice the first concern of a Minister would be to keep his Committee with him, to lead it if he were strong and capable; to follow it, if he were a man of timid character and moderate ability.

It may be necessary to answer certain objections which this scheme suggests. It will be said, perhaps, that secrecy could not be secured if all despatches were open to the members of the committee. That objection ignores the fact that all secrets are at present shared, in theory at least, among the members of the Cabinet, not to mention the higher officials at the Foreign Office. There is a better chance of finding discretion among eight or nine men than among twenty. Some leakage there would be, but is there none at present? The Committee would realise that its power depended on its own conduct, and it would doubtless require the resignation of any member who flagrantly and wilfully betrayed a confidence. It may also be urged that to concede so much power to a Committee representing all parties would be a departure from our system of government by majority. But the majority in the House would also have the majority in the Committee. Moreover, this objection ignores the fact that we have of recent years discarded the theory of party government in foreign affairs, and substituted for it a theory of " continuity." Finally, it will be said that the existence of such a Committee would destroy such control of foreign affairs as the whole House possesses at present. To those who realise how little control it does in fact possess. that will not seem a grave objection. The present system of questions, the present occasional debates, need not be interfered with. The final control of the whole House would remain unimpaired in the event of a disagreement between the Committee and the Minister. The House would, in fact, have conferred on certain elected delegates a real authority, in the place of a nominal control which it cannot at

present render effective. The only serious inconvenience would be, so far as I can foresee, that a
member of the Committee, who was in opposition
on any serious issue to the Minister, would have to
fight him in the whole House—if he could fight him
there at all—with his hands tied. He could not
freely use in public debate the confidential knowledge which he had acquired in Committee. But
after all, it is better to be able to make private use
of full knowledge, than to fight publicly but in the
dark, with no real knowledge at all. A confidential
Committee would not offer a perfect system of control. But the reasons which prevent Parliament
from developing an effective public control over the
details of diplomacy are likely to be permanent.
It is wiser to recognise that this latter ideal is in our
day unattainable, and to seek for the best substitute
within our reach.

There are certain other minor points on which a
democracy jealous of its rights would insist. The
diplomatic service, both within and outside the
Foreign Office, ought not to be as it is at present, the
close preserve of the upper class, jealously guarded
by a system of nomination. The Levantine Consular
service, which is filled by open competition, shows, if
I may trust my own observation in the Near East,
a much higher level of ability and competence than
the more aristocratic diplomatic service proper.
A consul in Salonica invariably knows much more of
Turkey, its people and its languages, and is usually,
in addition, an abler man than the distinguished
person who draws an immense salary for presiding
over the Embassy at Constantinople. Our Am-

bassadors, moreover, are rarely men of human and popular sympathies. Our consuls, on the other hand, in this capable Near Eastern corps, are usually as humane and generous by temperament, as they are intelligent and well-informed. The spirit of our diplomacy would gain in liberality and in humanity, as well as in ability and in the habit of hard work and careful study, if the service were recruited by open competition and its higher posts filled on the ground of merit alone. The ornamental side of diplomacy is rapidly becoming obsolete. Treaties and alliances are no longer made by the gay arts of the courtier. On the other hand, the advantage of appointing such a man as Mr. Bryce to such a post as Washington is apparent. Neither a courtier nor a trained diplomatist, he has none the less won the confidence of the American democracy, and immensely improved the relations of the two peoples. His personality means something to American citizens. Much might be gained by sending men of eminence in letters or politics to represent us in every country where public opinion is a real factor in diplomacy. Another proposal which may deserve a passing mention is that the Foreign Office should issue a weekly gazette, containing certainly all the despatches which could with safety and propriety be issued, and possibly also an occasional editorial article to explain our policy. We depend at present for our official information on Blue-books devoted to special subjects, issued at infrequent intervals and usually too late to be of much real service. If the same material reached us promptly in weekly instalments, its value would be immensely enhanced. For any interpretation of the British Government's policy, we and our European neighbours must depend on the *Times*, which is usually, but not always, inspired, and often pours into the official draught some liquor from its own cellars.   The editing of these leading articles would be an anxious task, and perhaps the Foreign Office, which at present finds dumb secrecy an easier part than cautious and temperate speech, would shrink from this bold suggestion.   But the advantages to be gained by the prompt periodical publication of official information are sufficiently obvious, nor would this practice carry with it any apparent risks.   Half the unrest in Europe comes from the effort to divine the real thoughts of a Government through the rare speeches of its members, the still rarer appearances of its Blue-books, and the daily, but not always authoritative pronouncements of newspapers which it inspires but cannot fully control.   To issue such a weekly diary would create confidence by a wise publicity, provide a prompt method of removing misunderstandings alike abroad and at home, and contribute at the same time to build up, by the provision of full and accurate information, an instructed public opinion.

It is only by concentrating on such proposals as these, but more especially on the creation of a permanent Committee for foreign policy, that a democracy may hope to exert a steady influence on the factors which make for peace and war, govern the growth of armaments, and limit our opportunities for humane service in the world.   In vain do we seek by spasmodic agitation to resist some sudden encroachment of militarism, to oppose a war already begun, or to unmake a treaty already ratified. These things depend on the main lines of our foreign policy, our permanent alliances, our understandings and misunderstandings, our rivalry with this Continental Power, our obligations to the other, and the posture for the moment of the struggle for ascendancy in Europe. These larger matters of policy are debated rarely on platforms and never in Parliament. Until we can by some means control them, our agitations beat in vain against occult forces and secret obstacles, whose presence and power we dimly discern.

CHAPTER VIII

THE CONTROL OF FINANCE

PSYCHOLOGY possesses a fascinating unsolved problem. Are we sad because we cry, or do we cry because we are sad ? Are we merry because we laugh, or do we laugh because we are merry ? There is often the same difficulty in international politics in distinguishing cause from effect. Does finance follow the flag, or is the flag dragged in the wake of finance ? No generalisation will altogether cover the facts. The bondholders pulled the flag after them to Egypt, and with the Gladstonian Government for standard-bearer, it went, vowing its reluctance, and protesting that its stay would be brief. It seemed, on the other hand, to be a political and sentimental impulse which carried the flag further into the Soudan. The discovery that its sands may be watered and made to bear cotton was an afterthought, which can hardly have visited the minds of the journalists who wished to " avenge Gordon " and the soldiers who hoped to forestall Marchand. The explanation of the remarkable solidarity between the diplomatist and the financier in most modern Empires is not to be sought in any crude labels. For each of them it is part of the providential order of the universe that patriotism should profit the governing class. That is why it is commonly the sincerest of all the disinterested emotions. It would be as false to say that the diplomatist is the sordid tool of finance, as it would be to say that the financier is the disinterested purse-bearer of patriotism. They belong to the same social world ; they each submit to the vague influences which cause the world to turn its interest now to this corner of the earth, and again to that. Each has his own formula to cover what he does. The financier knows that in pushing his business he is incidentally buying power for the empire. The diplomatist is convinced that he is serving his country by promoting " trade." However we explain it, the understanding between the City and Downing Street is admirably close. The City does not invest where investments would hamper our foreign policy ; the Foreign Office will stand by the City where it has invested. To demand the " control of finance " will seem to some readers superfluous, and to others chimerical. It is both, and it is also an object to achieve. In one sense it exists. With rare exceptions, a British financier will not use his money in any affair which has, or may acquire a political colour, without the approval of the Foreign Office. Our Foreign Secretary does not need the formal veto which a French Ministry possesses over the quotation of foreign securities on the Bourse. The general astonishment at the daring of an English banker who did venture recently to float a Chinese loan in London against the wishes of the Foreign Office, was an eloquent witness to the usual custom and the general feeling. Persia was successfully prevented from borrowing in London, though she had found a banker willing to accommodate her. Perhaps the most curious instance is supplied by the history of Russian loans. Before the Crimean War they were several times issued in the London money-market. From 1854 to 1906 the City boycotted Russia. The loan of the latter year followed the hints in Sir Edward Grey's speeches, and the evidently inspired articles in the *Times* which foreshadowed the conclusion of the political understanding then in process of negotiation. The services of finance and diplomacy are mutual, and in the modern world they have become indispensable to each other. It is an immense reinforcement to diplomacy in dealing with a debtor State to know that it has, in effect, behind it the exportable capital of a wealthy nation to give or to withhold. If any Power or group of Powers held the monopoly of the world's money-market even for a few years, and used it with a conscious political purpose, they would in the end dictate to Russia, China, Turkey, and the Latin-American Republics. We habitually classify Powers as Conservative or Liberal, as military or naval, as industrial or agricultural. But there is a classification as vital as any of these for an understanding of world-politics—the division into creditor and debtor States. It is her unequalled stores of capital for export which keep France, in spite of her stationary population and the relative decline of her military strength, in the front rank of the Great Powers. It is her absolute dependence on the import of foreign capital which has forced autocratic Russia into two unnatural associations, the first with Republican France, and the second with her Imperial rival, Britain. It is the financial power of Paris and London which assists the Triple Entente to maintain itself against the compacter military force of the Triple Alliance. It is the aspiration of Germany, a relatively new country which accumulates capital hardly fast enough for its own internal needs, and much too slowly for its over-seas ambitions, to obtain access to the closed money-market of Paris, that explains much of the unrest of Western Europe. Under the alternate bullying and cajolery of German diplomacy towards France there is often discernible the underlying thought that a rough wooing might bring about the fruitful marriage of German enterprise with French thrift.

It is impossible in all this intricate play of motives and forces to say where the pressure of finance ends, and the control of diplomacy begins. There is no antagonism, and there is no subordination. The British reconciliation with Russia appeared on the surface to be purely political, a strategical move dictated by the posture of the struggle for a balance of power. But the knowledge that an understanding with Russia would provide a profitable outlet for British finance must have furnished a powerful secondary motive, and the influence of Lord Revelstoke and the interests which he leads, was undoubtedly a force which helped to reconcile middle-class opinion to the change in our traditional policy, French statesmen were ostensibly buying the Russian army for eventual use against Germany when they concluded the Dual Alliance, but we may feel sure that the French banks, which control the French press far more directly than any one interest controls our English newspapers, did their part in preparing a connection which has been worth incalculable sums to them in commissions and profits of flotation. If the reader asks for a more recent illustration, there is the Mexican crisis. It may have been, and probably was, a train of purely disinterested and even doctrinaire reasoning which induced President Woodrow Wilson to oppose the Dictator Huerta. But without suspecting that the Standard Oil Trust, which has long been at feud, first with Porfirio Diaz, and then with General Huerta, directly influenced either Dr. Wilson or Mr. Bryan, it did undoubtedly help to make the public opinion which approved their policy. They could not have acted against it ; a fortunate concurrence of humanitarian views with financial interests enabled them to act with it. It was, one supposes, the influence of the rival British Cowdray group of financiers which made our own Government well-disposed both to Diaz and to Huerta, though in the end this influence was not powerful enough, after the initial stages of the crisis, to set our diplomacy in direct antagonism to that of the United States. The mischief of this relationship is not that finance invariably dominates diplomacy ; in point of fact that is not an assertion which could be maintained. The mischief is rather that the relationship is uncertain, obscure, secret and capricious. There is no avowed control of finance by diplomacy. It is rather that the right hand and the left of the same organism normally work in response to the brain of the same governing class. In the conversations which decide policy the financial groups, well-informed and alert, are always early in the field, and against their claim to represent a national interest, there is no popular influence, equally alert, equally well informed, to balance their pressure. Finance may be on occasion the subtle master of diplomacy. It may be also an invaluable instrument. To provide against the danger and to ensure the use, it seems essential for a modern State to possess an avowed and public means of control. It ought to be possible in the national interest that a Foreign Office should be able to do avowedly and publicly what ours does privately and semi-officially. Finance, as we have seen, relies on diplomatic support in all its dealings with States like China, Turkey, and Mexico. That is the basis for control. The power of sanction and veto exists already, but in a form so covert and irresponsible that public opinion is unable to control it, and can hardly question it. It is not in order to strengthen the bureaucratic authority of the Foreign Office that one desires formal control, but rather to make the Foreign Office itself accountable for its acts. These sanctions and vetoes are among the most important transactions of public policy. They ought to be subject to review by some such body as the Committee of the House of Commons proposed in the last chapter. They depend at present on conversations between financiers and public servants conducted, no one knows how, between the four walls of a room. The only way to convert them into responsible acts of an avowed policy, is to introduce in this country legislation, on the lines of the French model, which lays it down that the assent of the Government is necessary before a foreign security may be quoted on the Stock Exchange.

A single illustration will suffice to show the advantage which this power of control would give, on occasion, to those who desire that British policy should serve a high international purpose. There was a moment when the action of British finance was the decisive factor in the Russian struggle for constitutional freedom. It is rather difficult for Englishmen to realise how important the attitude of the rest of Europe is to Russia. Our foible is a certain disdain for foreign opinion : we can afford this luxury, for we are independent of foreign finance. Russia is sensitive because she depends as absolutely as any Latin-American Republic upon her repute in Western markets. She must float by far the greater part of her loans abroad. She cannot even provide from her own resources for the municipal enterprise of her cities. Her undeveloped coal and iron and petroleum fields all await the fertilisation of foreign capital. If we can conceive for a moment what German opinion would mean to us, if we had to float Consols through the Deutsche Bank, if Manchester had to go to Berlin for money to build her tramways, if a South Wales coal mine were awaiting the good opinion of some financier in Hamburg, we shall be able to realise dimly why and how much the good opinion of the English people matters to the Russian Government. Credit is a delicate possession. So long as British investors thought of Russia either as a hostile empire dangerous to ourselves, or as an unstable autocracy menaced by revolution, it was in vain that the Russian financier brought his proposals to the City. Prudence, patriotism and humanity were all against him. The change in the opinions of the moneyed classes began when the Conservative press advocated a *rapprochement*, when the *Times* ceased to give prominence to news damaging to the Autocracy, and when it was known that an agreement over Persia was in process of arrangement. There was no mystery about the reasons for this change of attitude. Sir Edward Grey had said that it was necessary to restore Russia to her rank as a Great Power in order to redress the balance in Europe. In plain words, our diplomacy wanted Russian support against Germany, and France was urging and engineering the reconciliation. The early months of 1906 were the critical moment for Russian finance, and it happened to coincide with the critical moment in the development of her constitution. While she was endeavouring to secure a loan of one hundred millions in Western Europe, the elections for the first Duma were about to be held. The Constitution was still a sheet of paper. Everything turned on the ability of the Duma to assert itself, to control the bureaucracy, to make itself the supreme power in Russia. There was one obvious method open to it. It must possess control of the purse, and that meant at the moment control over this foreign loan. If the loan were concluded before it met, the bureaucracy would meet it with its war-chest full. For a few months or weeks European public opinion was potentially the master of Russia's destinies. It professed full sympathy with the constitutional movement, and it had the means of giving its sympathy effect. The Russian Liberals (Cadets) were at one with the Socialists in urging that the granting of the loan should be made conditional on the consent of the Duma. This would have involved a delay of two or three months, but it would have enabled the Parliamentary majority to drive its bargain with a Tsar who had already repented his concessions. Fresh from their sweeping victories at the polls, the Liberals and Socialists might have said to the Tsar's Ministers : " We have Russia behind us, and we have Europe behind us. Your coffers are empty ; your credit is exhausted. Concede our full rights of responsible government, and we will vote your taxes and sanction your loan. Deny our rights, and we are convinced that neither in London nor in Paris will you find the money to finance your oppressions." But the great loan had already been floated in Paris and London by March, 1906, and in May when the Duma assem. bled, it found itself confronted by a Government which had nothing to fear from Russia, and nothing more to hope from Europe. Europe had enabled it to pay its Cossacks. For two generations we closed our money-market to the Tsars. We opened it three months too soon. Had we waited those three months, as the Russian Liberal press implored us to wait, the progressive parties must have triumphed. The Cossack can do little, unless the financier stands behind him. But no Parliament can effectively wield the traditional weapon of supply, if foreign banks have first provided for the despot's needs. The decision, in this instance, rested with London. The Paris banks, weary of the burden of supporting the tottering Russian chaos, had made it a condition of their supporting this loan, that English banks should share the profitable burden. It lay with the English banks on their side to insist on the brief delay required to obtain the Duma's assent. It may be said that " business is business " ; one cannot fairly expect a banker, when he is offered a large commission for floating a loan, to weigh all the consequences which his action will have for the liberties of a foreign nation. Perhaps not. But the bankers, one may be sure, consulted Downing Street, and Downing Street in its turn thought only of buying the dead weight of Russia to fling into the scales of a balance of power. Even from that standpoint it miscalculated : a free Russia would be a more trusty friend and more valuable ally than a Russia enslaved, oppressed, and busied with unending internal strife. But such foresight is as rare among diplomatists as disinterestedness among bankers. The decision in what was really an act of European policy, fraught with the gravest consequences for human peace and freedom, ought to have lain neither with the diplomatists nor with the bankers. Had it come before a Parliamentary Committee, some members at least would have listened to the appeals of the Russian progressives, and insisted on postponing the loan.

This illustration might be continued at will. When once the Russian bureaucracy had found its way to the British market, it knew how to establish itself. With steady and open official encouragement, with the aid of the financial press, and of the special Russian supplements of the *Times*, Russia has become popular as a field for British investments. One firm alone boasts in an advertisement that between November, 1909, and October, 1911, it placed Russian bonds worth £4,891,700 on the English market. Such transactions have two aspects. On the one hand, our propertied class was acquiring a stake in Russia. On the other hand, our good will was becoming increasingly important to the Russian bureaucracy. Banquets, official visits, and Royal courtesies were steadily employed to raise the temperature of opinion to the point at which money flows. And this went on while two Dumas were dissolved, the franchise gerrymandered, Finland enslaved, and Persia over-run. Even from the narrow standpoint of diplomatic technique our procedure was singularly inept. With all our buying, we never bought Russian loyalty, nor prevented her from coquetting with the German rival. Yet the cards were all in our hands. Whatever else Germany can do for Russia, she cannot lend her money. Had we made terms before we lent, had we even checked the flow of gold, we could have won some measure of control over Russian policy. If France had backed us (and we were earning her backing during the Moroccan crisis), it ought to have been possible to say to Russia, " No more money until Persia is evacuated." Persia, after all, is a luxury for Russia ; money is a necessity. When Conservative diplomatists retort to those who would have our diplomacy pay some regard to the interests of liberty and humanity, " Would you have us go to war for Persia ? " (or for Finland or Macedonia,

as the case may be), there is a simple and effective
answer, " War is an obsolete barbarism. In the
modern world finance is a more effective weapon.
At any moment, France and Britain, if they were
really at one, as they professed to be, could deal with
Russia or with Turkey as they chose. Shut the
doors of the banks, and these despotisms would be
helpless."

What is true of the impolicy and immorality
of allowing and encouraging the export of British
capital to assist a tyranny in its enterprises against
liberty, is even more obviously true of the use of
capital to assist a foreign war. It has been cogently
argued that if the munitions and provisions intended
for a belligerent army are contraband, money exported for its use is equally so, and that the lending
of money to a State engaged in war is a flagrant
breach of neutrality. There is no obvious answer
to this argument, and it would seem to follow that
the open flotation of loans in neutral markets for
the benefit of belligerents ought to be rigidly
forbidden. It is not so certain, however, that the
reform in law is worth making. It is on the eve of
war that such loans are usually contracted, and this
could be dealt with only under a general Act by
which all foreign loans require the sanction of the
Foreign Office. Europe made or pretended to make
some futile efforts to prevent the outbreak of the
Balkan wars. They failed because they were
insincere. Russia, as we now know, so far from
wishing to prevent the war, had actually arranged
it by presiding over the formation of the Balkan
League. At the very moment when she joined the

concert in declaring that none of the Allies would be allowed to keep the territory they won, she had set her seal to a treaty of partition, and accepted the post of arbiter in the division of the territory. It is such duplicity which makes concerts ineffective. Either of these wars could have been prevented, if the French banks had been forbidden to finance the combatants. They were not forbidden, because Russia willed it otherwise. Our own finance was comparatively, perhaps wholly, innocent. The case is worth citing only as an illustration of the importance of securing first of all that diplomacy shall control finance, and secondly that public opinion shall control diplomacy. More and more, finance is becoming the arbiter of war and peace, the master of despotisms, the unseen agent which might, by a bloodless intervention, check the ambitions of the world's rulers and relieve the sufferings of oppressed races. Looking back upon the records of recent years we can see how it might have been used to prevent Russian aggression in Persia, to save the Duma, to control the aberrations of Turkish policy, to prevent the outbreak of a shameful war. The tool lies ready for the grasp of a European democracy strong enough and united enough to use it. Together the three Western Powers could use it to control the world. But the first step in the realisation of that dream is to make it our servant at home.

The control of finance, where the dealing of British banks with foreign governments is concerned, is not the most difficult aspect of our subject. In practice it exists, though in a covert and unavowed form. In theory it would be a natural extension of the existing law. The meaning of the foreign Enlistment Act and of the orders which enforce neutrality in war-time, is that in his dealings with foreign governments a good citizen is expected to subordinate his own personal interests to those of his country. The State, when once it has begun to protect and even to aid the financier in his operations abroad, has the right to regulate them. At any moment these operations may compromise us, lead to a demand for intervention, bring us into conflict with other Powers, and require the use of the prestige or even of the actual force of our Navy. Operations which may have such consequences cannot be regarded simply as the private acts of a private trader, of which the State need take no cognisance. We enter more difficult and contentious ground when we turn to the larger question of the export of capital abroad in the form, not of loans, but of railway building, mining ventures, and other enterprises which usually involve some direct dealings with foreign governments. The evils and risks of this peculiar modern development of " trade " have been dealt with in a previous chapter. Whatever view the reader may take of it, this at least is clear, that it differs in kind from the older and more familiar type of trade, the exchange of goods. It differs at both ends. Send a shipload of goods abroad, and the benefit of the transaction must be counted not merely in the merchant's profit, but in the wages of workers who made the goods and the sailors who carried them. Send a supply of capital, and no one save the investor (and a few bank clerks) shares in the direct gains.

Capital accumulates too rapidly, and the inducement to send it where labour is cheap, tends to
prevent its employment at home, limits the supply
of capital at home, and helps to make it relatively
scarce and dear. A further consequence is that
in order to support and promote its safe and profitable investment abroad, the whole nation is taxed
and its policy encumbered, to maintain the armaments which are increasingly an insurance for the
foreign investments of the few. The direct profits
of the trade in capital so vastly exceed the direct
profits of the trade in goods drawn by the moneyed
class, that our national policy has evolved from
what the Germans call " Manchesterism " to
Imperialism.

This is, of course, a partial presentment of the
facts ; there is another side. The peculiarity
of this modern trading which begins with lending,
and is conducted throughout on an elaborate
credit basis, is apt to be overlooked. It is not
" trade " as Cobden's world understood it, nor as
Lancashire still understands it. It has its own
special risks and mischiefs, and if the distinction
has been unduly emphasised in these pages, even
an exaggerated statement of it may have its uses.
It would be a mistake, however, to ignore the
connection between the export of capital and the
trade in goods. The former process prepares
and facilitates the latter, opens new markets,
unlocks latent resources, and hastens a movement
of population and goods which would at the best
have come slowly without it. Because money
has been lent to Canada, India and Argentina to

build railways, the seas are laden to-day with the ships which carry our food supplies from these countries. On the produce of the tropics and the colonies we depend for most of the raw material of our manufactures, and for many of the staples of our daily life. Had the colonists or the natives of these countries been left to accumulate their own capital unaided, and to build their ports and railways slowly as their own resources permitted, this trade would to-day be incomparably less in volume than it is. All this is so well known and so universally recognised, that it is hardly necessary to lay stress upon it. It would, moreover, be misleading to use language which recalled the primitive fallacies in the history of economics. We have long outlived the notion that the sending of capital abroad involves a diminution of our wealth ; nor is there in the end anything but a gain to the world's wealth and a saving of the world's labour from a process which stimulates production where it can be most economically carried on. It is not from the protectionist standpoint that the process is here criticised. There is, moreover, this to be said in mitigation of any criticism. It is a process of which the evils diminish with the lapse of time. While a new country is being " penetrated " or conquered, we must witness uncompensated mischief, which involves us only in diplomatic conflicts and increased armaments. As years go by the need passes for special military efforts ; and other Powers recognise the accomplished fact, and benefits of one kind or another begin to figure on the credit page of the national ledger. The permanent mischief remains as a dead weight on the national debt, and a standing annual addition to the Navy estimates. The evils of the process are a necessary and inevitable accompaniment of capitalistic civilisation. They cannot be ended or avoided. The utmost we can do is to enquire how far they can be regulated and limited, so that the minimum of injury shall result to ourselves, to native races, and to our European neighbours.

A peculiarly gross scandal has recently led to some discussion of the need for a means of controlling British companies which operate with British capital abroad. The organisation which had imposed in the Putumayo region a system of virtual slavery, as cruel and as wasteful as anything which King Leopold created on the Congo, was a British company with British directors, and an office in the City. Public opinion discovered, as the revelations went on, that no device exists by which British financiers, whose agents have imposed slavery on a primitive race by massacre, torture, and rape, can be either punished or checked, provided they confine their cruelties to foreign territory. Public opinion was moved, and a suggested remedy, in itself, natural and simple, will shortly be proposed to Parliament. It is, in a word, that British subjects who in future lend their names and their capital to companies engaged in such criminal ventures, shall be liable to prosecution and imprisonment in this country, wherever the scene of their vicarious crimes may have been. The proposal embodies a salutary principle, and it marks the first recognition of the fact that British capital exported abroad is in some

sense an emanation of ourselves, a function of the
national life which ought to be subject in some
degree to British law and national control. But the
criminal law is a clumsy means of control. It is
only in the rarest and the grossest cases that it could
be successfully set in motion. One has only to
conceive the difficulty and expense of obtaining
evidence in the heart of Africa or South America
and transporting the witnesses to London, to realise
how seldom the thing could be attempted. The
defence would never be at a loss for hired or terror-
ised witnesses, who would swear that the worst of
its agents was regarded by the natives as a beneficent
deity, and the jury, ignorant of the local conditions,
and ready enough to believe that if wrong was done,
the directors in England were not to blame, would
seldom be eager to convict. No fair-minded man
had any doubt about the Putumayo atrocities, but
evidence which would convince a historian is not
always enough for a court of law. For one gross
case like this there are a score of cases in which
exported capital, while it may avoid crude, bloody
crime, is, none the less, guilty of grinding exploitation, which only a lawyer could distinguish from
slavery. The nightmare horrors of the Putumayo
could take place only in the remotest regions
of an unsettled and almost untrodden wilderness.
They are not common, nor are they apparently
very profitable, and they tend to cure themselves
by their own excess. The system known as *peonage*
is, on the other hand, general throughout Latin-
America, and the capital by which it is worked is
often foreign and sometimes British. It is the rule

in Mexico and Brazil, and probably in all the
more backward Republics of South America.   The
victim, usually a native, but sometimes a white
or a half-breed, incurs a debt to the planter or
merchant, and by the Latin-American law of debtor
and creditor, which knows no Truck Acts, becomes
in effect his slave until the debt is paid off.   It
never is paid off ; the planter keeps the books.
Under this transparent fiction of debt, slaves
are bought and sold, villages broken up, peasant
landowners reduced to the level of serfs, and tribes
carried off to distant scenes of oppression.   Children
are bought and sold, and young women driven into
commercial prostitution.   All of this is a typical
expression of Latin-American civilisation.   But
foreign capital venturing into these regions adapts
itself to its environment, and does in Mexico as
the Mexicans do.   It turns the rather slovenly,
inefficient oppressions of the lazy Spanish landowner
into a competent and extensive system, conducted
with a ruthlessness and on a scale which transcend
the habits of the country.   The spectacle is not
one which a European democracy ought to watch
with indifferent eyes and folded arms.   If the
people of Mexico or Brazil developed a capitalistic
system of their own, then however gross its evils
might be, the process ought clearly to be allowed
to follow its own natural evolution.   For purely
Mexican wrongs, the Mexicans themselves must
find the remedy. But the European financier
goes forth equipped with resources taken from our
stores on a career of conquest and exploitation,
protected by our flag and backed by our prestige.

Our moral responsibility for what he does is as clear as was the complicity of our fathers when they allowed the slaver and the buccaneer to fit out their ships in Bristol harbour. The mischief is far wider than any extension of our criminal law could control, and it assumes multitudinous shapes. To-day British capital is migrating to Russia. It finances a Siberian gold-mine, and presently we read that the workers, who had revolted against intolerable conditions, have been shot down literally by the hundred. To-morrow it will be building factories in China, and the worst evils of our own nascent industrial era will be repeated under incomparably worse conditions.

It is not easy to prescribe a remedy, and honest thinking ought to admit at once that there is no adequate remedy. If one could regulate this process of the export of capital with an autocratic hand, one would like to exclude all foreign capital from weak and undeveloped States until they are strong enough to master it themselves, to make it their servant, and to subject it to Factory Acts and Truck Acts of their own. There is work enough for it to do in the newer countries which have a civilised government. Such a policy, however, would require a firm agreement among all civilised States, and it would postulate a degree of self-restraint and a sensitive humanity which exist at present in none of them. The utmost we can do as yet is to formulate our standard, to study methods of control, and to introduce them by degrees. At present we are faced by the fact that the Palmerstonian doctrine of the rights of the

Civis Romanus is the undefined principle of our foreign policy. Our diplomacy acts on the principle that it is its duty to promote and defend the interests of the British investor and concessionaire abroad. If we could begin the world anew, or if we were strong enough to reverse an established practice, we probably ought to meet this principle with a direct negative, and instruct our embassies and consulates that British subjects who invest capital or seek concessions abroad do so entirely at their own risk. The result would be an automatic regulation of the export of capital, which would achieve most of the results which we desire. Capital would not go to disturbed, unsettled and uncivilised regions, because the risk of being robbed by the native government would usually overbalance the chance of exploiting native labour profitably. In dealing with the more intelligent of these " native " States, it is possible that the subjects of a Power which did not protect them might enjoy a positive advantage. China, for example, pays her debts and keeps her bonds without external pressure. If she knew that she might favour British capital without risking diplomatic intervention, and without finding that areas which it was developing had been ear-marked as a British sphere of penetration, it is certain that she would prefer to deal with British financiers, if she were free to choose. The answer to this argument is, of course, that she would not be free. Other Powers would take advantage of our abstention to force their own capital by their own methods on China. It is clear that the policy of abstention could not be recommended as

necessarily good for British business, unless it were
adopted by our chief competitors as the result of
an agreement. That is not, however, a fatal objection. On the contrary, the nation as a whole has
the right to say that it does not choose, for the sake
of profits to finance, to involve itself in the competition for concessions and spheres of influence in
China, a competition which must bring in its train
some aggravation of the struggle for a balance of
power, and some stimulus to the accumulation of
armaments. We have an immense estate to develop.
It is no hardship to ask British capitalists, if they
must have the protection of the British flag, to
confine themselves to an intensive cultivation of
the vast Empire which we possess already. If
that does not content them, the whole world is
open to them, provided they face its risks without
expecting the support of our diplomacy. There is
nothing chimerical or Utopian or impracticable
in suggesting the reversal of this Palmerstonian
doctrine. The Tory party was opposed to the
Civis Romanus formula before Disraeli and Mr.
Chamberlain had taught it the new financial Imperialism. Nor is there any reason why Liberals
should cling to it. They dislike criticism of the
export of capital at present, because they suspect
those who indulge in it of a mercantilist or protectionist bias. That is entirely to miss the relevant
point. The main point is simply that the backing
of investments by diplomacy means inevitably
an increase of the armaments which are the diplomatist's last word. When that has been realised
by any party which sincerely cares for peace and

can shake itself free of the financiers who maintain
the party funds, it will begin the reduction of armaments by the simple step of reversing the Palmerstonian doctrine. Armaments are an insurance
for our exported capital, and they will continue to
grow so long as we allow our diplomacy to be used
to serve finance. The surest way to stop their
growth is to instruct our Ambassadors that they
must never again assist a financier who is endeavouring to obtain a concession.

There is at present no force in our political life
strong enough to carry a reversal of the Palmerstonian maxim. For this reason, and also because
some means are needed by which existing investments can be controlled, it may be well to attempt
a sketch of some less heroic alternative policy.
British capital operating abroad is in a position
comparable to that of the traveller who applies for
a passport. Passports are not granted as a matter
of right. In theory, and to some extent in practice,
they are regarded as valuable titles to protection
which are granted only to respectable applicants.
If a man or a company wishes to trade or lend
money abroad under the cover of our flag, it is
obvious that if we intend in any degree to protect
or recognise his business, it must be open to investigation, and it must conform to such rules as the present
standards of international morality may lay down.
It we are going to protect or assist the operations
of private finance at all, we have a right at least to
stipulate that it shall not engage in any form of
veiled slavery, or by *quasi*-political activities
embarrass our diplomacy. The first step is clearly

to make some measure of surveillance possible, by
requiring British businesses which operate abroad
to apply for registration. A careful register, subject
to annual revision, ought to be kept at the Foreign
Office or the Board of Trade, of all the capital owned
abroad by British subjects, whether in the form of
loans, concessions, mines, railways, factories, or
share investments. The keeping of such a register
would be no light task, and a fee for registration
proportionate to the capital involved would naturally be imposed to meet expenses. With the proceeds of these fees it would be possible to improve
the consular service, and to maintain a staff which
could report on the conduct of business, and investi-
gate charges of slavery and kindred offences. The
register would naturally distinguish two classes of
undertakings—those which merited recognition and
some measure of official protection, and those to
which recognition was refused. This classification
would be much less difficult than one might at a first
glance suppose. The greater part of this exported
capital goes to British colonies or dependencies,
and this would be registered without question or
examination. It is amenable there to British law
and British administration, and we need invent no
new machinery to deal with its activities. Nor
need we concern ourselves closely with companies
operating only in fully civilised regions—the United
States and Western Europe. There are some other
parts of the world so barbarous and unsettled, or so
fatally involved in unfree conditions of labour,
that no company operating in them ought to be
recognised. The debatable area, where recognition

might either be granted or refused, would still be considerable, and would include Russia, Turkey, China, Persia, the Portuguese colonies, and most of Latin-America. If the first task of compiling the register were entrusted to the officials of the Foreign Office, it would obviously be necessary to provide some Board or Commission, composed of non-official persons, before which appeals might be heard. Certain bodies, such as the Aborigines' Protection Society, ought also to have the right to state their case against a company, as the Societies for the Protection of Animals and of Children may do against an individual in a police-court. Certain general principles might be defined from the outset, or would gradually be established by precedent. It is easy to say in advance what some of them would be. No business ought to be recognised which offended in any one of the following ways :—

(1) By slavery or any of the disguises of slavery, by sweating or systematic ill-treatment of employees, or by tolerating conditions unfavourable to health.

(2) By usurious dealing with a native State, *e.g.*, by such terms as the bondholders imposed on the Khedive Ismail.

(3) By political activities, such as the financing of a revolution or civil war, as English financiers are said to have done (perhaps falsely) in Turkey and Mexico.

(4) By assisting a State at war or about to go to war, with money or arms.

Experience would certainly bring to light other

principles which ought to govern the recognition and non-recognition of British enterprises abroad. A " recognised " company would have the right to ask for protection in the conduct of its business ; how far that protection would go in any given case must, of course, depend on general considerations of policy. An " unrecognised " company, though no one could prevent it from trading at its own risk, would find the doors of our legations and consulates rigidly closed to it. The register must, of course, be public, and its contents open to the inspection both of investors and of the representatives of foreign governments. Adventurers would sometimes evade this machinery where the stake was high enough. But it can hardly be doubted that this method of control would prove to be effective. The first question which any careful investor at home would ask, would be whether the company which invited his support was " recognised," while abroad, the unrecognised company, if it had overcome the first difficulty of obtaining capital, would find that its inferior and disreputable status exposed it to continual suspicions and humiliations at the hands of reputable firms and foreign governments. Once on the list, a firm would know that if at any time it were tempted to ill-use its native employees, or to speculate in revolutions, it risked the loss of its favoured position. The registration fee (which ought to be an annual charge) might become a valuable instrument of fiscal policy. When it is generally realised that the Navy is largely an insurance for the investments of the propertied class abroad, the conclusion will be drawn that it ought to pay its full share of the cost, if possible, directly. That might be attained either through an annual registration fee, or by imposing a higher rate of income tax on the profits of foreign investments. This possible development of the register of exported capital need not be elaborated here.   The case for the register is that it supplies a simple and automatic means of controlling capital abroad.   Any use which might be made of it as a means of providing revenue ought to be secondary and incidental.

This proposal of a control over foreign investments exercised through a classified register, is put forward as the only logical development of the momentous innovation which Palmerston introduced in the theory and practice of diplomacy.   He bestowed nationality on money.   He lent the shelter of the flag to investments.   We have seen how the whole evolution of Imperialism has proceeded from this premise.   From the coercion of Greece because a Levantine moneylender had a claim against her, we have advanced to the modern practice of using diplomacy to back the financier who is engaged in concession-hunting.   To some of us this whole development seems wrong and mischievous from start to finish, both in morals and in economics. It is a question, however, whether a principle which has helped in half a century to transform a large part of the earth's surface can be reversed.   If the Empire intends to proceed on this principle, as no doubt it does, the reformer will endeavour at the least to define it and to regulate its action. We do not seriously mean to place the whole resources of our diplomacy and our armaments at the beck and call of every usurer, every sweater, every concession-hunter who has taken the trouble to be born or naturalised in these islands. We back some ventures at present and ignore others, but what the principle of selection may be, is a mystery hidden from unofficial persons. The argument of these pages is that the selection ought to be drastic and systematic, that it should follow certain axioms of humanity and policy, and that its results should be publicly known in such a way as to discourage and handicap disreputable enterprises.

The evils of an unrestricted competition for concessions and monopolies between rival financial groups backed by their Governments, are so notorious that diplomacy has found several typical formulæ for bringing them to an end. Some of them have been mentioned already, and it will suffice to pass them briefly in review. The obvious method of resolving such conflicts is the demarcation of spheres of " influence," " interest " or " penetration " within which each of the competing Powers enjoys a monopoly respected by the others. This method is open to two grave objections. In the first place, it is rarely adopted before a ruinous conflict has exhausted the competitors. For years or decades they carry on a trial of strength which affects not merely their local relationship, but their attitude to one another in Europe, and is measured year by year in their military and naval estimates. If we were to take the sum by which British and German armaments have increased in the present century, it would be possible to allocate the increase, roughly, somewhat as follows : 50 per cent. or less for the settlement of the question, Who shall exploit Morocco ? ; 25 per cent. or more for the privilege of building a railway to Bagdad and beyond it ; 25 per cent. or more for the future eventualities which remain unsettled—the fate of the Portuguese colonies in Africa, and the destinies of China.   In the second place, the delimitation of spheres of interest is almost inevitably fatal to the national existence of the country partitioned, and as inevitably adds a vast burden to the commitments of the Imperial Power. Persia furnishes the obvious illustration. Sir Edward Grey is clearly resolved that he will not allow himself by the march of events to be drawn into the assumption of any direct responsibility for the administration of the British sphere.   It is a laudable resolve, but Russia may at any moment frustrate it.   She deals with her own sphere on the opposite principle, and her sphere happens to include the seat of the central government. That government is already a puppet of Russian policy, enjoying only a simulacrum of independence. How much longer can a government which is not a government continue to rule the southern sphere ? Sooner or later a choice must be made.   Either Russia must withdraw, or some separate government under British protection must be created for the south. Turkey is drifting rapidly towards a dissolution in which the spheres which the Great Powers already claim will be formally delimited.   It is easy to predict what that will mean.   There will be first provincial loans, then provincial advisers, and finally a military control, under which each of these

" spheres " will become what Egypt already is, a dependency of a European Power.

The method of avoiding financial competition by marking off zones of monopoly, is clearly the worst which can be pursued. There are alternatives. Let us consider what methods might be followed if the Powers were sage enough to shrink from the terrific conflict which may one day overtake them for the partition of China. China is so thickly peopled that crude conquest presents few attractions. Even Japan could not settle her surplus population in a country where every hill is terraced and every field subjected to intensive cultivation. But there is here a field which capital is already eager to exploit, and every year diminishes the resistance of prejudice and inertia to its ambitions. The attempts to mark out spheres of influence have so far been tentative and unsuccessful. Our own claim to the lion's share, the Yangtse Valley, is admitted by no other Power, and it is doubtful whether the Foreign Office still maintains it. There are several principles which might be adopted if the Powers desired to avoid the jealous and dangerous struggle for concessions. In the first place, the simplest plan and the best would be the adoption of a self-denying ordinance by all the chief competitors. Let it be understood that British, French and German banks may compete among themselves for railways and loans, but that none of them shall receive any aid or countenance whatever from the embassies or consulates of their respective countries. If that could be decided, the allotment of concessions would be settled either by the merits of the competitors or more probably by their skill and audacity in bribing Chinese officials. One may doubt, however, whether any of the Powers has sufficient faith in the honour of its competitors to enter on such an undertaking. A second and more hopeful plan might be borrowed from the undertaking negotiated by France and Germany over Morocco. They agreed to promote co-operation among their subjects, who were to share in agreed percentages in the coveted opportunities for public works. A vast " pool " or syndicate in which all the rival financial groups were represented, might be left to internationalise all the opportunities of monopoly in China on a plan which would give to each its allotted share in the risks and profits. The scheme worked badly in Morocco, and indeed created the friction which led to the Agadir incident. Something of the kind existed in China while the alliance of the banks of the Six Powers subsisted, and it eventually broke down. By this method friction may be avoided among the Great Powers, but China would be subjected to an intolerable financial dictation, which would be none the less oppressive because it was cosmopolitan. There exists, however, in the Ottoman Public Debt, a model which might be followed elsewhere. Its council represents all the bondholders of every nationality, and usually maintains good relations with the Porte. If the railways of Turkey, China and Persia could be amalgamated, each in a single system under a cosmopolitan administration, the risk of partition and all the danger to peace, which this risk entails, might be removed. The obvious step is to confer on these syndicates of capitalists an international legal personality, which would enable them to sue or be sued before the Hague Tribunal. Some disinterested council nominated by the Hague should be interposed between the syndicate and the State in which it operates, so that the intervention of diplomacy may be as far as possible eliminated.

The problems raised by the export of capital have been considered in this chapter mainly from the standpoint of the creditor State, which sees its diplomacy involved in the process. We have found, so far, no solution which is satisfactory from the standpoint of the debtor nation. The inroad of foreign capital always means for it some loss of independence, and it has nothing to gain by agreements among competing Empires. It may, indeed, keep its independence by playing on their rivalries. Its shadowy autonomy vanishes when they come to terms. The pacifist and the nationalist are here divided in their sympathies. The former, thinking only of European peace, rejoices when Russia and Britain end their differences by the partition of Persia. The latter, seeing only that a nation has been destroyed, regards the agreement as a peculiarly evil development of Imperialism. Both are right, and both are wrong. The ideal expedient would preserve European peace without destroying the victim nationality. To propose that expedient requires an excursion into the realms of Utopian construction. We can propose nothing which seems feasible to-day, but a solution is conceivable which requires only an easy step in the organisation of the civilised world for peace.   The motives for the partition of Persia were rather political than financial.   The object-lesson of Egypt, where the occupation had its origin in debt, is a more typical instance of modern processes.   It happens that the Hague Conference has laid down a principle which is capable of fruitful extension for dealing with such cases as these.   The Drago Doctrine, put forward by Señor Drago, a jurist and statesman of the Argentine Republic, supported by the United States and eventually adopted by all the Powers, provides that no creditor State may use arms to enforce a liability upon a debtor State, unless a decision of the Hague Tribunal has recognised the liability and prescribed the method of payment.   This doctrine, even as it stands, is of immense value to minor but civilised States like the South American Republics, Portugal and Greece, which may find themselves obliged to defer payment of an external debt.   The Hague Tribunal would in such a case, if it realised its opportunities, act as a good County Court Judge would do at home— refuse to admit a merely usurious claim, and lay down terms and dates of payment which would admit of the debtor's recovery from any temporary difficulty.

But to defeat the more unscrupulous methods of the international usurer, this idea requires some amplification.   It may be necessary for a debtor State, some grades below the level of Portugal and Greece in civilisation, to mortgage some part of its revenues, and to accept, at least over part of them, some degree of foreign control.   That means, if the creditor country has also political ambitions, the almost certain loss of its independence. There are also States like Turkey which stand in need of expert advice for the reorganisation of their finances, but dread the consequences of admitting any foreigner, who may perhaps think more of the interests of European finance and of his own motherland, than of those of the country which employs him. To draw the full advantage from the international machinery at the Hague, there ought to be evolved a permanent Credit Bureau to which weak and timid States might apply. It might conduct enquiries into their solvency, lend them experts to reorganise their finances, help them to negotiate loans in neutral markets on fair terms, and in case of need provide the commissioners who would control their mortgaged revenues. It would act as a trustee or as a Court of Chancery towards its wards. It could have no political ambitions to further, and the country which applied to it need not tremble for its independence. Persia or Egypt, had this Bureau existed, might have turned to the Hague for help. If, in the end, owing to civil war, or the hopeless incapacity of native statesmen, forcible intervention became inevitable, it would lie not with any interested Power, but with the Hague itself, to take the initiative of summoning a European Conference to prescribe the nature and limits of the interference. It is even possible that the Bureau might be used as an arbitrator at the request of a State like China, hard pressed by the rivalry of Empires competing for concessions, to decide between them in its name, and to appoint a neutral adviser or board of advisers, who would stand between it and the greedy Powers in the allotment of its financial patronage.

A Europe which has organised itself for peace will be at no loss for expedients wherewith to reconcile the appetites of capital with the rights of nationality. A spectator of the moving cosmopolitan drama which is played, the world over, around this central motive of the export of capital, can readily invent attractive schemes for the regulation of the process. But such exercises tempt one to ignore the dynamics of the problem. The same primitive forces of greed which in earlier centuries inspired conquests and migrations are still strong enough to grip diplomacy and build navies. Our first task is to win at home the power to control this export of capital, to check it where it disregards the current ethical standards, to rebuff it where it would lead us into international rivalry, and at last to use it as the potent servant of a humane diplomacy. It can be forbidden to carry the devastations of slavery into distant continents. It can be checked in its usurer's practices upon simple States. It can be used, if it be firmly mastered, to starve into submission a semi-civilised Empire which meditates aggressive war, or draws from Western stores the funds to finance its own oppressions.

CHAPTER IX

ON ARMAMENTS

On the wall of a big room at the Admiralty there used to hang, and may still hang, an oddly decorated map of the world's seas. The decorations were movable points which indicated the varying positions of German merchant vessels. It was a map which could be used with great effect in conversation, and the effect was one which the Admiral whose pride it was, produced very willingly. Here he sat with the wireless installation on the roof above him, a genial, capable spider, with the world for his web. He knew every day the approximate position of every German ship. He knew a little more accurately where his own cruisers, scouts and commerce-destroyers and armed merchantmen were stationed. He had worked out to a nicety the orders which would radiate from the big poles overhead, if ever war were declared. The rapid arming of British merchantmen on the high seas played a great part in the scheme, and the official calculation promised that about four-and-twenty hours would suffice to make every German merchantman a British prize. The reckoning was probably optimistic, but it was delivered with great assurance, and the Admiral was convinced that the navy which

he commanded was an efficient predatory organisation.   It was a flattering dream to indulge, and
somewhere in the dimmer regions of the professional
consciousness there may have lurked the recollec-
tion that such a sweeping of the seas, if it could be
effectively carried out, would mean for the service
that accomplished it, wealth " beyond the dreams
of avarice."   For the King's regulations make the
value of a prize of war the " perquisite " of the crew
which takes her.   You may see in the Old Kirk of
Haarlem a superb monument to a fortunate Dutch
captain of the seventeenth century, who amassed
an untold fortune from the pillage of English ships.
The law of war still sanctions this legalised piracy.
The prizes are richer, and the machinery of capture
incomparably more effectual, but nothing else is
changed.

The British Admiralty has a costly skill in adver-
tising.   It advertised the " Dreadnought " and our
estimates show the result.   It advertised that
elaborate map, and the result was the growth of a
set determination among the middle-class of the new
industrial Germany, that a war which might cost
it its merchant fleet, should not be lightly declared.
The late Chancellor of Germany has put this from
his own standpoint in a few telling sentences.
(*Imperial Germany*, by Prince von Bülow, p. 18 of
the English translation.)

When in the spring of 1864 the English Ambassador in
Berlin drew the attention of the Prussian President of the
Council at that time to the excitement in England caused
by Prussia's advance against Denmark, and let fall the
remark that if Prussia did not cease operations the English Government might be forced to take arms against

her, Herr von Bismarck-Schönhausen replied : " Well, what harm can you do us ? At worst you can throw a few bombs (shells ?) at Stolpmünde or Pillau, and that is all." Bismarck was right at that time. We were then as good as unassailable to England with her mighty sea power, for we were invulnerable at sea. We possessed neither a great mercantile marine, the destruction of which could sensibly injure us, nor any oversea trade worth mentioning, the crippling of which we need fear.

To-day it is different. We are now vulnerable at sea. We have intrusted millions to the ocean, and with these millions the weal and woe of many of our countrymen. If we had not in good time provided protection for these valuable and indispensable possessions, we should have been exposed to the danger of having one day to look on defencelessly while we were deprived of them. But then we could not have returned to the comfortable economic and political existence of a purely inland State. We should have been placed in the position of being unable to employ and support a considerable number of our millions of inhabitants at home. The result would have been an economic crisis which might easily attain the proportions of a national catastrophe.

In these sentences Prince von Bülow explains the origin of the modern German navy, in so far as it is the creation of German public opinion. Our Admiralty was ill-advised enough to supply the advocates of a great German navy with an object-lesson and an argument by the seizure of the German liner *Bundesrath* during the South African War. With the anger and alarm created by that incident there began a revolution in German habits of thought, and the Reichstag, which had always hitherto resisted the ambitions of the Kaiser, was now with ease induced to vote large programmes, and to increase them periodically.

We need not suppose that the fear of the effect of the British doctrine of capture at sea was the chief motive of German statesmen in increasing the German Navy. Navies are valued by statesmen primarily as instruments of pressure held in reserve by diplomacy. Had the need of defending commerce been their guiding thought, the German Government would have made an attempt to ascertain whether on any terms the British Government could be induced at last to fall into line with the United States and other Powers, which have for a generation demanded the reversal of this barbarous doctrine. It has never taken that course, and there is some reason to believe that the German Admiralty has recently come to perceive the value of capture at sea. What is that value ? The power to destroy an enemy's commerce is at the first glance a tremendous weapon of menace or aggression. It would be devastating in action, and it is only a little less valuable as a threat. But in the balance it can be of advantage only to the stronger Power, and one may question whether even that Power could draw great profit from it, unless its aggression were sudden and unexpected. If, as Mr. Arthur Lee stated in a speech to his constituents while he was a Civil Lord of the Admiralty in Mr. Balfour's Government, we dispensed with a declaration of war, following the Japanese and Bulgarian precedents, undoubtedly our fleet could dispose of a great part of the German mercantile marine on the first day of the unforeseen opening of hostilities. With a more regular and honourable procedure the advantage would be less, for Germany can also use the resources of wireless telegraphy, and manifestly large numbers of her ships at the first warning would seek the shelter of a neutral port. The blow to the economic life of Germany which would follow from the suspension of her shipping trade, though very serious, would not be fatal. She can at need raise all the food stuffs she requires for her own wants, and she has railway communication with neutral States. The loss to her industry from the stoppage or interruption in the import and export of its raw material and its produce would hardly be felt in time of war, for the first consequence of mobilisation would be that all the mines and factories which depend on male labour would be forced to work half-time or even to close down. Export in any event would cease on the outbreak of war. The loss to Germany would be limited to the risk of the seizure of her ships at sea and their cargoes, and the extent of that loss would evidently depend mainly on the suddenness of our aggression.

In attempting to answer the question, Of what value is capture at sea from the British standpoint ? we are faced by a sharp divergence between commercial and naval opinion.[1] Naval opinion is decidedly, though not unanimously, in favour of the doctrine. Commercial opinion, more particularly

[1] P.S.—Employment of the submarine has made it inevitable that the whole question of capture at sea should be reconsidered. The use of these craft has been rather an outrage to humanity than a serious menace to our commerce. But some further development of the submarine might easily reverse all our calculations and render a supremacy in surface-ships useless to the stronger naval Power. Herr Dernburg's declarations in America suggest that Germany has returned to her original position, and once more desires the abolition of the right of capture.

in such centres as Liverpool, is as decidedly against it. Parties are divided, and a leading Conservative like Mr. F. E. Smith, who speaks for Liverpool, is in agreement with Lord Loreburn, who has presented the case against capture largely from the standpoint of a Liberal who desires to civilise international relations. It would be superfluous to attempt to summarise at any length a controversy in which all the arguments are familiar. The Admiralty's case, in one sentence, is that the capture of an enemy's shipping gives to a Power which has no army capable of attack or invasion, the only effective means of injuring an enemy. That argument, as we have seen, requires some reserves. The injury, to begin with, would be overwhelming only if our attack were sudden and unexpected, or in plain words if it were a deliberate aggression made before the resources of diplomacy had obviously been exhausted, before mediation had been attempted, and without a formal declaration of war. Few British statesmen would in public agree with Mr. Arthur Lee in recommending such a brutality as this. Further, it is untrue that " capture " is the only means of injuring an enemy. In the first place all the German colonies are vulnerable from the sea, and so long as our main fleet commanded the Home waters, some of them could be seized and held, if we so desired it, by comparatively small forces of British or Indian troops. In the second place the destruction of Germany's fighting fleet would deprive her diplomacy for a decade or two of one of its main sanctions. The argument used by all statesmen that armaments are necessary to back diplomacy falls to the ground, if it be questioned that the loss of the German fleet would cripple her future action in world-politics. It is true that the fear of losing her mercantile marine must always make Germany reluctant to engage in a trial of strength with us. In that restricted sense, the maintenance of the doctrine of capture may help to prevent war. But the class which has most to lose is not the warlike class; the merchant community needs no such deterrent. To the warlike class in Germany, the Prussian ruling caste, the risk of losing colonies and warships would seem a graver misfortune than the loss of the mercantile marine. Moreover, if Germany did meditate aggression, she could with ease take precautions in advance against the greater part of this loss.

If the advantages claimed from a British standpoint for the maintenance of capture are problematical, the risks to which it might expose us are tremendous. However efficient and however powerful our navy may be, it cannot absolutely insure our mercantile marine against all risk of capture, and if the war broke out suddenly, its losses would be relatively heavy. The effect would be felt at once in the rise, first of insurance premiums, then of freights, and finally of prices. All the inevitable disturbance to banking and trade which any war must cause to any elaborately-organised modern community would in our case be aggravated by the doubt whether our food supply could be maintained uninterrupted and our factories steadily supplied with raw material. One may feel sure in cold blood that nothing worse than a momentary interruption of any of our chief sea-routes is possible. But it is less easy to feel certain that public opinion, with its indices in credit and prices, would remain perfectly steady when the inevitable incidents began to occur. Some panic, some stringency, some privation there probably would be at the best. On the other hand, if any of the more romantic dangers which the popular novelist is fertile in inventing were ever to occur, and our fleet were for a time taken by surprise, or outclassed by some new invention, or outnumbered by an improbable combination, it is obvious that our own chosen weapon of capture could be turned against us with deadly effect. If victory were delayed, if the fleet had for any reason to fight a prolonged battle for the absolute command of the seas, our dependence on imported supplies would reduce us much sooner than our antagonist to a position in which we must sue for terms. The case for capture, whether from the British or the German standpoint, is, in short, extremely problematical, and to maintain it at all is to take a gambling chance. Germany, as the weaker power at sea, could gain by it only if she began the war suddenly and treacherously, if she evolved some new and deadly weapon, or if she brought about some wholly improbable combination of forces against us. Under normal conditions, the only gain to her would depend on our nerves ; she might do just enough against us to make a panic, and against this small gain must be set the risk of a great though not fatal loss of wealth. We, on the other hand, stand to gain much, if the moment for attack were of our choosing, but much less if the war were forced upon us. Disasters and unforeseen combinations may seem improbable, but in balancing gains and losses, we cannot afford to forget that, should disaster ever happen, the stoppage of our sea trade and loss of our mercantile fleet would instantly force us into a humiliating peace, from which we should emerge to face economic ruin.

If this be a fair summary of the probable results from the doctrine of capture at sea, it is puzzling that the directors of the British and German navies should maintain it. It is above all puzzling that they should both maintain it. If it must have a decisive effect in war, that effect cannot be equally advantageous to both. With half the world's shipping under our flag, one might suppose that our clear course, if we mean to thrive by commerce rather than piracy, would be to press for every reform of international law which would protect commerce. The Germans, content to possess a fleet which stands to ours nominally as ten to sixteen, and really as much less, ought, one would imagine, to reject a weapon which can be wielded with a balance of advantage only by the stronger fleet. Is the case really so doubtful that two Powers which apparently occupy opposite positions can reach the same result, when that result is obviously not the course of safety ? We have to deal with shrewd and capable men ; it is clear that there must be a good explanation of this riddle. It stares us in the face. Capture at sea is maintained by both navies, because it supplies the prime argument by which industrial and peaceable nations can be induced to maintain great navies. As a strategical device it is of doubtful value to both, and if it is valuable to one, it must therefore be disastrous to the other. As a spur and lash to public opinion it is absolutely indispensable. The German Navy Act was passed by no other means, as the extract from Prince von Bülow shows. In our case we need only glance at current controversy. When Mr. Churchill and his friends, after securing a navy overwhelmingly and permanently superior to that of the only Power which could attack us, go on to demand more ships, what is their argument ? It is that we must consider our " whole-world requirements " ; we must remember that much of our corn comes to us from the Black Sea and India through the Mediterranean, and that commerce on its way to the colonies must be protected by local fleets. There is a good answer to this, but in all frankness it is a plausible, and at first glance, a weighty argument. In every country the instincts of civilised men are against armaments. We would nearly all of us, unless we have sons in the service or shares in Armstrong's, abolish armaments, if we could, or at least have less of them. There are few men who doubt in their better moments that war and armaments are absolute evils. Those whose interest or professional duty it is to maintain armaments, must force us to think that the evil is a necessary evil, and that we shall be ruined if we discard it. These capable minds study strategy. The more important part of strategy for them is not the alignment of embattled navies ; it is the management of public opinion. They are at war not with Germany but with the instincts of civilisation. The chances are that they never will be at war with Germany, but the battle against civilisation grows every year more difficult. The more one studies this enigma of the maintenance of capture, the more does the conviction impose itself that this monstrous and barbaric practice is upheld solely because public opinion would become unmanageable without it. That is why it is equally useful to Mr. Churchill and to Admiral von Tirpitz, to the stronger and also to the weaker fleet, to the Power with the greater, and to the Power with the lesser stake. It is in itself an affront to every civilised instinct. Modern peoples conceive of war as a quarrel between governments, but this is a predatory plot against the property of individuals. The individual naval officer is by this doctrine authorised to rob the individual merchant of his ship and its cargo, and to sell them for his personal profit. Such practices were once permissible and common in land warfare ; they are now rigidly forbidden. Every argument which tells for the capture of private proverty at sea, might be used as legitimately in defence of unlimited loot on land. One might just as plausibly say that if a nation knew that the price of defeat would be the sacking of its cities, the slaughter of non-combatants, and the violation of women, it would think twice before it went to war. But the deterrent never works in this way. No nation voluntarily goes to war in any circumstances unless it hopes to win. The expectation of loot was in more barbarous ages a potent incentive to war, and within certain limits one must suppose that the doctrine of capture acts in the same way, in so far as it acts at all as a motive.

But its real operation is not in making wars.   Wars
are not the world's chief danger to day.   What it
helps to make is the everlasting war of steel and
gold, the constant struggle with mounting budgets
and lengthening lines of armoured ships.   Abolish
the doctrine of capture, and at the first blow navies
might be vastly reduced.   We in this country would
have most to gain.   Gone would be our anxiety
about our long lines of communication and our
scattered fleets of food-carrying ships.   The talk
about " world-wide requirements," exaggerated even
now, would then have become patently foolish.
With this fear removed at once from our mind
and from those of the Germans, the problem of
naval armaments would be faced in a wholly new
atmosphere.   Our navy would have been restricted
to what ought to be its only function—the defence
of our coasts from invasion.   Our rivals, realising
that it no longer threatened their commerce, would
in their turn have to ask themselves why they
require a navy.   They can deal with an invader
when he lands, or while he is landing.   In both
countries the chance of defending vast navies on
the hypocritical plea that they are purely defensive, would have become less promising, and an
arrangement to reduce them would in every country
encounter less suspicion and less resistance.

Our opponents have their strategy ; we must have
ours. The first step towards a reduction of armaments
is to divide those who now support them.   They
fall into two classes.   Much the greater number
both in Britain and Germany is composed of those
who in their hearts neither desire war nor enjoy

paying for armaments. They act under pressure of a supposed necessity, the defence of commerce. To this class belong most of our merchants and manufacturers in the middle-class, and all of the working-class which is by custom or temperament Liberal or Conservative. To the other class belongs the caste which governs and finds employment in the Empire and the services, and the larger financial and investing world which sees in the navy an insurance for its capital exported abroad. It is this latter class, a large and growing class, which is the enemy. It is rich, capable, and influential, a formidable antagonist even when it stands alone. But at present it does not stand alone. It has cleverly contrived by the artificial and anachronistic doctrine of capture to rally to its side both in Britain and Germany, the peaceable middle class which wants no adventures, hates war and looks askance at armaments. Abolish capture and this class regains the possibility of following its natural instincts and its clear interests. Our problem is not, as pacifists too readily suppose, how best to influence disinterested opinion. No mass of opinion can under present conditions be disinterested, save that of the proletariat, which is nearly powerless. But the interest in defending its ships and cargoes from capture, which on the whole ranges the mercantile and industrial class on the side of armaments, is artificial and unnecessary. This class can be detached by the simple expedient of bringing the customs of sea-warfare into line with those of land-warfare, in a word, by abolishing the doctrine of capture. Before this Government fixes its policy at the next Hague

Conference, Parliament, if it respected itself, would insist on the preliminary discussion of this question. If the Radical Group and the Labour Party realised the vast importance of this issue they would not hesitate to declare in advance that they would back their opinion by a vote. The abolition of capture is of incomparably greater consequence than the reduction which may be brought about by agitation in the naval estimates of any one year. It is the key to all future reductions. A reduction at present is out of the question and never has been won. All that can be won by efforts that avoid this main issue is a diminution in the rate of increase. The centre of our battle is here, and the position will be lost, if our delegates are once more allowed to go to the Hague with the old instructions.

There is another step which might well be taken at once, in the hope of detaching interests from the forces which make the armed peace. Pacifists tend to argue that the armament firms are the only interest or the chief interest which maintains armaments and war. It has been the purpose of this book to show that the chief interest is something far more powerful, far more considerable, and much more widely diffused than the traders in war possess. It is the interest of the whole class which exports capital abroad. But it would be folly to ignore or minimise the direct interest of the trade. It is an interest which happens to be firmly entrenched in political circles, and as the exploit of Mr. Mulliner shows, it is a singularly alert and energetic interest. If public life continues to develop on the present lines, the great scandal of to-morrow

will be a discovery that the Liberal Party Funds
have been invested not in Marconis, but in Krupps.
The way to meet this evil is so simple that one need
waste little space in discussing it. Every one can
see it, and every one will see it, when they choose
to see it. The most rigidly individualistic Liberal
need not scruple to admit that there is one
monopoly which ought to be in the hands of the
State—the manufacture of arms. If the State
arsenals and dockyards forged our armour-plate
and built our ships, there would, at all events, be no
direct interest with a stake in the increase of armaments. There is no question that the State can do
it. It builds ships still, though in constantly diminishing numbers. Nor would there be any difference
in the quality of the brains employed. The great
firms are glad to engage our admirals as directors,
when their term of service is expired, and the great
naval architects are employed now by a firm and
then by the State. The obvious argument that
competition secures lower prices can no longer be
maintained, for the great firms have formed a close
ring. Indeed, the case for nationalisation deserves
to be considered, if only that the State may free
itself from the domination of this ring. It has become so powerful that the State now neglects to
keep its own arsenals, factories and yards employed,
and actually hands over to contractors work for
which it possesses itself all the necessary plant.
The first step is to insist that the existing yards and
factories shall be fully employed, and the next to
take over from private hands one or more of the
best equipped yards, so that the whole work of the

State may be completed by its own resources. Until this is done, we shall always suffer from the occult and interested pressure of a small but powerful group of contractors and investors whose profits depend on the maintenance and grow with the increase of our armaments. Were this done not only in Britain but in every country of Europe, there would be within a year a surprising diminution in the demand for armaments. Newspapers in some inexplicable way would lose their keenness in manufacturing scares, while the Navy League and the Flottenverein would be left lamenting the decline in their subscriptions.

The problems raised by the army are in our country of secondary interest, and they have at present comparatively little bearing on the relation of armaments to opinion. The whole conception of the Expeditionary Corps calls for criticism, but it is useless to attack it while our diplomatic position is what it is. This corps is governed by the idea that it may have to serve on the Continent as an auxiliary force to a French army defending the northern frontier against a German invasion. So long as our exclusive intimacy with France continues, and so long as we pursue the phantom of a balance of power, such a force will be necessary. Given these premises, it is, indeed, an absurdly small force for the purpose in question. It would, however, be an utterly excessive provision for our needs, if we entertained no thought of intervening in Continental warfare. Second in importance to the Expeditionary Corps stands the force which we maintain in India. Its size is really determined by our political policy there. As we continue the programme of the Delhi proclamation, our rule in India must become gradually less dependent on the sword in a white hand. The ideal of self-government, however slowly it is developed, must in the end mean that India will provide for her own defence and her own police. Every step towards the realisation of that ideal is also a step towards the time when the Anglo-Indian army may be reduced and even abolished. A party of reform which aimed at cutting away the buttresses of interest which maintain the present level of armaments, would turn its attention also to the native regiments in India. A system which refuses to Indian soldiers any rank above a subaltern's, means primarily that a great number of positions are kept in these regiments for British officers. These positions are among the perquisites of Empire, and their maintenance reinforces the caste feeling at home which tends to maintain and extend Empire. Open these positions to natives, and our own governing class will lose one small contributory motive which goes to make it Imperialist and militarist in sentiment. What is true of India is equally true of Egypt, though everything there is on a smaller scale. South Africa is another point at which an economy might be effected. A Dominion so absolutely self-governing that it cannot be checked even when it affronts every instinct of our race and every principle of citizenship by sending Labour leaders into exile untried, has no right to ask the Empire for a contribution towards its own defence. It has the protection of the navy, while it escapes the burden of taxation. It no more needs the assistance of the army than do Australia and Canada. It ought to be possible to withdraw these troops and to reduce the army by a number equivalent to theirs. These however, are minor questions, and their influence on opinion is slight. It is hardly possible to hope for any great change in the scale or cost of the army, so long as it remains primarily a force for service abroad in a scattered Empire.

Some pacifists are tempted to look in one form or another at proposals for the creation of a home defence force based on compulsory service. If it were possible to hope that this might become our principal and ultimately our only armed force, the scheme would be attractive, if it did not involve prolonged service in barracks, and would answer to a healthy ideal of a citizen's duty. One dreads, however, the use which would be made of it to inculcate conceptions of blind obedience, automatic discipline and social subjection. But the main objection to it is that it would certainly be, while our present political conditions endure, in no sense a substitute for the navy and the overseas army, but an addition to them, and a further burden piled upon the present cost of the armed peace. To give any countenance to this proposal at present is an excessively risky strategy, which may well lead, not to a decline, but to an immense increase in militarism. When the navy has been reduced to the comparatively modest dimensions which would suffice if capture at sea were abolished, when the army has been cut down by the abandonment of the struggle for a balance in Europe and the gradual emancipation of India, it will be time enough to urge that a citizen army would be the most self-respecting form of national defence. Paradoxical as it may seem, universal service in a citizen army, for short terms of service without the brutalities of military discipline, and with the minimum number of professional officers, is the true pacifist ideal. Professional armies, whether on land or sea, are an offence against democracy and against human dignity. But pacifists would do well to see their way to the drastic reduction if not the abolition of mercenary armies, before they begin to smooth the path for the creation of another force which under actual conditions would certainly be used to further ambitions that are not theirs.

We have dealt with certain aspects of the problem of armaments in which it directly touches public opinion. Clear away the artificial stimulus to the creation of great navies which the doctrine of capture supplies, remove the incentive which the traders in war possess to manipulate the moods and convictions of a democracy, and some of the superfluous obstacles will have vanished which now prevent the reduction of armaments. Allow that this has been done, and the question of ways and means still remains. Is it reasonable to hope for a limitation by agreement in the present condition of Europe ? If politics were governed by cold reason, it ought to be so. It is not the absolute strength of navies and armies which determines victory, but the comparative strength of the two combatants. If the ratio of the British and German fleets were really fixed at sixteen to ten fighting ships, the result would be the same, however far the reduction went. . Restrict the two Powers to eight and five capital ships apiece, and it is obvious that they would enter a conflict with exactly the same chances as they do to-day, when the Dreadnoughts built or building approach the forties and the thirties. It will be objected that the breadth of the seas, the length of our lines of mercantile communication, and the magnitude of the commercial fleet which our navy has to protect, establishes for us something like an absolute standard : we must have ships enough to be able to scatter a certain number over all the seas. This argument, however, would have little cogency if the practice of capture were abolished. One may admit that geography does for certain Powers establish something resembling an absolute standard. Russia must have two fleets, one for the Baltic and one for the Black Sea. France was in the same case, until her confidence in us (a confidence which rests, we are told, on no treaty), enabled her to withdraw all her fighting ships from the Atlantic, to concen-trate them in the Mediterranean. The United States has had in the past to consider both the Atlantic and the Pacific, though the Panama Canal will presently make them in effect one sea. With such geographi-cal factors to reckon with, it is obvious that for each Power there is a certain minimum. Russia (to take the clearest case) builds in the Black Sea solely against Turkey ; in the Baltic she has to consider Germany, and her obligations to France. Theoreti-cally the balance of naval power would be the same in Europe if all the fleets were simultaneously reduced by one-half or by nine-tenths. This allur-ing yet elusive truism inevitably haunts the minds of pacifists. The interests of contractors and younger sons may be the chief reason why we never wake up one morning to learn that this beneficent operation has been carried out by some magical impulse of common-sense. But it is not quite the only reason. There is the troublesome geographical difficulty. There is also, above all, the financial disparity between certain Powers. There is an advantage for a rich Power in raising the scale of preparation for war. To put the matter crudely, we know very well that if fleets once sank to eights and fives, Germany could afford by a sudden effort to raise her five to ten. On the other hand we reckon that while the actual numbers stand at the forties and the twenties, she lacks the means to exceed her present limit. If geography lays down a minimum for every Power, finance limits the maximum. The same thing is true of armies. In one sense every European Power has reached the maximum, because they all long ago adopted universal service for every able-bodied man. But the term of service varies in length, and in poor countries the full legal term is not always exacted. When France last year raised the term of service from two to three years, in order to have a larger force always with the colours on her eastern frontier, she took a course to which Germany might retort in kind. If the Germans should in their turn raise the term of service, their superiority would once more be crushing. But the French reckon on their financial advantage, and speculate on the reluctance of Germany, deeply involved in naval expenditure and hard pressed so reconcile her taxpayers to their burdens, to take to drastic a course. It may turn out that the French reckoning is at fault, but in a desperate strait it seemed a hopeful gamble with chances. It is such considerations as these which maintain the present level of competition in the war of steel and gold. There is for some Powers an advantage in forcing the pace and raising the scale, and that is the main reason why it would be chimerical to propose, in the present posture of the struggle for a balance, that the world's fleets should be halved, or the service-time of conscript armies fixed (let us say) at a year. That is no reason for desisting from such proposals. But it is well to realise in advance the objections (often unspoken), which they are certain to encounter in the minds of the world's rulers.

It is still a new experience for Englishmen to think in terms of a Continental system. The present generation grew up in " splendid isolation," and the fact which has impressed itself on all our minds in recent years has been not so much that we are a member of the Triple Entente which is at issue with the Triple Alliance, but rather that we are involved in a ruinous naval rivalry with Germany. Inevitably all our thoughts about the reduction of armaments turn to the navy, and base themselves on Anglo-German relations. It is a dangerously insular habit of thought. For good and evil we are embraced in a Continental system, and if we mean to treat separately with Germany, we must begin by quitting this system. While we remain within it, we cannot afford to neglect the views and interests of our partners. By all means let us quit a combination which we ought never to have entered, but what we do should be done deliberately and openly.

More than once proposals for reduction have been publicly and officially made on our side, and on each occasion they have called forth vehement and not unreasonable protests from the French press. The French see in any arrangement which would permit Germany to economise on her navy, a plan which would enable her to spend the more upon her army. In plain words, if she were to cease her spendthrift building of Dreadnoughts, there would be nothing to prevent her from raising the term of service with the infantry by six or twelve months. The French attitude is frankly egoistic, but so is ours. The worst of such egoism is that it can only aggravate the European unrest. We profoundly desire a relief from our own naval expenditure, but as good Europeans we cannot wish that the result should be an acerbation of the military rivalry on the Continent. It may be well to add that it was not for this reason that our proposal failed. Mr. Churchill's " Naval Holiday " met with no response in Germany, first of all because he was content to make his " offer " in public here—with the manifest intention of disarming his Liberal critics, and took no steps whatever (so Admiral von Tirpitz has stated) to convey it officially to the German Government. It failed, secondly, for the even simpler reason that it was, in plain English, a thoroughly dishonest offer. While he undertook to cease building against Germany for a year, he reserved to himself the right to accept ships from the colonies, and to build ships for use in the Mediterranean. The Germans know very well that in case of need both the colonial ships and the Mediterranean ships would hurry under forced

steam to join the North Sea fleet. The same exceptions vitiate Mr. Churchill's 16 to 10 ratio.

While the present grouping of the Powers continues, the problem of armaments cannot be split up
into a Franco-German and an Anglo-German problem. It is a European problem. Every Power is
under obligations to its allies or partners, and
separate arrangements can hardly be considered,
unless these alliances and understandings have first
lapsed. It follows that the naval problem cannot be
treated in isolation from the military problem. If
armaments are to be arrested or reduced by agreement, the understanding, one is inclined to think,
must embrace the Six Great Powers, and it must
cover armies as well as navies. Possibly the most
hopeful proposal which could be put forward would
not attempt to lay down rules for the building of
ships or to define the terms of military service. It
would look broadly at the expenditure upon armaments for sea and land. It would provide that for
a term of years no increase should be made by any
Power above its present armaments budget under
either head, or, better still, that these totals should
be reduced by a certain percentage. Even this is
not a wholly satisfactory formula. No two Powers
reckon their expenditure on exactly the same system,
and confidence could hardly be preserved unless
loans to meet current expenditure were rigidly forbidden. But the chief difficulty would not lie in
defining the formula. It would begin when the
Powers looked anxiously round to discover whether
rivals were not evading the agreement to maintain
armaments at the present level. When one begins

to reckon, not in terms of single Powers but in terms of groups, there are clearly two ways of increasing one's military resources. One may add a few corps to one's own army, or one may acquire an ally. If after concluding an agreement not to increase his own Budget, Mr. Churchill were to persuade the Malays or the Canadians to build Dreadnoughts for him, the Germans would rightly feel that they had been cheated. It was the suspicion that the Balkan League was really an auxiliary force attached to the main Slav army of Russia, which was adduced by Germany as a reason for increasing her army in 1913. Sweden or Roumania might conceivably attach themselves to the Triple Alliance. The Young Turks have been in a chronic position of comfortless detachment ever since the Revolution, and have offered themselves in turn to each group. Spain is or was a semi-detached partner of the Triple Entente. In short, an agreement among the Great Powers to arrest or reduce armaments would be subject to grave suspicion, so long as the struggle for a balance of power continues. If one group added to its strength by acquiring even a minor ally, its rival would feel that it could no longer be expected to refrain from balancing this gain by increasing its own armaments.

The moral is that armaments depend upon policy, and in our day not on the policy of single Powers, but on the aims and conduct of coalitions. One readily discerns certain preliminary steps which must be taken if we would prepare public opinion for their reduction. The aim of this book has been to analyse the permanent material factors which explain the competition in armaments. We found the main cause in the effort to adjust the balance of power in such a way that the capital of the Powers which attain a balance favourable to themselves, may be exported with advantage to distant regions where it will enjoy a monopoly. It need not surprise us to find that when we attempt to solve the problem of armaments in isolation, we are promptly confronted with a more difficult issue. It will not be solved until Europe substitutes the ideal of a Concert for the attempt to reach an unattainable and unstable balance of power.

CHAPTER X

THE CONCERT OF EUROPE

In the early phases of the Peace Movement, Arbitration seemed to be the one remedy that was needed for the nightmare fear of war and the sedentary incubus of armaments. Young movements are always hopeful, and it is only after long years of disappointment that they realise the whole extent and complication of the mischief with which they are contending, and revise the expectations which they founded on their first prescription. The defects of arbitration as a substitute for war are better understood to-day, and indeed most writers and speakers who use the word now have come to give it a broad and general meaning, which covers any appeal to reason. It is the antithesis to brutal force, and it is generally understood to include mediation or indeed any settlement by the intervention of disinterested parties. The obvious difficulties are sufficiently familiar. There is no means, while we continue to think of States as isolated units, by which a reluctant Power can be brought to accept arbitration or even mediation. Mr. Kruger proposed it before the South Africa War, and there was no appeal open to him from the refusal of the British Government. The media-

tion of Russia on the eve of the second Balkan War
had actually been accepted, in word at least, by all
the Balkan States, when King Ferdinand and
General Savoff suddenly began hostilities by what
they doubtless considered a bold Bismarckian
stroke. The other obvious difficulty, that one
party or the other might disregard the findings of
the arbitrator, is probably less serious. From the
moment that arbitration had been accepted, passions
would subside, and few States would enter the
international Court unless they intended to obey it.
So long, however, as governments reserve points
of honour and vital national interests as questions
unfit for arbitration, this expedient cannot be
regarded as an established substitute for war.
The honour of nations is a tempting theme for
satire, but this reservation does, in fact, point to
the real inadequacy alike of arbitration and of
mediation.

Arbitration is a judicial process, and it cannot
in international affairs achieve more than the
civil law accomplishes in a civilised State. We trust
our courts to interpret statutes, to adjudicate on
contracts, and to deal with money claims. But
we do not allow them to legislate for us, or to
determine national policy. A Court may decide
whether John Smith owes £100 to Patrick Kelly,
but it is not allowed to determine whether a nation
of Smiths owes Home Rule to a nation of Kellys.
The same manifest limits apply to arbitration in
international affairs. There is a great range of
disputes which are judiciable, but it includes rather
questions which might with ill-will be used as a

pretext for war, than questions which any two nations in their senses would seriously consider worth a war. It is probable that the limits of arbitration, in the strict sense of the word, have been reached already, and that civilised nations will usually resort to it when disputes over judiciable questions arise between them. One may and ought to arbitrate about the interpretation of the wording of a treaty, about the delimitation of a frontier which has in any sense been fixed in the past by usage or agreement, about liability for debts, about compensation for injuries, and about such international police cases as the North Sea outrage and the Casablanca broil. But it would be a rash claim to say that any one of the recent wars could have been settled naturally and properly by judicial arbitration. Could a Court of Jurists have examined the title of Spain to rule in Cuba and the Philippines, determined whether a degree of oppression existed which justified revolt, and finally pronounced on the right of the United States to intervene? These are questions which transcend law. They are questions of morals and sentiment, and where they touch interest, it is the interest which no contracts can define. Between Russia and Japan, in the dispute over Manchuria and Korea, a Court could only have said that both of them were interlopers and that neither had a shadow of legal right. It would have been as hopelessly beyond its depth in the Moroccan, the Persian, or the Balkan questions. It might indeed have settled the interpretation of the secret treaty of alliance and partition between Servia and Bulgaria, but any civil Court in such a case would declare that such a contract, for the division of another country's territories, is against public morals and therefore null and void.

Where arbitration is manifestly inapplicable, there remains, fortunately, the method of mediation. A mediator differs from an arbitrator mainly in this, that he is not bound by legal principles. His decision will not make a precedent or govern future cases. He renders no judgment. He acts by the light of common sense, and will usually content himself with proposing, as a friend of both parties, a compromise which will do substantial justice, so far as possible, to both their claims, and avert war by saving what they are pleased to call their honour. Oddly enough, though the Hague Convention actually enjoins upon neutral Powers the duty of offering mediation to avert a quarrel, there has been no successful instance of its use in our day. The Tsar's action in the Balkan quarrel was rather mediation than arbitration, and it failed to prevent war, presumably because both sides were confident of their ability to win in a trial of strength, and also because neither of them trusted the impartiality of the Russian Government. It may be premature to doubt whether mediation as a means of avoiding war has a future before it. It certainly has no past. It is an untried procedure, and there clearly are some reasons why States which have a vital issue at stake should be reluctant to rely on it. A jurist is at least expected to act on fixed principles which he applies to a given case. But a mediator must interpret not international law, but international

morality.   It is a large trust to repose in a foreign
monarch or in the minister whom he may name
to act for him.   It is not easy in such cases to
discover a neutral who will inspire equal confidence
in both parties.   The result, if this method of
settling disputes became common, would usually be
a compromise which neither party would consider
satisfactory.   To dictate a settlement which may
have to be bold and far-reaching, to sanction,
conceivably, some rather novel and revolutionary
principle in international politics, and perhaps
to send one of the disputants empty away, it is
clear that there must be a strong and independent
mediator, whose decisions inspire respect, a mediator
powerful enough to ignore the discontent of the
unsuccessful State.   It will rarely happen that any
single Power satisfies these conditions.   The ideal
mediator, in short, is no one Power, but a Council
of all the Powers.   Such a concert or Council of
Powers is comparable not to a Court of Law or to a
private mediator, but to a Federal Government or
Council, which is expected to take broad decisions
of policy in the name of the common good.   It
has to decide, where there is no question of legal
right at issue, what solution will best serve the
interests of humanity as a whole.

It may seem to require a bold faith, in the last
pages of a book which has traced the egoism of
contemporary Powers, to suggest that the world's
final hope of peace depends on bringing all these
egoisms together into a Council, where they must
struggle together to elaborate a disinterested solution.   Unluckily for the idealist, the Concert exists

in name, and has a history. " Where " the
student of history may ask, " where from the Congress of Vienna to the Council of London, has it
justified this touching faith ?   Did not the Congress
of Vienna amuse itself by defying those aspirations
of nationality which a series of triumphant revolutions was to justify ?   Did not the Congress of
Berlin hand back to Turkish misrule those provinces
which have only now been ' liberated,' after a
generation of misery and two wars of unexampled
horror ?   Did not the Conference of London preside
over the frustration of its own decisions, and sit
idly by, while war followed war to advertise its
impotence ?   A pretty device for preventing wars,
forsooth.   It has been in history nothing but the
instrument for scattering the dragon's teeth.   The
recognised function of a Concert is to prepare the
wars of the day after to-morrow."   The indictment
is only too well founded.   One listens to it uncon-
vinced, as one listens to denunciations of any
institution which blunders humanly, while destiny
still points to its function.   In such terms as these
a cold critic of history might have denounced the
Parliament towards the close of the Stuart period.
" Did it not make a civil war ?   And when it once
more raised its head, it was to make a revolution.
A pretty instrument of civil peace, forsooth.   It
makes the laws and conspires to overthrow them."
In just such terms as this men used to speak of the
Republic in France.   But we do not doubt to-day
that both institutions are guarantees of civil peace.
One cannot speak with enthusiasm of any chapter
in the record of the Concert, but it is commonly

said, and generally believed, that the Conference of London at least achieved the considerable feat of preventing an outbreak of war between the Great Powers. If that is to ascribe to it a too active *rôle* and a degree of authority which it hardly possessed, it would certainly be true to say that when Austria and Russia were on the brink of war, each dreading war, and each shrinking from making concessions directly to the other, the Concert supplied them with a formula and a procedure that rendered concessions honourable and easy. Two Powers which might never compromise, if they were left alone face to face, may readily show a reasonable disposition, without loss of prestige, when they consent to become members of a common Council which claims to base its decisions on a regard for the common good. How far Sir Edward Grey, with the aid of Germany, acted as a mediator, how far Austria and Russia really settled their differences directly under the soothing influence of the formula of a Conference, no outsider can know. The general belief ascribes much to Sir Edward Grey's good offices, and he has himself attributed much merit to Germany. In either case, it is clear that the Conference did achieve precisely what a Concert ought to achieve. The creation of a free Albania stands to its credit. If the second Balkan War broke out, that is not a proof of the futility of the Concert. The discredit for that disaster belongs, in so far as any one outside the Balkans is to blame, primarily to Russian diplomacy. One need not assume that if Sir Edward Grey had invited the disputants to refer their quarrel to the London

Conference under his direction, he would have failed, as the Tsar did, to avert war.

A philosophic historian will demonstrate with much conviction, after the fact, how inevitable was the evolution which constituted the modern national State out of its minor components. We do not doubt that it was a beneficial and necessary process which made the United Kingdom, or consolidated Italy, or built up the German Empire from its constituent States. We, who are involved to-day in a much slower and as yet less conscious process, may still see, perhaps with less assurance, before the event, that factors are at work which are moulding a Europe that will learn to act as a unity. One need not speak of the dream of a United States of Europe, though it may possibly be some federal organisation so closely knit as to deserve that name, which will in the fulness of time emerge. A measure of unity much less compact than that would suffice to make wars obsolete, and to end the folly of competing armaments. The minimum which is required for such an end is an organisation based on the model of the London Conference, but less restricted in its scope and more permanent in its aims. What was done for the Balkan crisis must be done in every crisis which threatens to embroil the world. We need not trouble ourselves to consider where it will sit, nor who shall summon it, nor what statutes, if any, will guide it. An institution which grows in response to a need will prove itself in action, and can evolve under the pressure of circumstances. The only indispensable condition for its growth is the European mind, which recognises that a common ideal of civilisation demands its organs, and is intolerant of chaotic strife. Amid the fears of the world and the alarms of war, in spite of predatory interests, and the indolent scepticism of little minds, we can discern factors which are making for this evolution. Of the factors of opinion it is hardly necessary to speak—the disgust with our present plight which is the common mood of most educated minds, the puzzled, compromising, yet wholly sincere good will which is the usual profession of Liberal parties throughout Europe, the conscious indoctrinated sense of class-solidarity which knits the Socialists of all advanced countries in a vast league of peace. But beyond all this, there are non-moral forces which are working towards the same end. It becomes with each year and each decade more difficult to regard any considerable and dangerous issue as the affair of two Powers alone, who may be left to " fight it out " with their blood on their own heads. Every Power in Europe is, to begin with, a member of a Group, and even if the issue in question does not oblige the others to share in the hostilities to which it may give rise, they cannot afford without an effort to see their partner pre-occupied, weakened by a struggle, and perhaps defeated. To that extent the system of alliances, which seems at a first glance only to dig a chasm in Europe, does make for a certain perverted and paradoxical solidarity. If the Powers are as yet incapable of a broadly European outlook, if they do not realise the fraternity which in every issue would make them the brother's keeper of any member of the European family, each is of necessity

its ally's keeper.   Three Powers, at least, are to-day
world-Powers, with interests or ambitions so wide-
spread that nothing which can happen anywhere
can find them quite indifferent.   The stoic *nil
humanum a me alienum puto* is a moral ideal
beyond modern diplomacy.   But a Power comes
near it in effect when it declares that every human
issue touches its interests.   Our own country, by
reason of its trade and its scattered possessions,
has been for many generations the type of a world-
Power.   France by the intricate permeation of her
investments is in the same case.   Germany has
in our day claimed this status, and built a navy
to enforce it.   If Russia's interests are not world-
wide, they do at least cover a vast area.   The
Moroccan question was the test case which demon-
strated that in the modern world it is henceforth
impossible for two Powers to settle a considerable
issue without considering the views of their neighbours.   After that experience the choice is clear.
It lies between such perils and confusions as the vain
attempt to exclude Germany from the settlement
caused in fact, and a frank recognition from the
start that " world-politics " are a matter for the
Concert to settle.
  Midway in the Moroccan quarrel, the Kaiser,
in one of his more truculent speeches, remarked
that nothing must happen in the world " without
Germany."   This claim to be consulted in every
world-event may be, and doubtless in the Kaiser's
mouth it was, simply an expression of political
high spirits.   But the maxim is capable, in the
Kantian phrase, of being universalised.   It lays

down the basis on which a real Concert of Europe might be founded. Let us say rather that nothing should happen throughout the world without the consent of all the civilised Powers. We should, perhaps, exclude America, since the Monroe Doctrine makes it a self-contained continent. We may also admit that, for practical purposes, the Concert will not in every instance be the same. Japan has no status in a European, nor Austria and Italy in an Asiatic question. But the meaning of our principle is clear. There ought to be no change in the *status quo*, which means the acquisition by any Power of rights over another State, however backward or weak, without the consent of the general body of civilised opinion. It is obvious that this principle, and this principle alone, can set a check upon lawless aggression, appease the rivalries of predatory Powers, and create a tribunal to which the weak may appeal. It will be objected that this means the constant meddling in questions which do not concern them of Powers which have no real " interest " in some given region of the earth. When Germany claimed a voice in the Moroccan affair, Britain and France retorted that she is not a Mediterranean Power. A like answer would doubtless be returned if she were to obtrude her opinion at some phase of the Persian crisis. But, to our thinking, an opinion gains in value precisely in so far as it is disinterested. What a monstrous theory it is that Britain and Russia, simply because they have considerable material interests, political, strategic, and mercantile, in Persia, should have the right to dispose of the destinies of its people.

Just because they are bound to think of their own interests, rather than the good of the Persian people, are they incapable of fulfilling their assumed task.   British financiers have lent money to Egypt, and therefore British administrators are held to be the proper persons to conduct the education of Egypt.   There could be no more immoral or unreasonable proposition than this.   John Smith, let us suppose, has been made bankrupt for a debt to some Amalgamated Dynamite Trust, and has gone to the mad-house in despair.   Does it follow that the Trust should be made the guardian and tutor of John Smith's children ?   We can usually find in modern diplomacy a precedent for any principle, even for the wider and humaner principles. There was, in 1905, a phase of the Turkish question when the Powers were discussing who should take the initiative or the main responsibility for the reforms in Macedonia.   Austria and Russia, because they are the neighbours of Turkey, claimed to be the " interested " Powers, and demanded the right on that account to carry through a scheme of their own.   Lord Lansdowne, in a memorable despatch, challenged this claim, both in theory and in its particular application, and vindicated the right of the disinterested Powers to a parity of control over Macedonia.   He was emphatically right.   Austria and Russia, because they were interested, were certain to pursue only their own interests.   The other Powers have occasionally allowed some fitful regard for the interests of the peoples of Turkey to influence their policy.   The Concert of Europe is a very slow and very fallible instrument of justice. It has sanctioned many a wrong, ignored many a misery, and proved itself in crisis after crisis, nerveless, lethargic and unintelligent. But with all its faults it is a check upon the ambitions of any single Power ; it cannot be captured by any one national group of financiers, and it has, on occasion, at least affected to listen to the pleas of the subject races or lesser States whose fate hung in the balance.

The fundamental basis in the theory of a Concert is that interests must not be confused with rights. No Power has any rights over another people. The Moors, the Persians and the Bosnians alone have rights in Morocco, Persia and Bosnia. To an act of barter between interested Powers we must refuse the sanctity of law. If change is inevitable in the status of any people, it is the Common Council of the civilised world which alone can sanction it. We must go on to say that the formation of alliances among the Powers is an act of treason to this ideal of a Concert, because they stand in the way of any decision based upon the merits of the case. The Concert ought to decide what would be best for Morocco, Persia or Bosnia, as the case may be. It cannot do this if Britain is pledged to think only of what will be best for France, and Austria only of what will be best for Germany. Groupings of Powers are, of course, inevitable. But they should resemble rather the coalition of parties in a Parliament than the old-world dynastic alliance. Their basis must be a community of principles and opinions. On one condition only should we reluctantly approve of a temporary alliance. If any

Power or group of Powers seeks to evade the control of the Concert, refuses to submit common European affairs to its judgment, defies the decisions reached at a Conference, or seeks to impose its will on others without a mandate from the Common Council, it would be legitimate to combine against it, to " isolate " it, and to make it impotent for evil. Let this principle once be acknowledged and the chief motive for armaments is gone. Armaments are the means by which Powers seek to obtain immunity and opportunity for expansion. But if expansion itself is dependent on the consent of the Concert, armaments have lost half their utility. It would, of course, be folly to suppose that the acceptance of this principle of the supremacy of the Concert would at once create harmony, and bring about a reduction of armaments. But it would at once achieve this —it would make a standard for the conscience of the civilised world, it would provide an objective test by which the loyalty of any policy might be tried, and above all it would supply a common ground on which all the parties of peace might take their stand. It would conduce to a gradual slackening of the European tension, a gradual loosening of the existing alliances, and in time create an atmosphere in which a proposal for the reduction of armaments, and eventually some scheme for the creation of a loose Federal Council to decide the common affairs of Europe might at least be considered.

To sketch Utopias which as yet have only a few stones of their foundations in reality is apt to be a demoralising exercise of the fancy. But from any statement of the ideal we return with a sharper sense of the faultiness of the actuality. A Concert we cannot have while the Powers are divided in two unnatural groups, which struggle for a balance without even a political principle to make an intelligible division between them. These groups may come together at present for deliberations which have a show of friendliness, but a real debate is impossible so long as the attitude of each Power is fixed by its alliances. An allied Power in the last resort must always be prepared to say " my ally, right or wrong." A disinterested arbiter in this strife can never be found. It would, however, be an error to regard even this state of things too pessimistically. No alliance is always equally valid and equally observed. Great Britain broke away in some degree from Russia and France when she assisted in the creation of Albania. Italy, to some slight extent, held aloof from the Triple Alliance during the conference over Morocco at Algeciras. The most fateful of all these developments has been the recent approach of Britain to Germany through several phases of the Balkan crisis. Each was resolved to keep the peace ; neither had much direct national interest in the questions at issue. Inevitably they acted as moderators, and acted together. The approach has survived the immediate occasion, and it may prove to be permanent. The leisurely adjustment of the questions of conflicting interest which hinge on the Bagdad railway and certain matters touching African colonies is not yet concluded as these pages are written, but it is said to be morally complete, and if that be so, it ought to leave a lasting impress on Anglo-German relations. Nothing has been wanting but good will during the last decade for the conclusion of such an understanding.   There is much to criticise in the manners and morals of German diplomacy, but a Power bent on " real " rather than sentimental ends is a Power with whom one can always do business, if the will to adjust conflicting interests is felt on both sides, as it now is.   One rejoices that these very limited occasions of friction have been cleared away, but it is an even greater gain for European peace that some parallel adjustment of minor Franco-German difficulties has taken place simultaneously.[1]

When Anatole France and Jean Jaurès were in London early in this year (1914), the one thing which they both said with urgency and iteration was to appeal to England to act as the mediator and common friend between France and Germany. Jaurès referred to Mirabeau's dream of a moral

[1] P.S.—These speculations on the prospect of a reconciliation between Britain, France and Germany may seem ironically absurd to-day.   They did none the less fairly represent the facts on the eve of the war.   In his last interview with our Ambassador the German Foreign Secretary said that the Chancellor's aim had been " to make friends with Great Britain, and then through Great Britain, to get closer to France."   Our Ambassador agreed that our relations with Germany were " more friendly and cordial than they had been for years." (White Paper No. 160.) I have left these pages unaltered, because I believe that the hope of a permanent peace in Europe still depends mainly on a reconciliation among the three Western Powers. It seems difficult to hope for this, unless there is an internal change in Prussia.   The surest way to prevent such a change would be to impose harsh or penal terms on Germany, which would cause the whole people to rally round the military caste for the organisation of revenge.

union of the French, British and German peoples
to secure the peace of Europe. That was indeed
a hope in which the whole generation of the Revolution used to indulge, before Pitt revived the doctrine
of the Balance of Power. Thomas Paine even
predicted that ten years would see the end of war
through such a coalition, though he substituted
the United States for Germany. After a century
of disillusionment the dream revives. It is a bolder
and more far-reaching conception than the too
narrow ideal of an Anglo-German understanding on
which English pacifists have concentrated. An
Anglo-German understanding of the conventional
pattern we probably could have to-morrow, and
might have had ten years ago. The obstacle to it
at the opening of the century was, as Prince von
Bülow has clearly shown, the suspicion that our
diplomacy meant to use it against Russia. An
understanding of that type, for the division of
someone else's country into spheres of " work " or
" influence " or " penetration," and for the frustration of some rival diplomacy, would add nothing
whatever to the peace and security of Europe. It
would only lead to some new adjustment of the
Balance of Power. When we think of peace we must
learn to think as Europeans. The real problem of
the creation of a Concert is primarily the problem
of the removal of Franco-German enmity, and so
far as outside forces can promote it, it is British
influence which seems naturally designed to bring
it about. If a firm habit of co-operation were
created between these three Powers, the two triple
groups would have ceased to confront each other as

hostile coalitions, and the alliances among the six Powers which provide for mutual defence in the event of war would gradually grow obsolete, though they might continue to exist. A natural grouping of the more advanced Western Powers would have been formed, and as concrete questions came up for decision, it would assert its reality over the cross-grouping of the older associations, because it would have behind it the sentiment of the three democracies. There is nothing impossible or illogical in the co-existence of two different systems of grouping. The Western Group would be an *entente* for peace. The other trinities are groups for war. Events would show, as the years went on, how vastly more important is peace than war. The aim should be rather to create a Western party in the Councils of Europe, which would act, in the broad sense of the word, as the Liberal party, and nothing would prevent the association of Italy with it, when she has tired of asserting her virility in futurist adventures. It would expand naturally into a broad European association as Austria progressed in the task of putting her house in order, and the Russian people asserted itself with success against its bureaucracy. But it would be fatal to the hope of a Concert that such a Western Group should start with the idea of breaking up the existing systems and setting another of the same kind in their place. It ought to be a group designed to promote the settlement of common European questions by the methods of a Concert ; it must not be an alliance formed to attain national ends by the methods of the balance.

The immediate obstacle to the formation of a

Western Group is not the question of armaments ;
that is not more than an expression and a consequence of the practice of the doctrine of a Balance.
Nor is it any longer the waning Anglo-German
antagonism. It is something more human and
more lasting than the frivolous and factitious
rivalry of British and German Imperialism in distant
regions of the earth. It is, in a word, the French
sentiment over the lost provinces. It is hard to say
how far that sentiment survives. It lives, like all
national idealism, by a connivance of courage and
cowardice. Any adventurer or rhetorician may
play openly upon it. Any army contractor may
exploit it. But few dare to combat it openly outside
the Socialist ranks. It is stronger among the old
than the young ; time is against it. It is rarely
met by the direct demand that it shall be solemnly
renounced ; rather it encounters the accumulating
proof that it cannot be hopefully cherished. The
masses who resent three years' service renounce it
as effectually, when they shrink from that sacrifice,
as the thinkers who oppose it in words. Nor is it
a sentiment which really serves the interests of the
greater world of French finance. The efforts first
of the banker-premier Rouvier, and then of M.
Caillaux, to conclude a comprehensive understanding
with Germany on a basis of finance, were a proof
that the present interference of sentiment with
business, by which the French money market is
closed to German enterprises, is felt to be irksome
and unprofitable. The pressure of material factors
is always at work to wear away the vitality of a
mere sentiment in politics. Now it is the investor

who would like to share in German ventures, or even
does on occasion surreptitiously share in them.
Again it is the business world which joins the pacifists
in asking, timidly and fitfully indeed, for a more
reasonable Franco-German tariff.   It is not exactly
a heroic spectacle—this dwindling of a brave and
vivid emotion under commercial influences.   But
even this prosaic process is a translation in crude
language of the fact that a sentiment must find its
place and its proportion in the whole universe of a
nation's concerns.   It may never be renounced, but
it may well be buried.   It is not a passion fierce
enough to sweep aside the restraints of prudence
and the calculations of probability.   Undoubtedly
when the alliance with Russia was first contracted,
there were Frenchmen who hoped and believed
that Russia could be induced to march with France
in a war of revenge.   That illusion has long since
faded, and sober Frenchmen realise only too clearly
that the first concern of Russian policy is to keep
the peace with the German neighbour.   So far from
desiring to aid France in any war of aggression,
the concern of Russia is rather to hold back her
impetuous right arm.   To-day the doubt is even
whether Russia would loyally back her ally in a
war of defence, and if her loyalty were above suspicion, military students ask themselves of what
service a Power could be whose mobilisation would
hardly be completed before the decisive actions of
the Franco-German campaign had been fought out.
There were moments when our own country seemed
to the ardent hopes of French nationalists a possible
substitute for Russian aid.   But closer study has

revealed our profound reluctance to create a conscript army, and without it what effective help could we render in a land war ? Little by little, as alliances have proved a vain hope, and the numerical disparity of the French against the German armies grows each year more evident, the material impossibility of a war of revenge has impressed itself on the national consciousness. The dying sentiment can scarcely now inspire an honest hope. An adventure it has never fired. Its utmost power is negative : it avails to delay reconciliation, and to frustrate all efforts at disarmament.

If it is difficult to measure the present force of the sentiment of the *revanche* among Frenchmen, it is even harder to arrive at the truth about the opinions of the people of Alsace and Lorraine. The German Empire has made little progress in the work of assimilating these conquered populations. If German culture has made some progress, it has not displaced French culture, nor seriously weakened the sentiment of affection towards France. Indeed, a new sense of resentment against the Prussian spirit of orderly force and regulated brutality has been engendered by a bitter experience, and has strengthened the original sympathy of this Germanic people for the French. Prussian efficiency has its limitations, and it has behaved in its handling of the Alsatians with a baffling want of intelligence ; one might indeed plausibly guess that the rulers of Prussia did not wish to win the Alsatians by conciliation ; they preferred to alienate them while they could master them. One contemplates in this spectacle perhaps the most melancholy instance of

human folly.   Had Bismarck refrained from annexing, or had he annexed only what was necessary for
strategic reasons, it is possible that European civilisation would have entered this century free from the
fears that arm it, fetter it, and beset it to-day.   It
is even probable that if he had done what Liberalism
did in South Africa, if he had conceded to the
Reichsland within a few years of its annexation the
full status of a sovereign State in the Federal Empire, the problem of Alsace would have disappeared
from the consciousness of Europe a generation ago.
The sufferers for this failure of statesmanship are
not merely in the first place the people of Alsace,
and after them the nations of Germany and France,
armed and regimented to maintain or to undo this
unceasing conquest.   The evil which sprang from
this one act radiates in unceasing mischief to all
the ends of Europe.   It affects the Russian conscript in a Siberian barracks.   It is felt in London
when we measure our fleet and contrive our expeditionary corps.   It is the one historical cause
which now affects the struggle for a balance of
power, the only important legacy from the past
which complicates the modern strife for distant
fields of exploitation.   In a retrospective Utopian
mood one can imagine what would have been the
ideal destiny of these provinces after the war of 1870.
If some all-powerful philosopher-king had presided
then over an awakened Concert, he would have
erected Alsace-Lorraine into a neutral but independent State, German by race, French by culture,
destined by its affinities to mediate between the
two peoples, and by its situation to serve as a

barrier between their armies. With a continuous belt of neutral territory stretching from Belgium through Alsace to Switzerland, another Franco-German war would have become an impossibility. But these are dreams. The question of to-day is whether this Alsatian question is in reality insoluble save by war.

The probability is that its gravity is immensely exaggerated, and for a quite intelligible reason. When one reads the eloquent pages which Prince von Bülow has devoted to the expression of his opinion that the French will never forget 1870, will never cease to work for the recovery of Alsace, and will never tolerate a reconciliation with Germany, one may not be convinced, but one is troubled and impressed. The impression gains a new clearness, when one reaches the further chapters in the same book (*Imperial Germany*), which argue that Prussia must never surrender her leadership in the German Empire, that Germany must remain an essentially military State, that responsible Parliamentary government would be its ruin, and that a military State requires a strong monarchy. The connection of the two sets of opinions can hardly escape the least suspicious reader. It was by no meaningless theatrical gesture that the German Empire was founded on drawn swords in the Hall of Mirrors at Versailles. Buried beneath its foundation-stone is the treaty which gave it Alsace. It exists on the dual basis of the German will to hold these provinces and the French will to recover them. To the German nation this basis is unnecessary. A full democracy requires no such stimulus to its corporate life.

The thing which must be founded on hate and greed is the domination of the Prussian land-owning and military caste.   Every institution of the Empire is designed to maintain its profitable and oppressive ascendancy, from the monstrous anomaly of the Prussian Three-class franchise to the anachronism of the Kaiser's personal rule.   This Prussian ruling class dominates, as the Spartans did, by maintaining even in peace the illusion of a continual state of war. That state of war is upheld primarily because Alsace is subjected to a daily and unending conquest. It is part of this illusion that France is ever watching for her chance to recover the provinces.   If the sentiment of the *revanche* did not exist, Prussia would have had to invent it.   She has invented it ; she has perpetuated it ;   she goads and exasperates it, even to-day, by such deliberate and organised provocations as the Zabern incident.   Germans must at all costs be made to believe that the Alsatians are ever ready to revolt, and the French ever ready to cross the frontier.   If by such partial acts of generosity as the recent concession of a faulty but still extensive system of Home Rule to Alsace, the Alsatians are lapsing into relative contentment ;   if by the flux of years and the pressure of other interests the French are forgetting their cherished sentiment of revenge, then the Prussian ruling caste must needs reopen the old wounds, and Colonel von Reuter, with the Crown Prince to back him, found the way at Zabern.   We are here in presence of a phenomenon comparable to our own doctrine of capture at sea.   The Prussian ruling caste will not allow the Alsatian question to slumber, because it is the best argument for their own military ascendancy. The first consequence of an evolution which should bury the Alsatian question in oblivion, would be the breaking of the Prussian yoke and the triumph of democracy in Germany, with all that this would mean for the decline of militarism and the reduction of armaments. So it is among ourselves; the abandonment of capture at sea would allow of a reduction of the navy. Every nation has its own chimaera, a nightmare which militarism deliberately breeds in its own Imperial studs. The German nightmare is the dread of losing Alsace. Ours is the fear of the loss of our shipping in war-time. Both of these factitious monsters could be hamstrung with one swift blow of commonsense. Abandon the doctrine of capture, and half the case for great navies would be destroyed; free Alsace, and Germany need no longer be organised for perennial conquest.[1] One may sometimes hear even from intensely anti-Prussian Alsatians the confession that a return to French rule has now become not only impossible but undesirable. While they still chafe under the rule of Prussian officials and Prussian soldiers, they have perforce built up with Germany, under the pressure of the protective tariff which inevitably diverted their trade from France,

[1] P.S.—An indefensible sea law and the question of Alsace-Lorraine are still the main obstacles to disarmament. Both may with good fortune be removed by this war. But the case for a *plébiscite* in Alsace is overwhelming. So long as territory can be transferred by the mere right of conquest, militarists will always argue that force may undo the work of force.

ties of commerce and credit which could not now be broken without catastrophic consequences to their industry. If Alsace were but granted such full autonomy as Bavaria or Saxony enjoy, it is doubtful whether a plébiscite would show a majority for a return to French rule.

The Alsatian question, in short, is no insuperable barrier to a Franco-German understanding. The French know that they cannot hope to recover the provinces by arms. The Alsatians are divided between sentiment and recent but powerful ties of interest. All that is required, if one may venture to prophesy where nothing can be certainly known, is that the mailed fist should relax its grasp, and that a homely local administration should take its place. So much has been conceded already, that it is not wholly futile to hope for this. When it happens a real Concert of Europe will have become possible ; it will indeed exist. But one may doubt whether Germany will be capable of such an act of grace, until the Prussian ascendancy has been undermined, and the spirit of the Prussian State itself transformed by the concession of a democratic franchise. In the last resort the triumph of a liberal civilisation in Europe awaits two internal events—the establishment in Russia of the Duma's supremacy over the bureaucracy and the Court, and the defeat of the Prussian squirearchy by the Prussian masses. Neither event can be indefinitely delayed, but until both these events are consummated, there will not exist in full consciousness and supremacy that sovereign ideal of self-governing nationality which thinkers presuppose when they dream of a United

States of Europe. That vision lies in the future, but some unforeseen internal changes might conceivably make it a by no means distant future. The steps towards it are not difficult strides. They are mainly two. The first of them is the promotion of such a degree of confidence, if not of cordiality, between Britain, France and Germany as would enable a council of the Powers to meet at frequent intervals on the model of the London conference, and to consider common European questions without inevitably breaking into two groups which neutralise each other. The second of them is the formation of a fixed opinion that no change ought anywhere to be made in the territorial *status quo*, no spheres allotted, no areas of penetration mapped out, without the assent of all the Powers. That opinion must be argued and preached and reiterated until it hardens into a canon of international law. When it is impossible for " anything to happen in the world " (to use the Kaiser's phrase) without the Concert, we shall at last have left behind the predatory phase of world-politics, with its inevitable accompaniment, the endless unrest of a struggle for a Balance of Power. Until that canon is imposed by public opinion and acknowledged by statesmen, there can be no end to the competition in armaments. The present method of barters and bargains between pairs of Powers may be a means of avoiding war, but it is nothing better than a ratification of bloodless conquests which have been achieved by the dry warfare of competing armaments. It is a method ruthless in its disregard of the rights of undeveloped peoples, and anti-social in its unconcern for the rights of third Powers. It does but measure the ability of the expanding Empire to take by force what it desires, against the ability of its rival to use force to restrain it. It is hopeless to declaim against the silent, half-conscious reliance of diplomacy upon force as its ultimate sanction. The hopeful method of dealing with this evil is to provide an alternative means of settling those questions which alone make an adequate motive for the accumulation of force. The essential is that such questions of the future as the destinies of Asiatic Turkey and China shall be settled, if ever they call for European intervention, by a Concert of the Powers. But this Concert will be no substitute for the armed bargaining of single Powers, unless its members enter it untrammelled by alliances, and free to act round its table on a disinterested view of what the common good requires. That is the ideal of a Concert, an ideal which seems to-day to be dismally remote. It is remote largely because it is not consciously grasped by the masses of thinking men who aspire to peace. By mere negotiation we shall not reach the reduction of armaments, nor shall we by arbitration abolish war. There is no solution save in the resolve that European questions shall be settled by Europe. When many wills are set to this end, when many brains are bent on its realisation, there will come that change in the intellectual atmosphere by which alone great reforms are achieved.

The mischiefs which oppress us to-day in the intercourse of nations will be exorcised only when clear and negative thinking has dispelled the megalomania that distracts us. The Powers struggle to-day over nothing vital, nothing homely, nothing relevant to our daily life. The great things in life, the high purposes for which nations exist, are not the struggle to mark out spheres of exploitation, the competition for the usurer's share in financing a dying Empire, or the question as to which national group of capitalists shall draw the profits of cheap native labour. It is a sophistication and a sentimentality which lends to this process the emotions of patriotism. There is in all of us an uneasy sense that this international struggle is distracting the mind of society, which ought to be bent on the civilisation of our own barbarous way of life, while it dissipates on the engines of strife the resources that would suffice to raise the casual labourer and the sweated woman worker to a human level of comfort and freedom. That vague distress, if it is to help us forward, must be translated into a searching curiosity, and developed into an indignant scepticism. It is not enough to desire peace. The generation which attains peace will have won it by an intellectual passion. It must feel the waste and the degradation of our present fears so deeply, that it will think its way through the subtleties and the secrecies which render plausible the present misconduct of international affairs. It will find, when it has faced its problem, that it is not national necessities but class-interests which condemn us to the armed peace. It will realise that in this vast competitive process, by which capital is spreading itself over the globe, there is no motive which can require, no reason which can excuse the hostility of nations. Let a people once perceive for what purposes its patriotism is prostituted, and its resources misused, and the end is already in sight. When that illumination comes to the masses of the three Western Powers, the fears which fill their barracks and build their warships will have lost the power to drive. A clear-sighted generation will scan the horizon and find no enemy. It will drop its armour, and walk the world's highways safe.

CHAPTER XI

A POSTSCRIPT ON PEACE AND CHANGE

A NATION at war believes what will conduce to
victory, and truth is what it is expedient that it
should believe. Each people in this universal
war is convinced that it is fighting on the defensive,
and each people is persuaded that the whole responsibility for this co-operative crime falls upon its
adversaries. Defence is the first necessity, but
apart from the necessity of defence another direction
of thought was prompt to reveal itself as the war
went on. Each of the combatants defined the
positive objects for which it strove, and the
imagination of all the belligerents, sometimes
in a mood of sincere and exalted idealism, elsewhere in a grasping and pedestrian spirit, began
to reconstruct the world. Few of these positive
objects were mentioned during the preliminary
negotiations. They must none the less have been
present, if only in the sub-conscious mind, to all the
statesmen of Europe, on the eve of war. No
Government makes war save in the hope of victory,
and half the attraction of victory is in the gain
which it will bring. The ambitions which dreamers
and schemers had conceived in modesty and secrecy,
were proclaimed on the outbreak of war to the
sound of the trumpet amid the clash of steel. A

war is made less by the dispute which may occasion it, than by the allurement of the positive ends which the combatants hope to realise. A statesman may make war with perfect sincerity because he believes that no other choice is open to him. But he is the readier to believe that it is necessary to fight, when he is also convinced that it will be profitable to fight.

The first of the objects which all the combatants proposed to themselves was somewhat vague. Each side desired safety for the future, and each was convinced that safety could be attained only by breaking the power of its adversary. No one avowed that he aimed at predominance for himself, but everyone meant to destroy the predominance of another. (1) The Allies declared that they must be freed from the menace of German militarism, while Germany sought relief from the menace of Russian Panslavism and British " navalism." (2) Many of the positive issues of this war can be grouped round the idea of nationality—the future of Alsace and Poland, the destiny of the Southern Slavs, the completion of Italian unity, the re-settlement of the Balkans, and, German progressives would add, the liberation of the Finns and other non-Russian peoples of Russia. (3) Some issues are Imperial and Colonial—the future of China, where Japan has already pegged out her claims, the status of Egypt and Cyprus, the ownership of Constantinople, the partition of Turkey, the redistribution of tropical colonies and spheres of influence all the world over. (4) German spokesmen dwelt from the first on questions which affect their trade. Early in the war they talked of constituting a vast Central European Zollverein or Customs Union. They now insist rather on obtaining access to the exclusive Colonial markets of other Powers, by breaking down the system under which many colonies give a preference to the trade of the mother country. (5) Lastly, there are claims and suggestions which aim at future security on land and sea—the reduction of armaments, the abolition of capture at sea, the neutralisation of straits and ship canals. Not only is this a vast range of questions, but most of them are of real importance, and some of them raise large and general issues of world-policy which only a congress could settle. They are more than mere " disputes " between single Powers. It is on the other hand only the questions of nationality which deeply affect the daily life of some small fraction of the European masses, and these questions would probably not have been raised had not Imperial issues lain behind them. Not one of these questions, nor all of them together, is worth this hideous waste and carnage. But they are not accidental or frivolous issues.

To obtain an insight into the psychological causes of this war, let us look at the " dispute " which occasioned it. It was not a large or unmanageable issue. Austria, after the murder of the Archduke, could have obtained from Serbia reparation and guarantees, without undue difficulty. The Hague Tribunal might have investigated the facts, and Sir Edward Grey's proposed conference could have found a formula of conciliation. War might have been averted, if Austria had delayed her precipitate bombardment of Belgrade, and if Russia had postponed her general mobilisation. The negotiations failed for the simple reason that the trivial police matter of the Archduke's murder was not the real question at issue, and the well-meaning efforts of diplomacy sought to avert war by ignoring the real ground of quarrel. The moment war broke out, the Archduke's grave was left in peace, and with a sense almost of relief we lapsed into frankness and faced the real facts. What was at stake was the national destiny of the whole Serbo-Croatian race, and the still vaster clash between the German economic penetration of the Near East and the Slav ambition to attain racial unity and political power. The war in the East brought to full view all the forces which had been working for the break-up of Austria, and the mastery of Turkey. The plain fact about the South Slav problem, is that it can be settled only by a fundamental change, and in one of two ways. If all the Serbo-Croats and Slovenes can be united in an independent kingdom, the world will have rest from this cause of disturbance. The same result would follow if all the Serbs and Croats, including those of the kingdom, were united within the Austrian Empire under a system of Home Rule. We shall begin to grasp the real nature of our European problem, when we realise that as Europe was constituted in 1914, a fundamental solution of this one question was hardly conceivable without war ; nay, more, given the system of alliances, it was hardly possible without a general war. Sir Edward Grey's Conference might have drafted formulae, suggested apologies, defined guarantees. But it would have proposed

neither the abandonment of Serb provinces by
Austria, nor the amalgamation of Serbia in Austria.
It would in short have left the South Slav problem
not merely unsolved, but no nearer a solution. At
least, the reader may object, it would have prevented
war. For how long ? Perhaps until Serbia had
recovered from the exhaustion of the Balkan
wars, until Russia had completed her strategic
railways, and France reaped the fruits of her return
to Three Years' Service. A war averted is only
a war postponed, so long as living forces still press
for organic change, and Europe lacks the organisation which can impose change without war.

An analysis of other questions which await settlement in this war would lead us to the same conclusion. Few of them were urgent. Nations
can wait for decades without yielding to the temptation to make a war. But these issues work,
even when they make no war. France has never
raised the question of Alsace since 1871, but that
question has none the less dominated her foreign
policy. She did not ally herself with Russia with
the deliberate intention of forcing on a war of
revanche with Russian aid. But she did calculate
that sooner or later a European war would occur,
and then, in association with Russia, she would
stand a chance of recovering her lost provinces.
The German military caste looked forward to a war
for the acquisition of " places in the sun," but it
understood that it would have to wait for a pretext
which would enable it to persuade the German
democracy that its war was not simply aggressive
and predatory. It is a truism to say that France

would not be fighting to-day in a Slav quarrel
unless she had desired to recover Alsace, nor Germany
unless she had coveted colonies and spheres of
influence, nor Russia if she ever ceased to aspire
to the leadership of the Near East and the ownership of Constantinople. The chief psychological
cause of war was, after fear, the fatalistic belief that
fundamental change is possible in Europe only as a
sequel of war. That belief had unluckily only
too good a warrant in European history. The
militarist assumed it as an axiom, while we who
opposed militarism were reluctant to face it, and
made the most of the precarious successes of diplomacy in dealing with secondary questions. The
big changes in the structure of Europe followed the
congresses of Vienna and Berlin at the end of the
Napoleonic and Russo-Turkish wars, and other
changes hardly less considerable came about as the
result of a series of wars from Louis Napoleon's
Italian campaign down to the two Balkan wars. The
massive lesson of European military history could
not be ignored ; large changes are the sequel only
of war. The failure of several efforts to achieve or
regulate large changes without war, was no less
conspicuous. The first Hague Conference failed to
reduce armaments, and the second to deal even with
the limited problem of capture at sea. The Conference of London allowed the Balkan settlement
to follow the unhampered dictation of the victors,
and without a protest saw its own recommendations
defied. All Europe realised instinctively from that
object lesson, that change means war, but the
pressure making for change was none the less so

strong that all the Powers prepared with redoubled zeal for war. The long time-fuse which regulates the explosion of the mines below the smooth surface of European civilisation had burned itself down during a generation of peace. New issues had accumulated, and Europe was still without the organisation which can bring about fundamental change by other means than war.

The perception of this connection between change and war has for a century influenced all European diplomacy. The number of statesmen who have in modern times consciously planned war is very small. The accepted canon of responsible diplomacy had come to be that its first object was to prevent wars. So far was it from yielding to an adventurous disposition, that the average characteristic of most European diplomacy has been an almost Chinese conservatism. Its first instinct when confronted with a situation that demanded drastic change, was always to proclaim the maintenance of the *status quo*. There were few limits to the patience with which it endured the wrongs and martyrdom of others. It had never brought itself to propose an adequate remedy for the misrule in Macedonia and Armenia, and on the eve of the Balkan Wars it once more mumbled over the phrases by which it had been used to consecrate things as they are. It made an ideal of immobility, and when events did force it to act, it proposed palliatives, but never remedies.

Behind this conservative practice lay the still more conservative theory of the Balance of Power. That singular fetish of statecraft is a survival from

the eighteenth century. It belonged to the same
order of ideas as the balance of the Constitution
which pre-revolutionary thinkers so profoundly
admired in the England of the days before Reform.
King, Lords and Commons were all engaged in
checking one another, and the balance in England
was so perfect, that it was difficult to conceive
that anything could happen at all. Change was
eliminated, and the stability of our institutions
seemed achieved. To the modern mind this idea
of a balance attained by counter-acting forces is
nothing but an archaic curiosity. The idea that
different classes or estates should spend their
forces in so checking each other as to render change
and movement impossible, would seem to all of us
a tragi-comic futility. In politics as in biology we
know that life means change. So far from dreading
change, we regard our modern constitutions as the
means by which society may constantly and safely
adapt itself to new conditions. While every fully-
civilised State has passed in its national life from a
mechanical to an evolutionary habit of thought,
diplomacy has remained in the eighteenth century.
It is recruited from the satisfied class ; it clings to
its aristocratic tradition ; it has kept its profession
a secret mystery, and its guiding conceptions have
never been permeated by the evolutionary ideas
which leave transformed every other domain of
human thought. It still conceives of Europe as
our great-grandfathers thought of England—a
system of balanced forces, of countervailing checks,
which work to perfection only when the dead
mechanism is at rest. The Six Great Powers were

engaged in checking each other, precisely as the Three Estates were expected to do in the English Constitution. No one, if the balance was preserved, could infringe the recognised rights of another, but it is equally true that no considerable grievance could ever be redressed, and no large change compassed. The dread of change was in each case a dread of violence. Change in England seemed to mean revolution, and change in Europe meant war. The nemesis for this conservative theory of the Balance lay inexorably in war. The society which lives must change, and if its organisation cannot enforce fundamental change without violence, then war is as inevitable as revolution.

There is to-day a danger that pacifists may repeat the mistake of diplomacy. The horror of war possesses us so strongly that we are apt to conceive our problem too simply as the prevention of war. Our problem is larger; it is to provide for international change without war. No solution is adequate and none stands a chance of acceptance which opposes only prohibitions and negations to the impulses of the average healthy mind, possessed with the sense that there is something which it wants, and confident in its power to win it by force. That is to repeat the fallacy of the simple-minded man of law and order who tries to prevent revolution by strengthening the police. First let us assure the nation stifled by some historic wrong or inspired by some legitimate ambition, that the changes it desires can be attained without war, and it will then be superfluous to forbid war. No nation desires war, but some nations desire change. The

concrete form which our thinking inevitably takes
while this war goes on, is the construction after it
of a permanent League of Peace, which might
direct its united forces against any Power which
breaks the harmony of Europe. Some defensive
organisation we must have, but what is it to defend ?
The *status quo ?* The settlement which may be
dictated by the victors at the close of this war ?
It is easy to imagine a League of this type which
would become as reactionary as the Holy Alliance.
If peace should come to mean the perpetuation of
any settlement, the stereotyping of any established
order, the writing of an imperious *Ne varietur* across a
map of the world, it will sooner or later come into
clash with the living forces, the restless energies of
mankind. For a time it may repress them, until in
its turn it is broken by the world's need of change.
We in this country have a wide outlook and a
broad experience of foreign affairs. But there is
one experience which we lack. We have no bitter
grievance, no unsated ambition, and alone of all
the nations engaged in this war, we entered it
with no imperious wish for some large change. We
have no lost provinces, no " unredeemed " kinsmen ; we have not felt ourselves " penned in "
as the Germans did, nor do we think that our
growth will be stifled and our trade hampered unless
we can acquire new " places in the sun." We are
sated with empire and have no temptation to disturb the peace. If we would understand the causes
of wars, we must endeavour to complete our experience by an effort of the imagination. We must
make an attempt to view the world's structure

from the standpoint of the unsatisfied nations. A settlement which made no provision for the future need of change, a defensive League which perpetuated the established order, might satisfy us. But how will it look to a proletarian State ? Take for the example the case of the Bulgarians. If the Allies win this war, and leave Macedonia in possession of the Serbs, as they very well may do, three Bulgarians in four would see in the League's command to disarm merely an intolerable act of tyranny. To abandon for all time every hope of winning freedom for their oppressed kinsmen, would seem not to the worst but to the best Bulgarians a surrender of their manhood. The settlement after this war may do much to better the case of those nations which have sided with the victors. But if it ends with a decided victory for either party, the settlement will inevitably be one-sided. It will redress some wrongs, and make or perpetuate others. It cannot satisfy every legitimate aspiration for change, and may not even realise the ambitions of the victors. In five or ten years new problems will be upon us, if not of nationality then of trade or colonisation or migration. In vain shall we preach disarmament, in vain shall we strive to prevent war, unless we have meanwhile created the organisation which can secure large and fundamental changes without war.

The distance which separates us from any closely-knit international organisation which can bring about change by legislation, may seem at the moment immense. Europe was never so deeply riven by hatreds, and when the struggle is over on the battle-field, it will continue in the press, and may even be prolonged by trade boycotts and tariff wars. The distance to be traversed must not be measured in years. The space to be crossed is a brief intellectual process. We may in the end come to understand that this has been as much a civil war as the American struggle of North and South, and that it must end in the same way, in the unity of a continent. The obstacle in the way is the pride, sometimes a proper sense of independence, sometimes an inflated megalomania, which dreads any diminution in the rights of the sovereign national State. No one would propose to sacrifice the form of the national State, its sentiment of patriotism, and its right to manage its internal affairs. But in its dealings with other States, how much of the substance and reality of sovereign independence still survives ? The great fact of our generation has been the creation of the permanent alliance. Temporary alliances for specific purposes are as old as States themselves, but the durable alliance, designed for peace as well as for war, working in diplomacy as closely as on the field, knit together by the financial ties of debtor and creditor, pursuing a common policy in economics as in strategy—this is a new phenomenon, and it dates only from the last quarter of last century. It has now gone so far that not even insular Britain can stand alone, and centripetal forces drive even the weaker neutrals into one group or the other. A Power which enters a modern Alliance inevitably surrenders something of its sovereignty. It binds itself at need to the principle " my ally, right or wrong." It

makes war and peace in common. No published
treaty provides any machinery by which Allies
control each others' policy, but the control is necessary, and is somehow, though imperfectly, contrived.
Italy expected to be consulted before the present
war broke out, and repudiated the obligations of
an ally because she was not consulted. Germany
more than once vetoed the forward policy of Austria
in the Balkans, and this war came about only because
in 1914 she authorised Vienna to press her quarrel
with Belgrade to extremes. German critics have
argued with some plausibility that the looser structure of the Triple Entente helped to bring about the
conflagration. Our own action was, they say,
incalculable, and if the Entente had been a more
disciplined Alliance, we might have averted war
by delaying the Russian mobilisation. There is
some point in these criticisms, though they involve
the deadly admission that Germany would and could
have kept the peace, if she had known that we
would be arrayed against her. If several nations
are so closely bound that the doings of one of them
may compel the others to go to war, their foreign
policy in time of peace ought to be subject to a
mutual control as absolute as their strategy in time
of war. Short of this no nation is mistress of its
own peace ; with such a control it has abandoned
some part of its sovereignty. The dilemma is
inevitable, and however it is solved, the old conception of sovereign independence is gone. Without control, Allies may drag each other into war ; with
control they are moving towards the ideal of
federation.

Alliances are intolerable and unworkable without mutual control. But this control will always be incapable of realisation while two rival groups confront each other in Europe. We dare not attempt to control our Ally beyond a certain limit, because it is always open to him to join the rival combination. The German Powers disapproved of Italy's adventure in Tripoli, but to check it would have been to drive her into the Triple Entente. We disapproved of much that Russia did in Persia, and of Japan's recent aggression upon China, but we could not interfere effectively, lest these Allies should cease to support us. An alliance under these conditions may involve not merely some surrender of vital interests, but also a paltering with principle. We may make war on an adversary when he violates the public law of Europe, but if we really required the support of an Ally, we should have to condone his misdeeds whatever he might do. If, to take an extreme imaginary case, Russia were to realise Swedish fears by attacking Sweden as Germany has attacked Belgium, or if Italy should insist on acquiring Slav territory in Dalmatia, we should still be compelled to avail ourselves of her aid. The system of alliances, in short, infringes at every turn our own liberty of action, our own power to determine our own course, but it does not by way of compensation fully provide for the salutary control of nation over nation, and above all it does not guarantee the public law of Europe. Such a state of things is so far from being satisfactory that it is not even tolerable. It is unthinkable that we should return to the national

X*

individualism of the last century. What Power
in the present condition of Europe would feel
secure if Alliances were dissolved ? What assurance would the victors have that the terms of the
settlement would be observed ? A coalition which
imposes terms must remain in being to enforce
them.   There is only one way of escape, and that
is to continue the process of evolution, to amalgam-
ate the warring groups, to create a single European system with an impartial machinery of mutual
control.   The group system is plainly a transition phase in a process of development from
isolated national states to a European Commonwealth.   What stands in the way ? Our hatreds
may bar the advance for a time, until we realise
that the pursuit of hate injures and burdens ourselves as fatally as it hurts the enemy.   The
illusion of sovereignty may hamper our action until
clear thinking and a survey of recent history have
taught us that in the modern world the unlimited
independence of sovereign states is as impossible
and as undesirable as the anarchical freedom of
individual citizens.

We may reach the same conclusion by another
road if we consider the change that has come over
the scope and character of European " disputes."
The notion that two Powers might fight out their
" differences " without affecting the vital interests
of others belongs to the past.   The system of
alliances has alone made an end of it. While that
system lasts, any war among the Great Powers
must be a general war.   Even when there is no war,
any aggrandisement of one Power commonly

gives rise to a claim for " compensation " from its neighbours. Every question, even a local territorial question, tends to affect more States than the principals to it. There has, moreover, emerged during this war a series of large and general questions which it would be grotesque to class among " disputes." The law of the sea and the regulation of colonial trade are as much at issue in this war as the fate of Serbia or Belgium. Such issues can be settled only by legislation, and when we have perceived this, it is plain that the world's peace and the world's provision for future change demand not merely arbitral courts and mediation in " disputes," but some organisation which can legislate. The Hague Conference could in a sense do that. But two defects in its constitution rendered it nearly useless. In the first place, it could legislate only when unanimity could be attained among the forty-four sovereign States of all grades and stages of civilisation which comprised it. In the second place it could neither impose its law upon a dissentient minority, nor could it assure the observation of a law even by those who had assented to it. We need a legislature for international questions, and a legislature is impotent unless it also possesses executive powers, or can call upon some other body which will act as its executive.

One need hardly pause to argue that the law of the sea must be rewritten after this war. Belligerents and neutrals are agreed in regarding the present anarchy as intolerable. The right of capture and the meaning of blockade both call for definition ; the development of the submarine has made all our traditions and calculations obsolete. It seems, moreover, useless to draft paper regulations : there will be no law at sea, unless neutrals can be organised to ensure its observation. One may have laws within a policed State, but hardly outside it. If there is ever to be a real law of the sea, we must create for its enforcement something that will in this limited respect correspond to a World-State. Closely connected with this subject is the provision and guarantee of free ports, and the regulation of straits and ship-canals. The struggle for territory will go on across the lines of nationality, unless the free communications of land-locked States are kept open.

It is not yet so generally recognised that the colonial questions which underlie this war call as imperatively as the law of the sea for international consideration. A redistribution of colonies will not end this competition, and might indeed aggravate it. The fundamental mischief is the belief of all the Imperial Powers that colonies and spheres of influence are " possessions " worth struggling for, worth acquiring and worth retaining even at the cost of war. We felt a shudder of repugnance when the German Chancellor's refusal last August to pledge himself not to annex French colonies, suggested the suspicion that, in declaring war, he was influenced by the hope of seizing some of them. But no Power is free from the reproach that it will use force for such ends. We were ready in 1906 and 1911 to go to war in association with France to back her claim to acquire Morocco. Russia has steadily expanded by military pressure, and Japan has just aggrandised herself in China by means of an ultimatum. So long as colonies are regarded as possessions and as indispensable outlets for national trade, the struggle will go on, until the distribution of colonies bears a closer relation to each country's power, to its population and to the vigour of its industry. Germans will remind us, when they talk of Morocco, that France has a stationary population, while theirs increases by a million a year, and that France has already two colonies of the same type (Algeria and Tunis) while they have none that is capable of settlement by white men. They will argue that the use of their central military pressure in Europe to win an empire beyond it, is morally no worse than our own command of the seas, by which we won and by which we retain our empire. On such lines of thought mankind is doomed to incessant warfare. They are, moreover, a brutal negation of the better impulse which teaches us to look on our unfree dependencies not as estates to be exploited, but as regions held in trust to be developed for the good of their immature inhabitants. That idealistic doctrine must, however, reckon with the fact that the economic policy of many colonies is designed to give an exclusive advantage to the trade of the mother-country. The French colonies and Asiatic Russia are conducted on this protectionist principle. Our own unfree colonies and those of Germany are open markets, but our self-governing colonies have latterly given to our exports a small unsought preference. Not less important than this question of open markets is the system by which all the Powers in effect reserve their colonies, pro-

tectorates and spheres of influence as monopoly
areas for the national capital, which seeks to export
itself, to build railways, to open mines and to found
industries. So long as these areas are reserved as
exclusive fields of national investment, so long will
the competition to secure them continue, and it
will seem profitable to the propertied class of every
Power to accumulate armaments, and on occasion
to use them. " Trade," said Cobden, " is a peace-
maker," and so it is when it is free. But the unfree
trading of the closed market and the concession-
area has been for a generation the most potent
cause of the armed peace. To remove this incentive
to militarism, we must advance to the organisation
of a genuine system of free trade, nor will it suffice
to break down tariffs, if we still employ diplomacy
to secure monopolies for national groups of capitalists. We are once more brought by this argument
to the conclusion that the world's peace demands
legislation. It is conceivable (as the New York Reform Club's memorandum proposes) that a congress,
after this war, might decide that non-self-governing
colonies must be opened, without any preference
for the Imperial Power which rules them, to the
trade of all the world. That might be secured without a permanent legislature, and even by a bargain.
If France, for example, regains Alsace, she might well
consent in return to open her colonial markets.
Such an arrangement would remove half of the
motives which now make for colonial expansion.
If a Power may trade freely with the colonies of
another, it need be at no pains to conquer them.
But this touches only half our problem. The

competition for concessions remains, and the colonies which are open to the merchant are still closed to the financier and the contractor. That is the case for the creation of a permanent authority which may labour to internationalise the export of capital. An undertaking that the finance of all the Powers should share on an agreed ratio in all railway or mining concessions in Turkey and China would go far to solve a part of our problem. Some similar arrangement might be reached even in Africa. Equity in this complicated and world-wide question could be preserved only by continual compromises, experiments and adjustments. This is work not for a single congress, but for a standing international authority.

If the world were quite ready to create the United States of Europe, we need only choose between the elaborate constitutions of the Abbé de Saint-Pierre and Immanuel Kant. For us the practical problem is rather to define the minimum which will suffice to enable civilised States to realise large international changes without war. We want to know how little we need sacrifice of national sovereignty and independence. But no scheme is worth the effort which any real advance would cost, unless it satisfies one test. Will it give to an aggrieved or ambitious State a prospect of attaining its legitimate ends so secure that it will desist from competitive armaments and partisan alliances ? If the way to gain a big and legitimate end is still by force, then our scheme will be only an otiose superstructure built on the volcanic foundation of the armed peace. Our object must be to ensure that the way for a nation to gain its ends is to appeal to the represented public opinion of Europe. We must give this opinion first a voice, and then an arm. It must be able first to frame and then to enforce its decisions.

There are two ways in which the common will may be executed. The direct and simple way is to use force, to brandish " the big stick," to coerce the dissentient minority. The simple way is the worse way, and a federation based upon it would be hard to create, and harder still to maintain. Our wars would merely have become civil wars. There is another way, and that is to base the League not upon force but on advantage. If it can offer to those who join it advantages so great that they will be supremely reluctant to quit it, it may safely require that while they remain within it, they shall obey its decisions. Secession must be permitted, but the way of the seceder can be made hard. The two conceptions are not rigidly exclusive, but it will make a vast difference which of the two dominates our planning and our advocacy. By force and threats we shall never constitute a League that will have the loyalty and devotion of Europe behind it. It must become a rallying point for the emotions of civilised men. Its success must depend on the advantages which it offers. Some of these, and the best of them, will be intangible—an enduring peace, progress without war, change without violence, the gradual permeation of our common life by the best thought of each friendly sister nation. But modern industrial society asks for cruder measures of advantage than these. We must not shrink

from meeting it on its own ground. Our League
will be the safer if its basis is rather economic than
military, if it is more obviously a Zollverein than
an Alliance. It must offer, whether by tariffs, by
the association of capital, by colonial privileges,
or by all these means together, advantages so clear,
that only a state bent on suicide would renounce
them. The sanction on which it relies to enforce
its awards, its decisions, and its laws must be rather
the withdrawal of these privileges than the use of
force. The procedure of its Council must be public,
so that Europe shall never again present the spectacle of nations at war in ignorance as to who is the
aggressor and who is fighting in self-defence. The
simple test of right and wrong for the democracy
in any future quarrel must be whether its government has obeyed or defied the common council of
Europe. When a way is open to obtain change
without war, when economic interest is enlisted
on the side of the preservation of the League, when
the masses can apply a simple test to detect the
aggressor, it may be possible to conduct the common
affairs of Europe without appeals to force. The
fundamental basis of any European League must
be the simple requirement that the seceder forfeits
its privileges. The military provisions which may
eventually form part of its constitution need be only
its second line of defence, held in reserve for an
emergency which the economic structure of the
League must render improbable.

There follows a rough tentative sketch of a constitution of such a League. The work of drafting a
workable scheme must be undertaken in co-operation

and by many minds, for it requires not only a scientific knowledge of political theory, but an expert acquaintance with the prejudices and aspirations of the nations which must constitute the nucleus of any League. This outline is intended only to illustrate the suggestions of the preceding pages. I have ventured to compose it because it seems to me that he best serves the common need in this downfall of civilisation, who refuses to despair and continues to construct. The enemy of all our peace is the man who by word or tone or gesture depresses hope and defers Utopia to a distant future. It will come when we will that it shall come. The choice is before us, and this war has taught us that our choice lies between Utopia and Hell.

APPENDIX

A SKETCH OF A FEDERAL LEAGUE

MEMBERSHIP is open to any civilised sovereign State, and all are invited. Self-governing colonies rank as Members. The term " civilised " must be defined, so as to permit the rejection or eviction of undesirable States. The right to secede is freely allowed. Eviction follows after due warning on any breach of the Constitution. An appeal on the interpretation of the Constitution lies to the Hague Tribunal.

The EXTENT at which the Federation should aim is not easy to determine. Many of its problems are world-wide, but a World-Federation would be unmanageable, nor would it constitute a unity which would appeal to the emotions. Perhaps three Federations might grow up, one Pan-European, one Pan-American and one Asiatic, which might be linked by treaty and by the reciprocal exchange of certain advantages. For us the immediate problem is a European League. It must include Germany as well as the chief Allies. Much would be gained by the admission of the United States.

DISPUTES among Members are referred, if justiciable, to the Hague Tribunal. Larger questions of " honour," " vital interest " or of general scope are referred to the Council of the League. A refusal to obey its decisions is equivalent to secession, and mobilisation by one Member against another entails instant expulsion.

THE COUNCIL

The COUNCIL of the League is comprised of deputies elected by the Lower House of each national Parliament on a basis of population (say one to five millions). The method of election is by proportional representation.

The alternative would be a Council composed of the nominees of the Governments. They would tend to be delegates who must obey instructions; such a Council could not deliberate freely, and the voting would follow secret bargaining between the Governments. The Council, as such, would therefore possess no moral authority as a representative body with peoples behind it, and would add no new element to the resources of diplomacy. Few States would like to be outvoted by the nominees of other Governments.

A middle course would be to create a small supreme Council or Senate of delegates of Governments, and an Advisory General Council or Lower House of elected deputies.

National groups elected by proportional representation would show some varieties of opinion. International parties would soon be created across them—a Socialist party, a Free-Trade party, a Conservative party standing for State rights, a Progressive party devoted to the extension of the federal idea. The public life of Europe would soon become an absorbing but peaceful struggle between these rival ideals, in which national divisions would be gradually ignored. No defeat, moreover, would be final. If some decision were generally disapproved in England, our resource would be by books, speeches, or official papers to bring over the rest of Europe to our view. One might devise checks and delays against the hasty action of a bare majority, and a Parliament must be entitled to recall and re-elect its delegates, but, on the whole, the best safeguard would always be the knowledge that a dissentient minority, if unfairly handled, may secede.

The EXECUTIVE work of the Council would, in the main, be performed by permanent officials, drawn at first mainly from the smaller European States. Their work would be controlled by several standing committees, elected by the Council from among its members and responsible to it. Each would be charged with a specific department. The Council would elect a President, who must not be the reigning sovereign of a Great Power.

THE FUNCTIONS OF THE COUNCIL

These demand exact and formal definition ; what follows is a mere hint. Generally the internal affairs of Member-States are declared exempt from interference. Two exceptions seem necessary, though even these must be protected from abuse. The States must surrender something, though not all or even much, of the power to impose tariffs. In grave cases also some interference to assure the rights of racial minorities may be justified. This might be provided for by a statute expressly guaranteeing certain specified minorities, or, better, by a general declaration. Action might also be taken in the gravest cases of oppression under the definition of a " civilised " State. The common affairs of the Federation must be defined by enumeration, subject to future additions as confidence grows and the international idea develops. We might now include :

(1) The police of the high seas in peace and war.
(2) The control of trade routes, ship canals and free ports.
(3) Trade with the unfree colonies of the Member-States.
(4) The control of the competition for concessions and spheres of influence.
(5) The control of dealings with bankrupt or anarchical minor States.
(6) The control, at least in principle, of emigration.
(7) International postal, telegraphic and railway arrangements, extradition, patent and copyright law.
(8) Some cautious development of the existing rudimentary arrangements for standardising national legislation as to dangerous trades, child-labour, the white slave traffic, etc.
(9) The protection in grave cases of racial minorities.
(10) The decision of disputes among Members on the initiative of any national group.
(11) Defence against external aggression.
(12) The consequent regulation of armaments.

The BUDGET of the Council, which would be trifling, would be met by matricular contributions from the Member-States, proportionate to their national revenues.

ECONOMIC POLICY

The key to the creation and maintenance of the League is its economic policy. Here we have in times of peace, the chief of the cruder motives for adhering to it, the chief obstacle to secession, and therefore the principal sanction for the decisions of its Council. The ideal would be a Zollverein, based on complete free-trade within the League and a tariff-wall against outsiders. To this, however, few States would consent to-day. Member-States may, however, be left free to impose their own tariffs in their home-

lands, provided they will agree to open to other Members
the markets of their unfree colonies, and to discriminate
in the home market against hostile outsiders and seceders.
The main points of such a policy would be :

(1) All Members must receive " most favoured nation "
treatment.

(2) The non-self-governing colonies of Members must be
open without preferences to the trade of other
Members on the same terms as the trade of the
mother-country.

(3) Short of free trade within the League some general
preference, say 5 per cent., might be given in
the home market by Protectionist Powers to the
trade of Members, but this is not essential.

(4) Some arrangement might be devised by which the
capital resources of Members should be open to
other Members. Certainly their Bourses must
not be closed to the quotation of approved securities of Member-States, as the French market
used to be to German ventures.

(5) The capital of Member-States will share in an agreed
proportion in certain joint enterprises—e.g., in
Turkish, Chinese or African railways.

(6) As a substitute for forcible coercion the council
may in extreme cases impose a prohibitive
maximum tariff on the trade of a hostile outsider
or an aggressive seceder.

Such a policy, if firmly administered would make it
hard for any aggressive outsider or seceder to maintain
himself in opposition to the League. It involves some
sacrifice of principle from free-traders, and some advance
towards freer trade from Protectionists. Peace is worth
much greater sacrifices than this, and the armed peace of
the past demanded more.

DEFENCE

The chief arm of the League would be its economic policy.
It is to be foreseen, however, than an aggressive outsider
or seceder might, on a capital issue, challenge the League
by an appeal to force. So long as this is possible, the League
must maintain such armaments as the state of Europe
requires. It might, however, be able at once to decree a
proportionate reduction. National armies and fleets, subject

to the exchange of plans and inventions usual between Allies, would at first be maintained. Eventually after some years or decades of successful life the League might create its own fleet, and its own technical military services, leaving Members to train and arm a militia.

The military Council of the League might consist of soldiers nominated by the Governments, under the control of the General Council.

The obligations of the defensive alliance would come into force only when a Member in a dispute with an outsider or seceder had from the first accepted the guidance of the Council in his management of his dispute. Short of this provision, a Member might require the Council to defend him in the practice of manifest injustice. The Council would require submission only in the case of disputes between Members. It would welcome it, without requiring it, in all other disputes. But a Member who had not submitted to its guidance would have no claim to its aid. Members might conceivably be allowed to join the League on its economic side and to take part in its Council without entering the Alliance or incurring any military obligation, and, indeed, such a provision would be necessary if neutral States are to retain their present status, and it might also attract the United States.

At the lowest such a League would mark an immense advance on the present type of secretive and incalculable alliance. Its economic policy would give it a sanction other than force. Its open and popular constitution would attract to it advanced opinion in the nations which remained outside it. Unless it were managed with unusual folly it could hardly fail to extend itself until it became a universal European League, and with each year that it survived it would create a loyalty to itself and a faith in its work which would make secession as difficult as is rebellion to-day in a well-governed State.

A NOTE TO CHAPTER I

P.S.—This chapter will seem to anyone who reads it during this war, to minimise the issues which underlay the struggle for a Balance of Power. Surely, it will be objected, the military power of Germany did threaten the liberty and even the territories of her European neighbours ? I still think that this view involves a misreading of Prussian

" Real Politik." Violent, non-moral and predatory it doubtless was, but its aim was not conquest in Europe, but expansion beyond Europe by means of a victory in Europe. So far as I can gather from good neutral observers who have visited Germany during the war, there was no serious thought of annexing Belgium ; it was regarded as a hostage to be bartered at the settlement. At the most, it was to be included in the German Customs Union, or Antwerp was to be made a free port. Herr Dernburg has insisted that in the event of victory Germany aimed mainly at two acquisitions, Morocco, and the recognition of Turkey as a German sphere of influence. It may seem cold-blooded amid the terrors of this war, to insist that it would never have come about save for these sordid colonial and economic issues. But the point is vital for the understanding of modern world politics. The long Moroccan struggle still seems to me typical. Like the Boer and Manchurian wars it turned on colonial ambitions. Nor can anyone who has read the brilliant despatches of the French Yellow Book (especially No. 5) doubt that it prepared the present war. German Imperialists meant to retrieve their diplomatic defeat over Morocco, preferably by a bluffing diplomatic victory against Russia, but, if necessary, by actual war.

Germany unquestionably pursued economic and Imperialistic aims. The other Powers were also influenced in some degree by similar ambitions. If the German Powers sought, by crushing Serbia, at once to free Austria from the risk of disintegration, and to open their way to the economic control of Turkey, it is equally true that Russia was bent on obtaining mastery over the Straits, not to mention Constantinople itself and Armenia. Russia was obliged to support Serbia, not merely for reasons of sentiment and sympathy, but even more because Serbia was the necessary barrier to German expansion in the Near East. The war began in a struggle for the hegemony of the Near East. Italy entered it largely because she claims a share in the partition of Turkey, and meditates acquisitions in Dalmatia ; most of her claims based on nationality could have been met without war. France is defending her colonies and especially Morocco. Germany is attacking and the Allies are maintaining the present distribution of colonies and dependencies. The stakes lie outside Europe, though the war is waged on its soil.

INDEX

339

THE LONDON AND NORWICH PRESS, LIMITED, LONDON AND NORWICH